CHRISTIE'S

Review of the Season 1984

CHRISTIE'S

Review of the Season 1984

Edited by John Herbert and Mark Wrey

PHAIDON · CHRISTIE'S

OXFORD

Distribution through Phaidon · Christie's Ltd.,
Littlegate House, St. Ebbe's Street, Oxford OX1 1SQ

British Library Cataloguing in Publication Data
Christie's review of the season.—1984
    1. Art—Periodicals
    705   N1
    ISBN 0-7148-8013-2

Distribution in USA and dependencies by Salem House,
99 Main Street, Salem, NH 03079

Design and layout by Norman Ball,
Logos Design, Datchet, Berkshire

Phototypeset in Compugraphic Baskerville by
J&K Hybert, Maidenhead, Berkshire

Printed and bound in The Netherlands by
Drukkerij Onkenhout b.v., Hilversum

Endpapers
SIR PETER PAUL RUBENS
Flemish, Siegen 1577 – Antwerp 1640
A Man threshing beside a Waggon, Farm Buildings behind
Black, red, blue, yellow and pale green chalk with
touches of pen and brown ink, on pale grey paper
10 × 16¼ in. (25.2 × 41.4 cm.)
Sold 3.7.84 in London for £756,000 ($1,013,040)
By order of the Trustees of the Chatsworth Settlement

Frontispiece
Augsburg ivory clock with silver-gilt mounts
Mid-17th century
26 in. (66 cm.) high
Sold. 5.7.84 in London for £842,400 ($1,170,936)
Record auction price for any clock

**All prices include the buyer's premium where
applicable. The currency equivalents given throughout
the book are based on the rate of exchange ruling at
the time of the sale.**

Contents

LEONARDO DA VINCI
Italian, Vinci 1452 – Cloux
1519
Caricature of a Man with Bushy Hair
Pen and brown ink
2¾ × 2¼ in. (6.7 × 5.5 cm.)
Sold 3.7.84 in London for
£226,800 ($303,912)
By order of the Trustees of
the Chatsworth Settlement

Foreword

JOHN FLOYD, *Chairman*

Twenty years ago in his introduction to the *Review of the Season 1964,* my predecessor, Peter Chance, wrote that 'Christie's sales during 1963/64 totalled £4,300,000 ($12,040,000), an increase of £550,000 ($1,540,000) on the previous year.' He added, 'So much has been written about the continued rise in prices for pictures and works of art ...' His younger colleagues of those days, who now provide the senior management and the basis of today's expertise, can tell the same story magnified a hundredfold. The 1983/84 season has been the most memorable in the Firm's long history.

Sales totalled £350.6 million ($463.6 million), an increase of 53 per cent on the previous year. Virtually every department in the London, Glasgow, New York and Continental European sale-rooms has contributed with substantially increased sale totals. New York continued its unparalleled progress, with sales increasing by some 70 per cent to $209 million (£158 million). New York prices and totals in sterling are, of course, boosted by the strength of the U.S. Dollar in relation to the Pound. However, it should be borne in mind that this factor acts as a disincentive to buyers and would-be buyers from Europe.

The most memorable sale of the season was the dispersal at King Street of 71 Old Master drawings from Chatsworth, which amassed a total of £21.2 million ($28.4 million). Did some sale-room veteran murmur, 'Shades of the Holford sale'? Described at the time, May 1928, as 'An outstanding event ... unique in the annals of Art', the Holford collection of 78 Dutch and Flemish pictures, including major works by Rembrandt and Van Dyck, sold for £364,094. The Chatsworth total is not merely a reflection of currency fluctuation, it is foremost a measure of the near insatiable demand for the finest works by masters of their art. Such is the confidence in the international art market of today.

When it is a question of sale totals, New York is not to be outbid. The autumn two-day sale of Impressionist, Modern and Contemporary Art at Park Avenue totalled $44.5 million (£29.7 million). Two major Impressionist paintings each sold for $3.9 million (£2.6 million); *La Promenade* by Edouard Manet, from the collection of Paul Mellon, and *Sucrier, Poires et Tapis* by Paul Cézanne, the property of the well-known Philadelphia collector Henry P. McIlhenny. The Magnificent Jewels of Florence J. Gould attracted no less attention when the collection totalled $8.1 million (£5.6 million).

Since the Firm was founded in 1766 by James Christie at premises in Pall Mall, almost within bidding distance of the present headquarters at King Street, it has had many unusual tales to tell. Not only have the last 218 years reflected the changing social history, scholarship and taste in the Fine and Applied Arts, they have also revealed numerous examples of 'finds', drama and the bizarre.

The current season was no exception. The vendor of the Chinese 14th-century underglaze-copper-red pear-shaped vase, sold at King Street for £421,200 ($606,528), had good reason to be satisfied. He had acquired the vase by 'lucky-dip' in the dispersal amongst members of

Noël Annesley, Director of Old Master Drawings, selling Raphael's study of a *Man's Head and Hand* for £3,564,000 ($4,775,760) at the sale of Old Master Drawings from Chatsworth on 3 July 1984, which totalled £21,179,880 ($28,381,039)

the family of his uncle's possessions thought to be of 'interest or value'! The most romantic story comes from Amsterdam, where our newest sale-room disposed of some 25,000 pieces of mid-17th-century Chinese porcelain recovered from an Asian ship sunk in the South China Sea at that time; the collection sold for a sum equivalent to more than £1.5 million. The most macabre item, the embroidered linen night-cap believed to have been worn by King Charles I at his execution on 30 January 1649, sold at South Kensington for £13,000 ($19,000).

'House sales', that is sales of the contents on the premises, have figured prominently throughout the year, when they were conducted not only in the United Kingdom but in Eire, Holland and the U.S.A. The sale at Elveden Hall, Norfolk, the property of the Earl of Iveagh, alone totalled £6.1 million ($8.6 million).

In the United Kingdom, negotiated sales to the nation of major works of art not only offer taxation relief to vendors but contribute largely to the preservation of the national heritage. Christie's are pleased to record the successful outcome of the negotiations with the National Trust to acquire Belton House in Lincolnshire, together with nearly £5 million worth of its historic contents. This is but one of a number of such transactions conducted during the year.

The following pages show the extent to which the international art market has grown today. They embrace the many facets of both traditional and newer forms of collecting and present a guide to current taste.

Negotiated Sales

CHRISTOPHER R. PONTER, LL.B.

During this year of record activity in our sale-rooms, it is satisfying that Christie's have also been successful in negotiating private sales to the nation of major works of art with a gross valuation of £16.1 million (this includes certain objects accepted in lieu of taxes). Such a healthy competitive market is essential to establish a truly international level of prices, and thus provide a fair guideline to negotiating values. However, before considering a sale at auction, many owners of pre-eminent objects do insist that we explore the possibility of private treaty sales to one of the major public collections – as they are very conscious of the heritage aspect involved.

To their credit, many curators of our heritage have responded to the challenge of utilising the *'douceur arrangements'* to ensure that the contingent tax liability is shared to the satisfaction of both the owner (or his Trustees) and the purchasing institution. Christie's record success in this area demonstrates that the system requires little modification (except where objects are offered to the nation on condition they remain *in situ*).

We are pleased to record the successful outcome of the negotiations with the National Trust (aided by the National Heritage Memorial Fund) to aquire Belton House in Lincolnshire together with nearly £5 million worth of its historic contents. Other transactions motivated in part to provide maintenance funds for the family home were the sale of the wonderful Bassano, *Christ on the Way to Calvary*, to the National Gallery in London from Weston Park (the home of the Earls of Bradford) and the sale of four pictures from the Bridgwater Collection to the National Gallery of Scotland, where they had been on loan since 1946. These comprised a fine Lorenzo Lotto, *Virgin and Child with Four Saints*, Jacopo Tintoretto's *Deposition*, almost certainly the altarpiece from the Bassi Chapel in the church of S. Francesco della Vigna in Venice, Gerard Dou's *Interior with a Young Violinist*, the earliest work by this artist to have survived, and Jan Steen's *School for Boys and Girls*, *c.* 1670.

A magnificent 13th-century Psalter, one of the few surviving English illuminated manuscripts of first rank, was sold to the British Library on behalf of the Trustees of the Duke of Rutland. Known to have been at Belvoir Castle since 1825, this Psalter is one of the finest examples of English book painting and contains the earliest examples of marginal illustrations of contemporary English rural life.

Other sales included a splendid Elizabethan piece, a Chinese Ming porcelain bowl with English silver-gilt mounts of 1579, and, also from the same family, a highly important Mary I parcel-gilt nautilus cup of 1557, the second earliest recorded English nautilus cup. These were acquired by the Victoria & Albert Museum.

In addition to the fine group of tapestries at Castle Drogo acquired by the National Trust last year, the Trust also received from the Government a very fine Venetian painting by Marieschi and two portraits by Joseph Wright of Derby to hang in their property Beningborough in Yorkshire.

Following the death of the 6th Baron Cromwell, his Trustees requested Christie's to negotiate the transfer of two important Canaletto paintings in lieu of tax. We are pleased to report that these two paintings, both representing churches by Andrea Palladio (1518 – 80), were allocated to the City of Manchester Art Gallery, where they will add to the existing important Venetian collection.

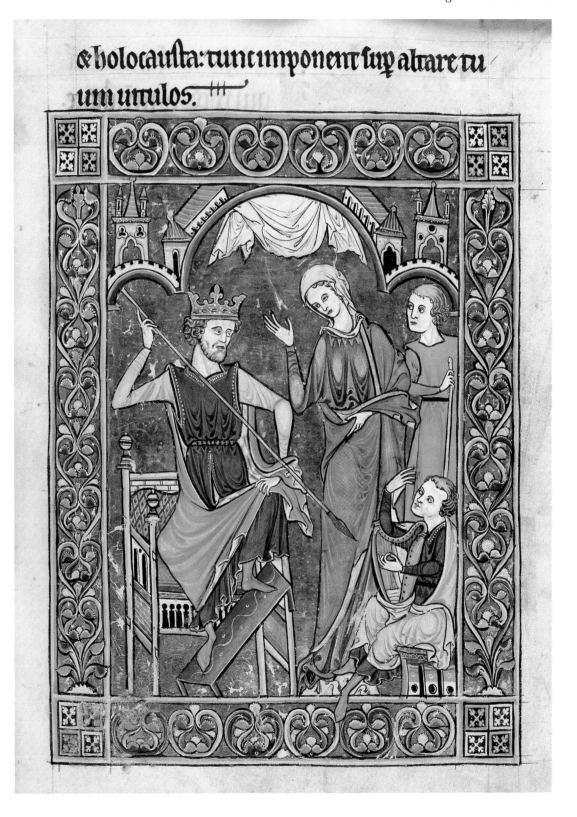

THE RUTLAND PSALTER
Illuminated miniature of the Boy David playing the Harp at the Foot of King Saul
Folio 55
Now in the British Library

LORENZO LOTTO
Italian 1480 – 1556
Virgin and Child with Four Saints
Oil on canvas transferred from panel
$32\frac{1}{2} \times 41\frac{1}{2}$ in. (82.5 × 105 cm.)
Now in the National Gallery of Scotland, Edinburgh

JACOPO BASSANO
Italian 1515 – 92
Christ on the Way to Calvary
Oil on canvas
Painted *c.* 1540
57 $\frac{1}{4}$ × 52 $\frac{1}{2}$ in. (145 × 133 cm.)
Now in the National Gallery, London

Chinese Ming porcelain bowl with English silver-gilt mounts of 1579
Now in the Victoria & Albert Museum

Pictures

NERI DI BICCI
Florentine School, 1418 – 92
Madonna and Child
Tempera on panel
Datable *c.*1470 on stylistic
grounds
35 ½ × 20 in. (90 × 50 cm.)
Sold 22.11.83 in Rome for
L.65,000,000 (£28,260)

Dürer and the Venetian Landscape: Some Points of Influence

ANDREW MORRALL

As a footnote to this year's *Genius of Venice* exhibition at the Royal Academy, it may be of interest to consider the evolution of the 'Giorgionesque landscape', and to do so in the light of the works of Albrecht Dürer which were circulating in Venice at the time when this new style was being formed. It might seem paradoxical to look to a German artist, known to contemporary Italians primarily as a producer of black-and-white prints, for influences on a school of painting for which colour was the main expressive medium. Yet Dürer's example was an important factor in the creation of this new style. It formed, to a significant degree, the syntax by which the Venetians could bring a more lyrical concept of landscape to expression.

Dürer's prints were available in large quantities in Venice during the early years of the 16th century. We have a vivid account by Vasari of the Bolognese engraver Marcantonio Raimondi, who met 'some Flemings with wood and copper engravings by Albrecht Dürer on the Piazza San Marco ... [and] began by imitating [them] ... which, for their novelty and beauty, were sought by everyone'. Seventy-four copied editions by Marcantonio alone survive today. Dürer himself corroborates this in a rueful letter to his friend Pirckheimer, written from Venice on 7 February 1506, when he says that the Venetian painters 'copy my work in the churches and wherever they can find them'. His prints could avoid the stringent guild regulations which forbad the importation of foreign paintings into Venice, and which helped to isolate Venetian culture from artistic currents elsewhere. This, together with Dürer's actual presence in the city between 1505 and 1507, gave his sophisticated and highly original designs a particular prominence which might not have occurred in different circumstances.

Dürer's influence is to be most concretely observed among the engravers of Venice and the Veneto. They copied directly and borrowed motifs with an astonishing freedom. In doing so they gradually adopted his methods of composition. This is very clear in the work of the Vincentine engraver Benedetto Montagna. An early work, his engraving of *St. Anthony* (Fig. 1), shows a format common to the Paduan School: a large frontally posed figure set in a rather bald perspectival setting that is visually uninteresting, expressive only of a pronounced recession. Yet already we find a curiously random selection of elements borrowed directly from Dürer: a dragonfly taken from Dürer's *Madonna and the Dragonfly* (B44); a thatched cottage loosely derived from those in Dürer's *Prodigal Son* (B28), and St. Anthony's pig taken directly from the same print. These constitute padding to an essentially Mantegnesque design. In later works, however, the whole nature of Montagna's composition changes to one that is entirely Düreresque. Dürer builds up his designs in terms of 'motifs', that is to say 'blocks' of trees, rocks, buildings and so forth, linked together by a tonal system which effectively subordinates the individual elements to an overall pattern of lights and darks. Space is indicated by an overlapping of those 'motifs' – like stage-flats – rather than by a system of perspective, and by a gradual lightening of tone as the distance recedes. This construction by 'motifs' necessarily gives emphasis to the picture surface, by which each 'block' forms a necessary element in the balance of the whole

Right

1. BENEDETTO MONTAGNA:
St. Anthony (Hind 4),
engraving

Far right

2. BENEDETTO MONTAGNA:
Virgin and Child in a Landscape
(Hind 22), engraving

composition. It thus confers a further aesthetic dimension on to the scene portrayed – an ornamental quality that complements the realism of the elements themselves. These principles were fully absorbed by Benedetto Montagna in works such as his engraving of the *Virgin and Child in a Landscape* (Fig. 2), in which there is a unified composition made up of 'motifs' – the trees, buildings, the human elements – which in technique, forms and construction is extremely close to the work of Dürer, without being in any way an imitation.

Benedetto Montagna and the other engravers were for the most part men of little originality, at best eclectics who derived inspiration from many sources. They may be said to be, as it were, the weather vanes of an artistic environment, clearly indicating by their very *lack* of originality the main influences to which Venetian artists were subject. That their conception of landscape forms, the arrangement of space, the disposition of light and shade and the overall aesthetic considerations of rhythm and balance were all affected by Dürer for the space of some 10 years bears testimony to the power of his influence.

The painters of early 16th-century Venice were similarly affected, though with artists of the originality of Giorgione and Titian one might expect to see such influences more wholly absorbed. Figure 3 shows a *Visitation*, now in Wiesbaden, by a North Italian painter, in which the buildings in the landscape are a direct transcription of those in the background of Dürer's engraving of the *Sea-Monster* (Fig. 4). This constitutes a literal example of a feature, derived from Dürer, that is to be found repeatedly in Venetian landscapes: meticulously observed rustic buildings, often in a state of romantic decay, as in Giorgione's Castelfranco Altarpiece, or atmospherically lit, as in Titian's *Noli-Me-Tangere* in the National Gallery, London. These buildings constitute one part of a wider approach to landscape learnt from Dürer, namely a meticulous rustic realism, where the settings constitute a direct rendering of the visible world – a concept very different from the 'copy-book' method traditional among the Venetians. Dürer's prints, moreover, reflect a view of nature that dwells on the down-to-earth aspects of farms and peasant-life, a view that was crucial to the development of the 'pastoral' element in Venetian painting, which recognised the power of placing elevated subject-matter in recognisable, everyday surroundings.

The painters, like the engravers, adopted Dürer's system of 'motifs' in an attempt both to give a new prominence to the landscape setting and to integrate the human with the natural elements simply and poetically. An early attempt at this can be seen in the Giorgionesque *Judgement of Solomon* in the Uffizi (Fig. 5), in which the 'motif' of the trees has been inspired by those in Dürer's engraving of *Hercules* (Fig. 6). It has been used in an attempt to unify the upper and lower parts of the composition, but has been imposed rather awkwardly on to a traditional Carpacciesque, stage-like foreground.

It is in Giorgione's work that one can trace most satisfactorily the evolution of a landscape idiom that owes much to Dürer. The 'Germanic' quality of his early *Judith* in Leningrad has often been commented on. The famous *Tempesta* in Venice, though, shows him at his most Düreresque. There is an analogous construction in terms of overlapping 'motifs', a similar linking together of elements into 'blocks' – the feathery trees on the left and the group of trees on the right leading down to the promontory of rock and enclosing the woman and child – that suggests direct cognisance of Dürer's prints, although not dependent on any single example. Giorgione's genius here lies in his command of *colour*, in his ability to suggest mercurial atmospheric conditions, something he owes to the tradition of Giovanni Bellini, with its emphasis on the effects of light. In his foreground landscape elements, however, he shows as yet a tentative quality, one that leans too much on a second-hand vocabulary of forms to be entirely convincing. In the *Three Philosophers* in Vienna of a few years later, this has completely gone, and in its place there is a new immediacy in his response to nature, and a greater command of his medium. Dürer's principles remain: a direct recording of natural *forms* – not merely of light – as well as such compositional features as the large tree-trunk silhouettes, the dramatic vista, the enclosing foliage; but they are now completely subsumed into a uniquely personal and poetic idiom.

Titian also used Dürer's prints on a number of occasions as the basis of his designs. The *Ecce Homo* in Vienna and the rather poor-quality *Last Supper* in the Escorial both depend on Dürer's woodcut versions of the same subjects as reference points. Much earlier in his career he drew from Dürer for his conception of landscape. The background buildings and landscape of his so-called *Sacred and Profane Love* in the Borghese Gallery suggest a knowledge of such prints as the *Hercules* (Fig. 6). We see here also another aspect of Dürer's art that Titian picked up in moving away from Giorgione's influence – the ornamental. Such elements as the gratuitously fluttering robe, the flattened sky with its burgeoning clouds and horizontal bands of colour, the dark silhouette of the bush, the ornate drapery, all have direct analogies in Dürer and contribute to a very similar sense of pattern and balance.

Just as in the 19th century the Japanese print opened up new possibilities of expression to Western artists, so Dürer, in his approach to nature and in his methods of composition, acted as a catalyst on the greater talents, allowing them to bring their more 'arcadian' and romantic idiom to expression.

1. G. Vasari, *Le vite de' più eccellenti pittori, scultori e architettori,* annotazioni e commenti di Gaetano Milanesi (Florence, 1878 – 85), vol. 5, pp. 399 ff.
2. W.M. Conway, *Literary Remains of Albrecht Dürer* (Cambridge, 1899), p. 48

Right
3. MASTER OF THE WIESBADEN
VISITATION: *The Visitation*
(Wiesbaden Stadtmuseum)

Far right
4. ALBRECHT DÜRER:
The Sea-Monster (Bartsch 71),
engraving

Right
5. FOLLOWER OF GIORGIONE :
Judgement of Solomon
(Uffizi, Florence)

Far right
6. ALBRECHT DÜRER: *Hercules*
(Bartsch 73), engraving

AGNOLO GADDI
Florentine School, documented from 1369, d. 1396
Christ the Redeemer, the Archangel Gabriel and the Virgin Annunciate
On gold ground panel
$26\frac{1}{2} \times 12$ in. (67.3 × 30.5 cm.)
Sold 6.7.84 in London for £102,600 ($134,406)
By order of the Trustees of the Doughty House Trust
Three panels originally forming the pinnacles of a dismembered altarpiece

GUIDO RENI
Bolognese School,
1575 – 1642
The Madonna and Child with St.
John the Baptist in an Interior
Oil on canvas
68 × 56 in. (172.7 × 142.3 cm.)
Sold 18.1.84 in New York for
$660,000 (£471,428)
A hitherto unrecorded late
work of the artist which was
identified by our experts in
New York

SIMONE DEL TINTORE
School of Lucca, 1630 – 1708
Still Life
One of a pair
Oil on canvas
28 × 37 in. (71 × 94 cm.)
Both sold 18.1.84 in New York for $242,000 (£172,857)
From the collection of Paul Mellon

ANTONIO CANALE, called CANALETTO
Venetian School, 1697 – 1768
A Capriccio of Buildings in Whitehall
Oil on canvas
20½ × 24 in. (52 × 61 cm.)
Sold 18.1.84 in New York for $682,000 (£487,143)
The painting is one of six commissioned from Canaletto *c.*1754 – 5 while he was in England by Thomas Hollis,
the English radical, sympathiser with the American Colonists and benefactor of Harvard

JACOPO AMIGONI
Neapolitan School, Naples
1682 – Madrid 1752
Venus and Adonis
Oil on canvas
84 × 58 in. (213.3 × 147.5 cm.)
Sold 6.4.84 in London for
£151,200 ($214,704)
Removed from Brownsover
Hall, Rugby, together with a
companion painting of *Cupid
and Psyche*, which was sold in
the same sale for £97,200
($138,024)

FRANCESCO SOLIMENA
Neapolitan School,
1657 – 1747
Venus at the Forge of Vulcan
Oil on canvas
$79\frac{3}{4} \times 59\frac{1}{2}$ in.
(203 × 151 cm.)
Sold 6.4.84 in London
for £205,200 ($291,384)
Possibly the picture
recorded as having been
ordered from the artist
*c.*1708 by the Procurator
Canale of Venice. The
Duchesse de Berry,
daughter of King
Ferdinand I of the Two
Sicilies, in whose
collection the picture is
first recorded, made
many of her purchases in
Venice.

JAN SANDERS VAN HEMESSEN
Antwerp School, *c.* 1504 – *c.* 1566
Double Portrait of a Husband and Wife, seated at a Table, playing Tric-Trac
Signed and dated 1532
Oil on panel
43¾ × 50¼ in. (111.1 × 127.6 cm.)
Sold 6.7.84 in London for £270,000 ($353,700)
From the collection of Mary, Countess of Crawford and Balcarres
Although not the earliest double portrait, this work, which remained unpublished until 1970, must have a good claim to be the earliest, near life-size double portrait executed in The Netherlands. Works by this artist are extremely rare.

PIETER BRUEGHEL THE YOUNGER
Flemish School, Brussels 1564 – Antwerp 1638
The Netherlandish Proverbs
Oil on canvas
44 ¾ × 62 ½ in. (111 × 158.5 cm.)
Sold 6.7.84 in London for £216,000 ($282,960)
The composition, in which 100 proverbs are depicted, derives from a painting by his father, Pieter Brueghel the Elder, in the Museum Dahlem, Berlin

CORNELIS CORNELISZ., called CORNELIS VAN HAARLEN
Dutch School, 1562 – 1638
King David routing the Amalekites, about to rescue his Two Wives
Signed and dated 1603
Oil on canvas
47³⁄₄ × 79³⁄₄ in. (121 × 203 cm.)
Sold 6.4.84 in London for £81,000 ($115,020)
The subject is taken from the 1st Book of Samuel, Chap. XXX,
Verses 1 – 20

Opposite
ABRAHAM BLOEMAERT
Utrecht School, 1564 – 1651
Lansquenets onlooking by a Tree
Oil on panel
34⁷⁄₈ × 35 in. (88.5 × 89 cm.)
Sold 29.5.84 in Amsterdam for D.fl.399,000 (£88,864)
Originally part of a larger picture which is in the
Indianapolis Museum of Art

ROELANDT SAVERY
Dutch School, Courtrai 1576 – Utrecht 1639
The Garden of Eden, with Eve tempting Adam
Signed and indistinctly dated
Oil on panel
33 ¼ × 55 in. (84.4 × 139.8 cm.)
Sold 6.7.84 in London for £118,860 ($155,706)
Painted in Utrecht and datable to the early 1620s

DAVID TENIERS THE YOUNGER
Flemish School, Antwerp 1610 – 90
An Alchemist at Work
Signed
Oil on canvas
28 × 34½ in. (71 × 87.5 cm.)
Sold 6.4.84 in London for £205,200 ($291,384)
This particularly fine work was making its fourth appearance at Christie's, having been offered in 1826, from the collection of Lord Radstock, in 1838 and in 1919. On the third occasion it was sold for 560 gns.

AMBROSIUS BOSSCHAERT THE ELDER
Flemish School, Antwerp 1570 – Utrecht 1645
Still Life
Signed in monogram and dated 1614
Oil on copper
11⅝ × 15 in. (29.5 × 38 cm.)
Sold 2.12.83 in London for £280,800 ($412,776)
Record auction price for a work by the artist

FRANS JANSZ. POST
Dutch School, Leiden *c.*1612 – Haarlem 1680
Landscape outside Mauritsstad, Brazil, with the Portuguese Residence, the Church and the Casa-Grande, the River Várzea beyond
Signed and dated 164(?)9
Oil on panel
15$\frac{1}{2}$ × 23$\frac{1}{2}$ in. (39.3 × 59.5 cm.)
Sold 6.4.84 in London for £129,600 ($184,032)
Painter, architect and engineer, Post paid two visits to Brazil at the time when a Dutch colony had been founded there

MICHIEL SWEERTS
Flemish School, Brussels 1624 – Goa 1664
The Plague at Athens
Oil on canvas
47¼ × 68 in. (120 × 172.7 cm.)
Sold 6.7.84 in London for £972,000 ($1,273,320)
By order of the Trustees of the Cook 1939 Settlement
Record auction price for a work by the artist
Traditionally considered to be the work of Nicolas Poussin and described in the most fullsome way by several 19th-century writers, this painting was identified as the masterpiece of Sweerts as recently as 1934. The activity of this rare Flemish artist, who later became a missionary and died in India, has only been re-established in the last 70 years. On a previous visit to Christie's in 1884 the picture remained unsold at 400 gns.

NICOLAS POUSSIN
French School, Les Andelys 1594 – Rome 1655
Venus and Adonis
Oil on canvas
39 × 53 in. (99 × 134.6 cm.)
Sold 6.7.84 in London for £280,800 ($367,848)
By order of the Trustees of the Cook 1939 Settlement
Long regarded as a copy or at best the work of a pupil, this painting has only recently been recognised as an early autograph work
painted *c.* 1627 – 8. It was last sold at Christie's in 1878 for 51 gns.

LUIS PARET Y ALCAZAR
Spanish School, Madrid 1746 – 99
A View of El Avenal de Bilbao
Signed and dated 1784
Oil on panel
23¾ × 32¾ in. (60.3 × 83.2 cm.)
Sold 2.12.83 in London for £81,000 ($119,070)
Now in the National Gallery, London
Paret was trained as a painter in Madrid, where he was influenced by Italian artists such as Tiepolo
who were working there. This picture dates from the later years of his career when he settled in Bilbao
and painted numerous sea views.

HUBERT ROBERT
French School, Paris
1733 – 1808
A Capriccio of a Fountain in
a Circular Colonnade set over
a Waterway, with a Boating
Party by a Quay
Oil on canvas
128 × 95 in.
(325 × 241.5 cm.)
Sold 6.7.84 in London
for £64,800 ($84,888)

SIR ANTHONY VAN DYCK
Flemish School, Antwerp
1599 – London 1641
A Grey Horse
Oil on canvas
32¼ × 27 in.
(80.6 × 67.5 cm.)
Sold 6.4.84 in London for
£129,600 ($184,032)
From the collection of Lord
Brownlow and the Trustees of
the Brownlow Chattels
Settlement, having been
inherited from Sir Abraham
Humje, one of the great late
18th-century collectors.
The painting is a study for
the equestrian portrait of the
Marchese Anton Giulio
Brignole Sale, executed by
the artist in Genoa.

GEORGE STUBBS
British 1724 – 1806
A Hound attacking a Stag
Signed and dated 1769
Oil on canvas
39¹/₂ × 50 in. (100.2 × 127 cm.)
Sold 18.1.84 in New York for $605,000 (£432,143)
By order of the Estate of Edgar Thom
Record auction price for a work by the artist
Now in the Philadelphia Museum of Art

JOSEPH MALLORD WILLIAM TURNER, R.A.
British, London 1775 – 1851
Bonneville, Savoy, with Mont Blanc
Oil on canvas
36 × 48 in. (91.5 × 122 cm.)
Sold 13.7.84 in London for £648,000 ($842,400)
One of two views of Bonneville exhibited at the Royal Academy in 1803; the other view is now in the Yale Center for British Art, Newhaven

THOMAS GAINSBOROUGH, R.A.
British 1727 – 88
A Rocky Wooded Landscape with Sheep by a Waterfall
Oil on canvas
$28\frac{1}{2} \times 36\frac{1}{2}$ in. (72.4 × 92.8 cm.)
Sold 18.11.83 in London for £70,200 ($104,598)

JOHN CONSTABLE, R.A.
British 1776 – 1837
Stoke by Nayland
Inscribed and dated on stretcher
Oil on paper laid down on canvas
$10\frac{1}{2} \times 8\frac{1}{2}$ in. (26.7 × 19.1 cm.)
Sold 18.11.83 in London for
£302,400 ($450,576)
By order of the Trustees of the
Mrs D.H. Maffett Will Trust
This view is similar to the
cornfield of 1826 now in the
National Gallery, London; it was
painted just before Constable's
marriage in 1816

Opposite
JOHN CONSTABLE, R.A.
British 1776 – 1837
East Bergholt Church
Oil on canvas
$21\frac{3}{4} \times 17\frac{3}{4}$ in. (55.2 × 45 cm.)
Sold 16.3.84 in London for
£102,600 ($149,796)
Probably painted in 1817, when
Constable made a pencil drawing
taken from almost exactly the
same viewpoint. This was shortly
after his marriage to Maria
Bicknell, whose grandfather was
rector of East Bergholt.

WILLIAM HOGARTH
British 1697 – 1764
Portrait of William Jones
Signed, inscribed and
dated 1740
Oil on canvas
50 × 40¼ in.
(127 × 102 cm.)
Sold 16.3.84 in London
for £280,800 ($409,968)
From the collection of
Viscount Parker
Now in the National
Portrait Gallery, London

SIR JOSHUA REYNOLDS, P.R.A.
British 1723 – 92
Portrait of Captain Philemon Pownall
Oil on canvas
87 × 57 in. (236 × 146 cm.)
Sold 16.3.84 in London for £129,600
($189,216)
From the collection of Mrs John
Bastard

Sporting Pictures

HENRY WYNDHAM

The H.J. Joel Collection of sporting pictures confirmed the tremendous surge in interest in paintings of this nature. Until recently, sporting art, which is virtually unique to England, was never taken seriously. Museums made no conspicuous effort to display the pictures and academics considered them provincial and uninteresting.

Times have changed. Exhibitions such as *British Sporting Paintings* at the Hayward Gallery, and this year's Wootton and Stubbs exhibitions, have all helped to re-establish the genre. Probably the most important factor has been the founding of the British Sporting Art Trust, which has not only helped to capture public interest but has also for the first time established several rooms at the Tate Gallery devoted entirely to Stubbs, Herring, Ferneley and their contemporaries. Coincidentally, activity in the sale-rooms has been ever increasing, capped by the Joel Collection, arguably the most important group of sporting paintings to come on the market since the Hutchinson House sale in 1951.

Illustrative of the progress since then was the highlight of the Joel Collection, *The Doncaster Gold Cup of 1838* by Herring and Pollard, which sold for £777,600 ($1,010,880), having made 900 gns. at Christie's in 1943. Dramatic but less spectacular increases in comparison included 'Birmingham' by Herring, which made £504 in 1956 and £51,840 ($67,910) in the Joel sale. Likewise, a Ferneley of *Captain Joseph Smyth-Windham with a Groom and Two Hunters* sold for the same price, having made 500 gns. in 1931. 'The Cur', by the same artist, sold for £216,000 ($280,800), a record for a work by Ferneley.

Much of the private interest in these pictures came from America, where Christie's held its fourth annual sporting sale in June, as always on the Friday before the Belmont Stakes. Since the first sale of this type in 1981 Christie's has sold over $11 million (£8.3 million) of sporting paintings, including the Harry Peters Collection in 1982. Prices have remained strong throughout, with great demand for works by Munnings, one selling for $357,500 (£197,573) in 1982. *The Horse Fair* by Herring, which sold for £24,000 at Christie's in London in 1976, sold eight years later for $412,500 (£292,553).

The market is very healthy, with probably more private buyers than in any other specialist field. There is no doubt that sporting art is very much a school to be reckoned with.

JOHN FREDERICK HERRING, SEN. and JAMES POLLARD
British 1795 – 1865; British 1792 – 1867
The Doncaster Cup of 1838 with the Earl of Chesterfield's three-year-old
colt 'Don John' beating Mr Orde's 'Beeswing', Mrs S.L. Fox's 'The Doctor' and Mr Robinson's 'Melbourne'
Signed, inscribed and dated 1839 by J.F. Herring
Oil on canvas
36 × 72 in. (91.5 × 182.8 cm.)
Sold 13.7.84 in London for £777,600 ($1,010,880)
Record auction price for a work by the artists
From the H.J. Joel Collection
Herring painted the horses in the foreground, and Pollard the stands and coaches, crowded with figures, in the background. 'The Druid', a popular 19th-century sporting journalist, claimed that Herring's racing scenes of this type were produced by using a sketchbook of ideal horses and jockeys with a few quick studies from life. The motionless quality of the galloping horses is summed up by Sir Nicholas Pevsner in *The Englishness of English Art*: 'where animal painting is at its best, where even the racing picture is at its best, there is no exacting action, but a curious stillness'.

JOHN FREDERICK HERRING, SEN.
British 1795 – 1865
Preparing to start for the
Doncaster Gold Cup, 1825, with
Mr Whittaker's 'Lottery',
Mr Craven's 'Longwaist',
Mr Lambton's 'Cedric', and
Mr Farquharson's 'Figaro'
Signed and dated 1827
Oil on canvas
18 × 36 in. (45.7 × 91.5 cm.)
Sold 13.7.84 in London for
£345,600 ($449,280)
Record auction price for a
work by the artist
From the H.J. Joel Collection

JOHN FREDERICK HERRING, SEN.
British 1795 – 1865
A Horse Fair on Southborough
Common
Signed and dated '1857 & 8'
Oil on canvas
39 × 69½ in. (99 × 176.4 cm.)
Sold 8.6.84 in New York for
$412,500 (£292,553)

JOHN FREDERICK HERRING, SEN.
British 1795 – 1865
Huntsman and Hounds
Signed and dated 1831
Oil on canvas
28 × 36 in. (71.1 × 91.4 cm.)
Sold 8.6.84 in New York for $154,000 (£107,092)

JOHN FREDERICK HERRING, SEN.
British 1795 – 1865
Partridge shooting at Six Mile Bottom
Signed, inscribed and dated 1833
Oil on canvas
22 × 30 in. (55.9 × 76.2 cm.)
Sold 13.7.84 in London for £151,200 ($196,560)
From the H.J. Joel Collection

JOHN E. FERNELEY, SEN.
British 1782 – 1860
'The Cur', a Chestnut Racehorse with a Jockey up, on Newmarket Heath, with Racehorses exercising beyond
Signed, inscribed and dated Melton Mowbray 1848
Oil on canvas
40 × 50 in. (101.6 × 127 cm.)
Sold 13.7.84 in London for £216,000 ($280,800)
Record auction price for a work by the artist
From the H.J. Joel Collection

The Proscribed Royalist, 1651

PHILIP HOOK

That curious mixture of youthful excess, high-minded seriousness, meticulous endeavour and prep-school bawdiness which characterised early Pre-Raphaelitism could not be better illustrated than in the painting of *The Proscribed Royalist*, a process which is well documented in Millais's letters of the time.

The picture was originally commissioned by Lewis Pocock in May 1852; he certainly received value for money in terms of the effort expended by the artist, who worked fairly constantly on the enterprise for the next 10 months. The subject had first to be settled. Looking for a follow-up to his great success with *A Huguenot* of 1851 – 2, Millais favoured another scenario involving star-crossed lovers. He toyed with Romeo and Juliet, but finally decided on a Civil War setting involving a Puritan girl who hides her proscribed Royalist lover in an oak tree. Once the plot was agreed, locations, costumes and models then had to be considered. In view of the thought and time which such questions occupied, the Pre-Raphaelite painter looks more and more like the modern-day film producer.

By 9 June 1852 Millais was writing to Mrs Thomas Combe, 'I have a subject I am mad to commence and yesterday took lodgings at a delightful little country inn near a spot exactly suited for the background.' The spot he had chosen was by one of the ancient oak trees on West Wickham Common near Bromley, Kent. It was a site to which he returned repeatedly throughout the summer in order to achieve that painstaking 'truth to nature' which was one of the first principles of the young Pre-Raphaelites' manifesto. By 21 October a note of frustration is evident from his letter to Holman Hunt: 'finished my background yesterday. Upon my word it is quite ridiculous. I have been 4 months about a wretched little strip of uninteresting green stuff.'

Models were a separate problem. The girl was Anne Ryan, who had sat successfully for *A Huguenot*. Millais wrote to Holman Hunt on 11 November, 'Today I have been drawing the girl's figure in the landscape. Yesterday it was too small and today too large. Tomorrow she comes again when I hope to get it between the two sizes */* I don't mean her legs.' The fact that this rakish footnote was addressed to Holman Hunt sheds new light on the painter of *The Awakening Conscience*. For the cavalier, the sitter was the painter Arthur Hughes, who posed five or six times in the Gower Street house where Millais had his studio. Millais even roped his mother in as wardrobe mistress. He records in a letter of 14 March 1853 that she was 'sewing away at a costume for a gay cavalier I am painting'.

Such letters, most of which are quoted in Malcolm Warner's excellent catalogue entry for the picture in the Pre-Raphaelites exhibition at the Tate Gallery earlier this year, provide an intriguing insight into the industry and discipline required of a Pre-Raphaelite painter at the most rigorous moment of the movement. The price realised for the picture, £842,400 ($1,246,752) in November 1983, is some recognition of its status and importance.

SIR JOHN EVERETT MILLAIS,
BT., P.R.A.
British 1829 – 96
The Proscribed Royalist, 1651
Signed and dated 1853
Oil on canvas
$40\frac{1}{2} \times 29$ in.
(103 × 73.5 cm.)
Sold 25.11.83 in London for
£842,400 ($1,246,752)
By order of the Executors of
the late Mrs Marjorie Mary
Yates
Record auction price for a
work by the artist

FREDERIC, LORD
LEIGHTON, P.R.A.
British 1830 – 96
*Old Damascus: Jews'
Quarter or Gathering
Citrons*
Oil on canvas
51 × 41 in.
(129.5 × 104.1 cm.)
Sold 25.11.83 in
London for £378,000
($559,440)
By order of the
Taxation Publishing
Company Limited
Record auction price
for a work by the artist

ALFRED MORGAN
British 1862 – 1904
One of the People, Gladstone in an Omnibus
Signed and dated 1885
Oil on canvas
31¼ × 42½ in. (79.3 × 108 cm.)
Sold 25.11.83 in London for £70,200 ($103,896)
Record auction price for a work by the artist

FILIPPO PALIZZI
Italian 1812 – 88
The Hunting Party of Ferdinand II of Naples
Signed and dated 1847 (?)
Oil on canvas
36 × 52½ in. (91.5 × 133.3 cm.)
Sold 23.3.84 in London for £34,560 ($49,421)
A version of the picture in the Pitti Palace, Florence

JOAQUIN SOROLLA Y BASTIDA
Spanish 1863 – 1945
La Vuelta de la Pesca
Signed
Oil on canvas laid on board
18 × 24 in. (45.6 × 61 cm.)
Sold 23.3.84 in London for £54,000 ($77,220)

MAX LIEBERMAN
German 1847 – 1935
Wannseegarten
Signed
Oil on canvas
$21\frac{1}{2} \times 29\frac{1}{2}$ in. (54.5 × 75.5 cm.)
Sold 25.11.83 in London for £62,640 ($92,707)

ALFRED DE DREUX
French 1810 – 60
A Grey Stallion
Signed
Oil on canvas
42 × 51 in. (106.6 × 129.6 cm.)
Sold 22.6.84 in London for £102,600 ($141,588)

ANDERS LEONARD ZORN
Swedish 1860 – 1920
Kaellbaecken vid Hemla
Signed and dated 1906
Oil on canvas
42½ × 33 in. (108 × 83.8 cm.)
Sold 27.10.83 in New York for $198,000 (£129,412)
From the collection of Mrs Myron Hammond, Connecticut

LUDWIG DEUTSCH
French 1855 – 1935
The Harem Guard
Signed
Oil on panel
31¼ × 23¼ in.
(79.5 × 59 cm.)
Sold 25.11.83 in
London for £91,800
($135,864)

FRÉDÉRIC DUFAUX
Swiss 1852 – 1943
A Regatta, Geneva
Signed and dated 1885
Oil on canvas
30½ × 49 in. (78 × 125 cm.)
Sold 23.3.84 in London for £64,800 ($92,664)
The regatta depicted is taking place at Les Paquis

ADOLPH FRIEDRICH
ERDMANN MENZEL
German 1815 – 1905
*Portrait of a Bearded
Man, Head and
Shoulders*
Signed with initials
and dated *5 Marz 55*
Oil on paper laid on
canvas
23 × 18¼ in.
(58.5 × 46.2 cm.)
Sold 25.11.83 in
London for £41,040
($60,739)

EDMOND GEORGES GRANDJEAN
French 1844 – 1908
Le Boulevard des Italiens, Paris
Signed and dated 1889
Oil on canvas
38 × 58 ½ in. (96.5 × 148.6 cm.)
Sold 1.3.84 in New York for $121,000 (£81,756)

FRITZ THAULOW
Norwegian 1847 – 1906
Les Eaux bleues
Signed
Oil on canvas
26 × 32½ in. (66 × 82.5 cm.)
Sold 22.6.84 in London for £81,000 ($111,780)

ARTHUR HUGHES
British 1832 – 1915
The Knight of the Sun
'Better a death when work is done than earth's most
favoured birth', G. Macdonald
Signed
Oil on canvas
40 × 52 in. (101.1 × 132.5 cm.)
Sold 22.6.84 in London for £172,800 ($238,464)
Record auction price for a work by the artist

CONRAD MARTENS
British d. 1878
A View of Sydney looking from the North Shore towards the City, Double Bay to the left and the Rocks to the right
Signed
Watercolour and bodycolour with gum arabic, unframed
18 × 26 in. (45.8 × 66 cm.)
Sold 26.10.83 in London at Christie's South Kensington for £48,000 ($73,440)
Record auction price for a work by the artist

JOHN SKINNER PROUT
British 1783 – 1852
From Sandy Bay, Hobarton
Signed and dated 1847
Watercolour
Sold 26.10.83 in London at Christie's South Kensington for £14,000 ($21,420)
Record auction price for a work by the artist

THOMAS BAINES
British 1822 – 75
Buffaloes driven to the Edge of the Chasm opposite Garden Island, Victoria Falls
Signed, inscribed 'Painted from memory in D'urban' and dated 'April 20 1874' on the reverse
Oil on canvas
20 × 26 in. (50.8 × 66.1 cm.)
Sold 29.5.84 in London at Christie's South Kensington for £90,000 ($126,900)
Record auction price for a work by the artist

THOMAS BAINES
British 1822 – 75
Koodoos, Luisi River, Zambesi Valley
Signed, inscribed and dated '1 Oct. 1874'
Oil on canvas
20 × 26 in. (50.8 × 66.1 cm.)
Sold 29.5.84 in London at Christie's
South Kensington for £60,000 ($84,600)

An American Heritage, Genre Paintings

JAY CANTOR

The reshuffling of political and economic institutions that followed the American Revolution had a powerful impact on the cultural life of the new nation, an impact that can be traced in the extraordinary and complex development of genre painting in the 19th century. Genre and figure painting, illustrated by excellent and sometimes rare examples in Christie's auctions of Important American Paintings and Sculpture in 1983/84, mirrored the gradual transition of America from a rural and agricultural nation to an urban and industrial giant.

Painters freed themselves from the tyranny of portraiture and turned to other aspects of American life in search of subjects that could represent the aspirations and accomplishments of a new democracy. Fledgeling academies and literary clubs fostered artistic training and engaged in theoretical discussions on what subject-matter would be appropriate to American life. Cultural nationalism was at a high pitch in reaction to the stinging European declaration, 'Who reads an American book?' In response, American artists of the 19th century, although still under the influence of Europe, turned increasingly to the problems of an American style and American subject-matter.

Genre and figure painting, as well as landscape painting, provided major areas of activity for American artists in search of a national style, and these fields were represented by major examples which set the record prices for the 1983/84 season. Thomas Cole's *View of Boston*, long misidentified as a view of Albany, New York, established the highest price at $990,000 (£702,127), followed closely by William Sidney Mount's painting *The Trap Sprung* at $880,000 (£611,111).

While American landscape painting has been widely chronicled, figure painting has received less attention, and examples in the 1983/84 season provide a comprehensive insight into this important field. Two canvases by John Lewis Krimmel, a German immigrant who worked in Philadelphia in the first decades of the 19th century, stand at the threshold of the genre tradition. Krimmel is considered the first serious genre painter working in America. *The Blind Fiddler* was painted in 1813 and *Blind Man's Bluff* in 1814, and they have not been exhibited publicly since 1820. These canvases rely on artistic sources typically used by early American painters: European engravings and the close study of plaster casts of antique sculpture. *The Blind Fiddler* is a copy after David Wilkie's painting, known to Krimmel through an engraving. Wilkie was the most brilliant practitioner in the English school of genre painting, continuing a tradition which traced its roots back to Hogarth in the 18th century. The comic and satiric overtones of English genre painting appealed less to the Americans, who found in scenes of everyday life a subject of admiration rather than snobbish amusement. Over the course of the 19th century, while styles and subjects changed, the reverence for the ordinary as a powerful expression of the political and social attitudes of a unique democracy informed much American work.

Genre painting reached a pinnacle in the middle years of the 19th century, as the earliest generation of painters matured and popular art institutions, such as the American Art Union

THOMAS COLE
American 1801 – 48
View of Boston
Oil on canvas
34 × 47 ⅛ in. (86.4 × 119.6 cm.)
Sold 1.6.84 in New York for $990,000 (£702,127)
Record auction price for a work by the artist

and the Düsseldorf Gallery, made paintings available to the public on a popular level. During the decades on either side of the Civil War, America probed deeply for fundamental values in the rural life of the nation. Farm and village life provided subjects for many of the best painters of these decades, ranging from William Sidney Mount and Eastman Johnson to Winslow Homer and Jerome Thompson. Mount occupies a special place in the chronicle as the most important pre-war painter of rural America. Only his contemporary George Caleb Bingham reached a similar level of prominence, providing for the life of the frontier a visual anthology similar to that which Mount created in describing the barns and taverns, parlours and farm lots of his native village of Stony Brook, Long Island. Mount studied briefly in New York but shunned the European study tour offered him and retreated to Long Island, where he concentrated on the labours and pastimes of his neighbours. In doing so he brought a fresh vision of rural life into focus, rendering his canvases in a rich artistic style. Mount took his compositional format from the scene as observed and imbued his canvases with a liveliness and spontaneity which also reflects his deep personal interest in music. Two paintings by Mount in the sale of 9 December, *The Trap Sprung* and *Bird Egging*, recall childhood diversions that were a significant aspect of his output.

Childhood was, in fact, a favoured theme of many genre artists, perhaps reflecting the youthful attitude towards a nation still discovering its potential, even as the shadowy clouds of sectional conflict were gathering on the horizon. The American painter's infatuation with youth and childhood pleasures is evident in Eastman Johnson's masterful drawing *The Picture Book*. The artist is in full command of the Rembrandtesque light and controlled modelling that was to characterise his best work. Recent study in Düsseldorf and The Hague had solidified his early competence and the quiet moodiness of this rendering continued as a dominant motif of his later paintings. Study in Europe had become a major component of artistic training for many Americans, and Johnson joined a community in Germany which included Albert Bierstadt, Worthington Whittredge, George Caleb Bingham, Richard Caton Woodville and Emanuel Gottlieb Leutze, among others. For many American painters, European study was merely a prelude, providing the chance to gain the tools of the trade so they might better deal with the close study of the American scene. Increasingly that scene was an urban rather than a rural environment, and already at mid-century, alongside the rural essays of such artists as Mount, others were exploring the streetscape of the expanding cities.

Two works by Lilly Martin Spencer are rare entries by a largely self-taught painter who grew up in Cincinnati. *The Young Husband: First Marketing* of 1854 and *Mother and Child* of 1858 document urban domestic life at the time. Spencer was the sole support of her family of 13 children, as her husband devoted himself to work as her agent and manager. *The Young Husband: First Marketing* is thus a true-life portrait of a rare role reversal in 19th-century America. It is also a document of the enormous capabilities of an artist whose work, like that of Mount, Homer and Eastman Johnson, found an extended audience through popular prints in the new chromolithographic process or in the increasing number of illustrated magazines. Many of the later genre painters and a host of important American artists of the 20th century learned their craft and gained early financial support working as illustrators feeding the demands of daily journalism and monthly serials. While some artists continued to show the rural aspect of American life, their pictures, when seen in the context of a gallery or one of the recently founded urban museums or in a great mansion, took on a humble and frankly nostalgic presence. They no

WILLIAM SIDNEY MOUNT
American 1807 – 68
The Trap Sprung (The Dead Fall)
Signed and dated 1844
Oil on panel
12⅞ × 17 in. (32.7 × 43.2 cm.)
Sold 9.12.83 in New York for $880,000 (£611,111)
Record auction price for a work by the artist

longer evoked optimism but seemed somehow a backward glance at a simpler past. This mood of reverie came to dominate much of the best work of the late 19th century.

Edward Tarbell's laconic composition *Quiet Afternoon* shows a world of lyric introspection, more Debussy than Brahms. Even William Merritt Chase's monumental depiction of childhood games converts the playful brightness of soft mid-century renderings to a more artful and contrived structure. Chase looks more to art than to nature and pays homage to Whistler and the Orient in his delicately balanced and elongated surface rendering. Where once naïve and localised interest informed American figural work, now a cosmopolitanism was to dominate. With new waves of European influence and greater ease of world travel, artists moved more frequently within international circles.

American painters in the international arena, including John Singer Sargent, Mary Cassatt and Whistler, achieved a status and respectability which had eluded earlier American artists. These artists turned the interest in the figure in new directions, abandoning narrative in favour of advanced aesthetic theories. Sargent's *A Bedouin Arab* in the June sale showed all the mastery on a small scale that he demonstrated with grand full-length portraits. It reached a staggering $269,500 (£191,134). In a gentler mood, Mary Cassett's pastel *The Conversation* set a new record for the artist of $495,000 (£351,063). Cassatt worked almost exclusively in France on the perimeters of the Impressionist circle, creating masterly oils and pastels of her close circle of family and friends. With the major reputation established by these expatriates, American nationalism was now measured by international acceptance. American painters caught up in the heady embrace of international culture at the turn of the century suspended their concern with the localised issues of an American style and an American subject. Only the renegades, the Ashcan painters, such as Glackens, Luks, Sloan and Henri, looked with a fresh eye at the new American scene. Their employment as illustrators for the daily journals deferred their serious consideration as artists with noble ambitions. They were, however, the true inheritors of the genre tradition begun a century earlier. They part company with that earlier band in their vision of America not as a unified whole with a distinct singular culture but as a polyglot, whose contribution to the world lay not in the quiet pursuit of rural virtues but in the restless energy that became necessary in an industrial world to guarantee not only success, but survival.

JOHN LEWIS KRIMMEL
American 1787 – 1821
Blind Man's Bluff
Signed and dated 1814
Oil on canvas
16½ × 22 in. (42 × 56 cm.)
Companion picture to *The Blind Fiddler*
Both sold 9.12.83 in New York for $308,000 (£213,888)
Record auction price for a work by the artist

WILLIAM MERRITT CHASE
American 1849 – 1916
Playing Horse
Signed
Oil on canvas
72⅛ × 36⅛ in. (183.2 × 91.8 cm.)
Sold 9.12.83 in New York for $385,000 (£267,361)

JOHN FREDERICK PETO
American 1854 – 1907
For the Track
Signed and dated 95
Oil on canvas
43½ × 29⅞ in. (110.5 × 75.8 cm.)
Sold 1.6.84 in New York for $506,000
(£358,865)

MARY CASSATT
American 1844 – 1926
The Conversation
Signed
Pastel on paper laid down on canvas
25 ½ × 32 in. (64.6 × 81.2 cm.)
Sold 1.6.84 in New York for $495,000 (£351,063)
Record auction price for a pastel by the artist

JOHN SINGER SARGENT
American/British
1856 – 1925
A Bedouin Arab
Signed
Oil on canvas
26 × 20¼ in.
(66 × 51.5 cm.)
Sold 1.6.84 in New York
for $269,500 (£191,134)
By order of the Trustees of
the Cholmondeley
Settlement, removed from
Houghton Hall, Norfolk

RALSTON CRAWFORD
American 1906 – 78
Industrial Landscape, Buffalo
Signed
Oil on canvas
Painted *c.*1937
25 × 30 in. (63.5 × 76.2 cm.)
Sold 9.12.83 in New York for
$187,000 (£129,861)
Record auction price for a
work by the artist

EVERETT SHINN
American 1876 – 1953
The Vaudevillian
Signed
Pastel on board
11⅞ × 18 in.
(30.3 × 45.8 cm.)
Sold 23.3.84 in New York for
$35,200 (£24,276)

ROBERTO ECHAURREN MATTA
Chilean b. 1911
The Disasters of Mysticism
Oil on canvas
Painted in 1942
$38\frac{3}{8} \times 51\frac{3}{8}$ in. (97.5 × 130.5 cm.)
Sold 29.11.83 in New York for $176,000 (£117,333)
Record auction price for a work by the artist

DIEGO RIVERA
Mexican 1886 – 1957
Mujer de Rodillas con Vira Soles
Signed and dated 1946
Oil on canvas laid down on masonite
59¾ × 47⅝ in.
(151.8 × 121 cm.)
Sold 29.11.83 in New York for $198,000
(£132,000)

Modern Pictures

CAMILLE PISSARRO
French 1830 – 1903
Le Pont de Chemin de Fer,
Pontoise
Signed
Oil on canvas
Painted *c.*1873
$19^5/_8 \times 25^5/_8$ in.
(50 × 65 cm.)
Sold 16.5.84 in New York
for $506,000 (£361,428)
By order of the Estate of
David M. Heyman

JEAN BAPTISTE CAMILLE COROT
French 1796 – 1875
Paysage à Mornex (Haute-Savoie)
Signed
Oil on canvas
Painted in 1842
15¾ × 24⅛ in. (40 × 61.5 cm.)
Sold 15.11.83 in New York for $330,000 (£220,000)
From the collection of Paul Mellon

EDGAR DEGAS
French 1834 – 1917
Danseuse debout, les Mains croisées
derrière le Dos
Stamped with signature
Black and white chalks on grey laid
paper
Drawn in 1874
$17\frac{3}{4} \times 11\frac{3}{4}$ in. (45×29.7 cm.)
Sold 16.11.83 in New York for
$154,000 (£102,666)
A study for one of the dancers in the
painting *Répétition de Ballet sur la Scène*
(Musée du Louvre, Paris)

EDOUARD MANET
French 1832 – 83
Portrait de Madame Brunet
Signed
Oil on canvas
Painted *c.* 1860 – 7
52 × 39¼ in.
(132 × 99.5 cm.)
Sold 16.5.84 in New York
for $2,200,000 (£1,571,428)
From the collection of Miss
Sandra Payson

EDOUARD MANET
French 1832 – 83
La Promenade
Oil on canvas
Painted in 1880
$36\frac{3}{8} \times 27\frac{3}{4}$ in.
$(92.3 \times 70.5$ cm.$)$
Sold 15.11.83 in New York
for $3,960,000 (£2,640,000)
Record auction price for a
work by the artist
From the collection of Paul
Mellon

EDOUARD MANET
French 1832 – 83
Fleurs dans un Vase de Crystal
Signed and inscribed
Oil on canvas
Painted *c*. 1882
21½ × 13⅞ in. (54.6 × 35.2 cm.)
Sold 15.11.83 in New York for $1,210,000
(£806,666)
From the Thomas W. Evans Collection of
The University of Pennsylvania School of
Dental Medicine
Thomas Evans was the artist's dentist and he
acquired this picture and *Nature morte à la
Brioche* (p. 89) directly from Manet. Both
pictures remained unrecorded until 1979.

EDOUARD MANET
French 1832 – 83
Nature morte à la Brioche
Signed
Oil on canvas
Painted in 1880
21⅝ × 13⅞ in. (55 × 35.2 cm.)
Sold 15.11.83 in New York for $1,100,000
(£733,333)

A London Suburb by Camille Pissarro

JOHN LUMLEY

La Route de Sydenham is a view of The Avenue, Sydenham, looking north-west towards St. Bartholomew's Church, Westwood Hill. The street is now called Lawrie Park Avenue, the name having been altered in 1886, and, as can be seen from the recent photograph, its character has also changed. In 1871 it was the widest of a group of streets, which had been made after 1854 when the Crystal Palace was re-erected at Sydenham, and at the centre of a new prosperous suburb, full of large villas, each standing on plots of an acre or more. It was a fashionable place, as Pissarro depicts. Today, though, the rich have gone; and their houses have followed, except for a few like Dunedin House, the white building in Pissarro's picture to the left of the church, which survives though now much altered, tile-hung and divided into flats.

Pissarro lived in Palace Road, Upper Norwood, a trim but much less fashionable street, only a short walk away across the pleasure grounds of Crystal Palace. He had moved to London with his family in the late autumn of 1870, in order to escape the chaos in France caused by the war with Prussia and the Commune in Paris. His friend, Monet, was already in London and it was here that they met for the first time Paul Durand-Ruel, a dealer in pictures and a man who was to play an important role in both their lives.

In a letter to the English painter, Wynford Dewhurst, written in 1902, Pissarro remembered, 'In 1870 I found myself in London with Monet … [We] were very enthusiastic about the London landscapes. Monet worked in the park, while I, living in Lower Norwood, at that time a charming suburb, studied the effects of fog, snow and springtime. We worked from nature.' (W. Dewhurst, *Impressionist Painting*, London, 1904, p. 31). But Pissarro did not really like London and was impatient to leave, when the news of the political situation in France improved. As he wrote to Théodore Duret, 'I am only here for a very short time. I count on returning to France as soon as possible. Yes, my dear Duret, I shan't stay here, and it is only abroad that one feels how beautiful, great and hospitable France is. What a difference here! One gathers only contempt, indifference, even rudeness; among colleagues there is a most egotistical jealousy and resentment. As for my private affairs, sales, are concerned, I've done nothing except with Durand-Ruel, who has bought two small pictures from me. My painting does not catch on, not at all, a fate which pursues me more or less everywhere' (letter, 30 May 1871, published in *Bulletin des Expositions*, Paris, 1931 – 2, III, and translated in part in J. Rewald, *Pissarro*, 1960, p. 22).

Although necessarily a subjective judgement, *La Route de Sydenham* is probably the finest of the 12 recorded London pictures of 1870 – 1. Indeed, it will be hard to find an equal to it among the whole of his work of the early 1870s, which may 'like that of Monet and Renoir, with good reason be described as the most purely impressionist in Pissarro's entire *oeuvre*'.

CAMILLE PISSARRO
French 1830 – 1903
La Route de Sydenham
Signed and dated 1871
Oil on canvas
Painted in April – May 1871
$18\frac{7}{8} \times 28\frac{3}{4}$ in. (48 × 73 cm.)
Sold 26.3.84 in London for £561,600 ($814,320)
Record auction price for a work by the artist
Purchased by the Trustees of the National Gallery, London

EDGAR DEGAS
French 1834 – 1917
Danseuse, pendant le Repos
Signed and inscribed
Pastel and black chalk on
board mounted on board
Painted *c.* 1880
30⅛ × 21⅞ in.
(76.5 × 55.5 cm.)
Sold 15.11.83 in New York for
$1,210,000 (£806,666)

EDGAR DEGAS
French 1834 – 1917
Deux Danseuses en Jupes vertes, Décor de Paysage
Stamped with signature
Oil on canvas
Painted *c.*1895
55 × 31½ in. (140 × 80 cm.)
Sold 16.5.84 in New York for $1,925,000
(£1,375,000)

HENRI DE
TOULOUSE-LAUTREC
French 1864 – 1901
Misia Natanson
Oil on board
Painted *c.* 1897
$29\frac{1}{8} \times 20\frac{7}{8}$ in.
(74 × 53 cm.)
Sold 16.5.84 in New
York for $423,500
(£302,500)
By order of the Estate of
David H. Heyman

Opposite
PIERRE AUGUSTE RENOIR
French 1841 – 1919
Femme au Chapeau blanc
Signed
Oil on canvas
Painted *c.* 1890
$21\frac{7}{8} \times 18\frac{1}{8}$ in.
(55.5 × 46 cm.)
Sold 15.11.83 in New
York for $1,265,000
(£843,333)
From the collection of
Paul Mellon

VINCENT VAN GOGH
Dutch 1853 – 90
Young Scheveningen Woman, knitting
Signed
Watercolour and gouache on
paper
Painted in December 1881 in The
Hague (Etten period)
$20\,^5/_8 \times 14\,^3/_8$ in. (52.2 × 36.5 cm.)
Sold 16.11.83 in New York for
$198,000 (£132,000)

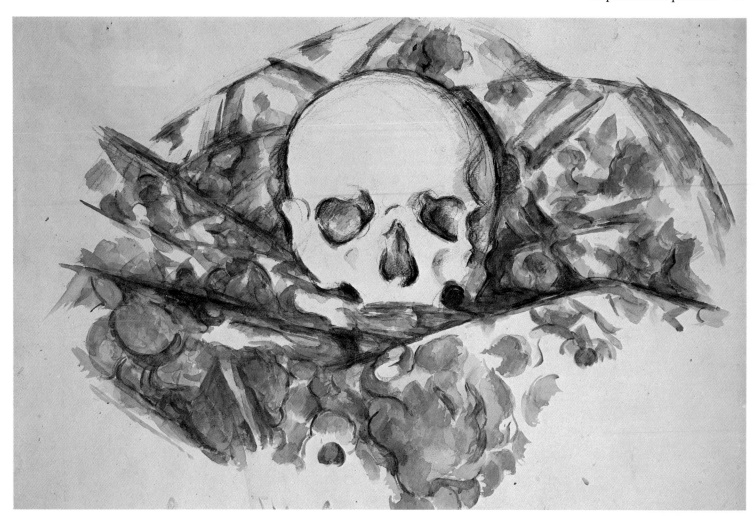

PAUL CÉZANNE
French 1839 – 1906
Crane sur une Draperie (recto); Arbres et Rochers à Bibémus (verso)
Watercolour and pencil on paper (recto), pencil (verso)
Painted *c.* 1902 – 6
12¼ × 18⅞ in. (31.2 × 48 cm.)
Sold 15.11.83 in New York for $550,000 (£366,666)
From the collection of Paul Mellon

PAUL CÉZANNE
French 1839 – 1906
Sucrier, Poires et Tapis
Oil on canvas
Painted *c.* 1893 – 4
$20\frac{1}{8} \times 24\frac{3}{4}$ in. (51.5 × 61.9 cm.)
Sold 15.11.83 in New York for $3,960,000 (£2,640,000)
From the collection of Henry P. McIlhenny

CLAUDE MONET
French 1840 – 1926
La Cathédrale dans le Brouillard
Signed and dated 94
Oil on canvas
$41\frac{3}{4} \times 28\frac{1}{2}$ in. (106 × 72.5 cm.)
Sold 16.5.84 in New York for
$1,265,000 (£903,571)

CLAUDE MONET
French 1840 – 1926
La Seine à Vetheuil
Signed
Oil on canvas
Painted *c.*1879
$21\frac{3}{8} \times 29$ in. (54.5 × 73.5 cm.)
Sold 16.5.84 in New York for $748,000 (£534,286)

PAUL SIGNAC
French 1863 – 1935
Le Port de Portrieux
Signed and inscribed 'Op.182' and dated 88
Oil on canvas
18⅛ × 21⅝ in. (46 × 55 cm.)
Sold 15.11.83 in New York for $396,000 (£264,000)
From the collection of Paul Mellon

Miró's Catalan Inspiration

MARILYN McCULLY

Joan Miró, who died last year at the age of 91, created an art that has become a familiar part of our own visual world. Although often private in meaning, his characteristic simplified forms, limited range of colours and organic line have universal appeal. To explore the seemingly infinite space of Miró's paintings is to embark on an odyssey that seems to begin in his imagination and arrive in our own; while in his sculpture, the same imaginative forms and humorous juxtapositions of objects seem to step out of his paintings into the world of three dimensions.

Miró himself said on several occasions that we must look to his homeland, Catalonia, where he lived the majority of his long life, to understand the sources of much of his imagery. Yet the departure for discussion about the meaning of Miró's work has usually been his life in Paris and his contact with the Surrealists in the 1920s (Miró lived in France from 1920 to 1931 and again during the Spanish Civil War). The story still to be written about Miró's life as an artist is that of his youth and artistic formation in Barcelona and in the Catalan countryside during the first two decades of this century, for there the inspiration for his approach to painting and his personal vocabulary of forms was born. That story is rich enough for a book, and this article seeks only to highlight those years and to suggest a few of the ways in which Miró's search for a pictorial language and style originated.

Barcelona, when Miró was an art student, was a lively city with unusual opportunities for artists. During the first decade of the century, the city's face was being changed by *modernista* architects like Antoni Gaudí, and the problems and the challenge of life in the city and in the new century were the subjects of its painters. The artist who gave this expression a radical new form was, of course, Picasso, and it was his success and his recognition in Paris that also inspired young Barcelona artists such as Miró in their search for a new art.

Miró (like Picasso) had begun his artistic training as a small child – drawing-classes at the age of 7 and then studies at the Barcelona art academy La Llotja. These were interrupted in 1911 by illness, and following a period of recuperation in the country at Montroig Miró returned to the city and began to attend classes at Francisco Galí's more liberal art school, where he met other artists whose aspirations to find a new artistic form were close to his own. Among them were Josep Llorens Artigas (the potter who championed Picasso in the 1920s and who would become Miró's collaborator on ceramic murals many years later) and the painter Enric Cristófol Ricart. In 1915 Miró and Ricart left Galí's academy and shared a studio not far from the flamboyant *modernista* music palace (designed by Domènech i Montaner) which had opened several years before and stood as a symbol of Catalan cultural pride.

Around the time Miró and his friend Ricart left formal art training, they began to frequent Josep Dalmau's art gallery on *carrer* Portaferrisa, which had won the reputation of being the centre of the Barcelona avant-garde ever since Dalmau had introduced cubist painting and Duchamp's *Nude Descending a Staircase* to Barcelona in 1912. Thereafter, Dalmau's was not only the principal exhibition space for foreign avant-garde artists, as well as some local artists, but

1. JOAN MIRÓ: *Village Landscape.*
1917. Pastel on paper,
22 × 17 ¼ in.
(56 × 44 cm.)
Fundació Miró, Barcelona

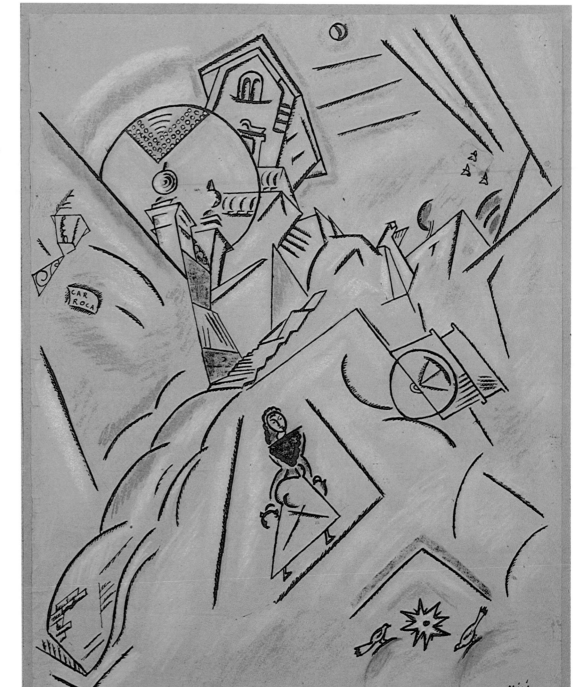

also their chief gathering place, particularly during World War I, when Spain remained a neutral country.

Barcelona, like Zurich and New York, became the temporary home during World War I for many artist-exiles, including Francis Picabia, Albert Gleizes, the Delaunays, Olga Sacharoff, Otto Lloyd and Arthur Cravan, among others, and their presence was of importance to young local artists such as Miró. Their exhibitions, experimental poetry and little magazines inspired Catalan artists and writers in similar endeavours. In 1917, for instance, with the help of Dalmau, Picabia published four issues of his Dada journal *391*, which included drawings, poems and essays principally by artists in the foreign community in Barcelona. Not only did this journal stimulate interest in their work, but it also drew attention to other important artists and writers of that time, including Guillaume Apollinaire. In its fourth issue *391* published Apollinaire's only coloured calligram, *L'Horloge de Demain*; his proto-Surrealist play, *Les Mamelles de Tiresias* (which directly influenced Miró[1]), was also privately produced in Barcelona in 1918.

These publications and the exhibitions of cubist and futurist-inspired paintings were especially important to Miró, whose developing style was affected not only by cubist space but by the typographical elements of new poetry. Miró's cover for the sole issue of the Catalan poet Salvat-Papasseit's tiny journal *Arc Voltaic* of February 1918 employed expressive typography with cubist-inspired drawing: the curvilinear elements of a nude are echoed both in a design of repeated arcs and also in the word 'voltaic' itself. Below the drawing, the aims of the journal read like a manifesto, 'Plasticity of the vertical, forms in emotion and evolution – vibrationism of ideas – poems in Herzian waves.' The words 'evolution' and 'vibrationism' in this case have specific reference to the artistic theories then in vogue in Barcelona propounded by two Uruguayan artists who were regular members of the Dalmau circle, Joaquín Torres Garcia (evolution = modern life) and Rafael Barradas (vibrationism = a style to convey the dynamism of modern life, based upon Italian futurism).

In another journal, *Trossos*, which was founded by the Catalan critic (and acquaintance and great admirer of Apollinaire) Josep Junoy, a drawing by Miró appeared accompanying a brief notice of his first exhibition in Barcelona, which was being held at the Dalmau Galleries in February – March 1918. Junoy (who undoubtedly wrote the notice) saw Miró's work as a new form arising from an essentially Catalan base:

> [Miró's paintings] attempt to awaken a new sensibility and to initiate a triumphal march towards a new classicism – the vitality of the *noucentistes* [the 'twentieth-century' artists of Catalonia] and the blood of the future – we at *Trossos* claim him as one of ours.

The drawing was based on a pastel of 1917 (Fig. 1) which demonstrates Miró's approach at that time. The strokes of blues, yellows, greens and white seem to radiate from linear elements, suggesting inspiration derived from Delaunay's shifting colour planes. (Robert Delaunay, known for what Apollinaire called 'orphic cubism', had exhibited at Dalmau's in 1916.) However, here line and the angularity of forms are primarily analytic cubist in inspiration and they occupy a relatively flat space with little perspective. The inclusion of representational forms – the birds at the lower right, the female figure in the lower centre and the architectural structures above – provides a curious mixture of simple representational notations in abstract surroundings. By referring to identifiable forms Miró perhaps appeared to Junoy to be sharing the *noucentista* painters' aim of a 'new classicism'. But from the very beginning these forms had taken on a notational character, almost like transfers or decals, which turned them into two-dimensional

2. JOAN MIRÓ: *The Farm.*
1921 – 2. Oil on canvas,
48¼ × 55¼ in.
(122.5 × 140.3 cm.). Private
Collection, U.S.A.

elements functioning more like typography and distinguished them from *noucentista* painting.
The seeds of Miró's style were thus already very much in evidence at the time of his first exhibition
in 1918.

By the end of the war, most of the exiles had left Barcelona – Miró, Ricart and Llorens Artigas
along with them – for Paris, which once more became the art capital of the world, and there
Dada and later surrealism challenged a new generation of artists. Miró, like Picasso before him,
had had to leave Barcelona to develop a fully personal style. In Paris he eventually gained
international recognition as a surrealist, but his roots still remained in his native Catalonia and
in the special set of artistic circumstances that had initially stimulated a new artistic vision.

In the early 1920s an important series of paintings based upon memories of the countryside
in Montroig shows how Miró's painting evolved at that time from a simplistic, almost Rousseau-
like, patterning of objects into a heightened dream-state, which is a prelude to his well-known
surrealist compositions of the following years. *The Farm* (1921 – 2; Fig. 2), for example, appears super-real, as if it were lit by high-intensity lamps rather than the Spanish sun, and, in
this way, gives the impression of being a memory image rather than an image after nature – very

3. JOAN MIRÓ: *The Wine Bottle.*
1924. Oil on canvas,
28¾ × 25½ in. (73 × 65 cm.).
Fundació Miró, Barcelona

much in the spirit of Apollinaire's 1917 definition of 'surrealism' (in the introduction to *Les Mamelles de Tiresias*), in which invention after nature creates a new reality. It is the combination of recollections of his youth with his conception of space and heightened colours and light that becomes the fundamental quality of Miró's best-known works.

The Wine Bottle (1924; Fig. 3) is a painting in which the space of the imagination – specifically the landscape of Catalonia – provides a visual field for Miró's forms, whose meaning resides in his experience; for us as viewers, however, they are compelling, often playful, signs that trigger our own imaginations. Hills subtly define a jagged horizon, while the three principal elements of the composition seem fixed in front of us: the bottle of wine (*vi* means wine in Catalan) at the upper left, a snake-like creature in the lower centre, whose red eye is like the bull's-eye of a target, and the imaginary insect at the upper right. All three share both foreground space (as if they were pasted on a transparent mirror) as well as the brown ground of the overall canvas.

Moreover, brush-strokes and line are also repeated in various areas of the composition, creating patterns which unify space; for example, the whiskers of the snake are echoed in the lines of the sky. In this way, the whole space is collapsed into one indeterminate location, and the most plausible reading for this collection of images is that it exists not only in front of our eyes but in the imagination of the artist.

Miró's work of the twenties and thirties was done primarily outside Catalonia. His well-known surrealist paintings of this major period of creativity seem increasingly similar, because his vocabulary of forms is reduced to a personal system of notation, but the endless variety of these and later works – both in painting and lithography – clearly demonstrates Miró's rich and fertile imagination. Experiments in sculpture in the thirties were particularly fruitful, and some of the most memorable images of surrealist objects are Miró's imaginative juxtapositions – sometimes found objects, sometimes organic forms. A study of Miró as a sculptor (particularly in his later years) is another chapter of his life that needs to be fully explored.

By 1936 Miró's imagery had taken on a violence that was conveyed both through his distorted, gesturing creatures and also through intense colour. Miró had returned to Catalonia for a few years in the 1930s and his work reflected the growing conflict in his homeland and the imminent civil war. In 1937 he returned to France and along with Picasso, who showed *Guernica*, Miró exhibited a major large work, *The Reaper* (now lost), in the Republican Spanish Pavilion at the Paris Exposition that year. The theme of *The Reaper*, according to Roland Penrose, was the heroic Catalan peasant who seemed 'to shout defiance [and] grew like a plant from the soil crowned by a crumpled Phrygian cap [the typically Catalan red *barretina*] and surrounded by a tattered star and large circular spots like explosions.'[2]

After the Spanish Civil War, unlike many other artists and intellectuals, Miró returned to Catalonia and continued to work there at a time when artistic life under Franco was severely restricted. The absence of foreign art journals and exhibitions during the 1940s meant that Miró's presence was the only link with avant-garde art for young artists (such as Antoni Tàpies). A full appraisal of Catalan art in these years will surely judge Miró as the central influence for artists of that decade.

Eventually Miró moved to Majorca, where he worked with greater freedom in an island retreat, and where his friend Josep Lluís Sert (who had himself chosen exile in the United States) built him in 1956 the studio in which he and his wife then settled. But Miró was not silent. He produced a large body of work in the last 30 years of his life, including various experimental formats (such as burned paintings), lithographs, sculpture, ceramics and much graphic work in support of Catalan culture (including posters, book and record covers). In 1975, along with his friends Joan Prats (whom he had known since 1917) and Sert, Miró helped establish the Fundació Miró, which both houses a collection of his own work and also functions as a study centre for contemporary art. In this light-filled building designed by Sert on Montjuich mountain overlooking Barcelona, Miró has not only given young Barcelona artists the opportunity (as he had had at Dalmau's) to meet, exhibit and see new art, as well as major twentieth-century masterpieces (recently Duchamp's *Nude Descending a Staircase* returned to Barcelona to be exhibited at the Foundation), but he has also left a living reminder to all of us of the life, dedication and great creativity of an artist who changed and enriched our own visual world.

1. Margit Rowell discusses the importance of Apollinaire for Miró in 'Miró, Apollinaire and *L'Enchanteur pourissant'*, *Art News*, October 1972, pp. 64 – 7.
2. Roland Penrose, *Miró* (London, 1970), p. 89.

MAURICE DE VLAMINCK
French 1876 – 1958
Paysage au Bois mort
Signed
Oil on canvas
Painted *c.*1906
$25\frac{5}{8} \times 31\frac{7}{8}$ in. (65 × 81 cm.)
Sold 26.3.84 in London for £367,200 ($532,440)
Record auction price for a work by the artist

ODILON REDON
French 1840 – 1916
La Barque Mystique
Signed
Pastel
Executed *c.*1900
20½ × 25½ in. (52 × 65 cm.)
Sold 5.12.83 in London for £118,800 ($174,636)

AMEDEO MODIGLIANI
Italian 1884 – 1920
Bambina con Trecce
Signed
Oil on canvas
Painted *c.* 1918
$23\frac{5}{8} \times 17\frac{7}{8}$ in.
(60 × 45.5 cm.)
Sold 16.5.84 in New York
for $1,650,000 (£1,178,571)
Record auction price for a
work by the artist

FERNAND LÉGER
French 1881 – 1955
Paysage avec Figures
Signed
Oil on canvas
Painted in 1921
36 × 25 ¼ in. (90 × 63.5 cm.)
Sold 16.5.84 in New York for
$462,000 (£330,000)

MARC CHAGALL
Russian/French b. 1887
Le Cosaque
Signed and dated 12
Gouache on paper
$17\frac{1}{4} \times 12\frac{1}{2}$ in.
$(44 \times 32$ cm.)
Sold 6.12.83 in London
for £97,200 ($141,912)

MARC CHAGALL
Russian/French b. 1887
Fleurs dans la Rue
Signed and dated 1935
Oil on canvas
35½ × 46 in. (90 × 117 cm.)
Sold 16.5.84 in New York for $605,000 (£432,143)
By order of the Estate of Herbert Segerman

FERDINAND HODLER
Swiss 1853 – 1918
Malojalandschaft
Signed and dated 1907
Oil on canvas
20 × 31 in. (51 × 79 cm.)
Sold 5.12.83 in London for £259,200 ($381,024)

EMIL NOLDE
German 1867 – 1956
Blumen
Signed
Watercolour on paper
$17\frac{3}{4} \times 13\frac{3}{4}$ in.
(45 × 35 cm.)
Sold 6.12.83 in
London for £54,000
($78,840)

PAUL KLEE
German/Swiss 1879 – 1940
Rote Säulen vorbeiziehend
Signed and dated 1928
Casein on paper laid by the artist on board
13⅜ × 18½ in. (34 × 47 cm.)
Sold 17.5.84 in New York for $176,000 (£124,823)
By order of the Estate of Stephen Richard Currier and Audrey Currier

PAUL DELVAUX
Belgian b. 1898
Une Rue; la Nuit
Signed and dated 1-47
Oil on masonite
48 × 96½ in. (122 × 245 cm.)
Sold 16.5.84 in New York for $286,000 (£204,285)
Record auction price for a work by the artist

RENÉ MAGRITTE
Belgian 1898 – 1967
Les Droits de l'Homme
Signed
Oil on canvas
Painted between
September 1947 and
mid-January 1948
57¼ × 45½ in.
(145 × 115 cm.)
Sold 26.3.84 in
London for £248,400
($360,180)

ALBERTO GIACOMETTI
Swiss 1901 – 66
Chariot
Signed
Bronze with light-brown patina
Executed in 1950
56 in. (142.2 cm.) high
Sold 15.11.83 in New York for $1,375,000
(£916,666)
Record auction price for a work by the artist
and for any 20th-century sculpture
From the collection of Mrs Fernand Leval

CY TWOMBLY
American b. 1929
Untitled (Grey Painting)
Signed, inscribed and dated May 1969
Oil and crayon on canvas
$79\frac{1}{2} \times 94\frac{1}{2}$ in. (200 × 240 cm.)
Sold 6.12.83 in London for £54,000 ($78,840)

JEAN DUBUFFET
French b. 1901
Service de Barbe
Signed and dated *juillet 59*
Mixed media on canvas
45½ × 35 in.
(116 × 89 cm.)
Sold 26.6.84 in London
for £135,000 ($184,950)
From the estate of the
late Karl Ströher,
Darmstadt

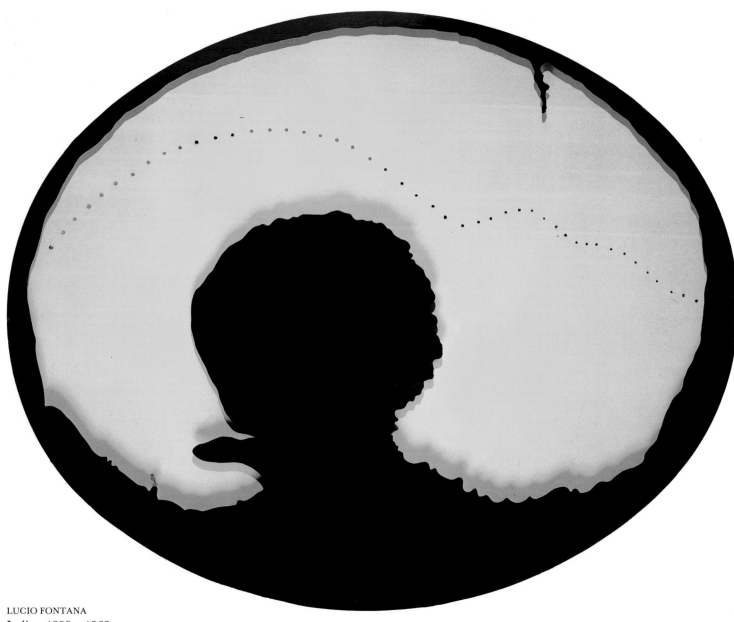

LUCIO FONTANA
Italian 1899 – 1968
Concetto spaziale – Teatrino
Signed and titled on reverse
Yellow 'cementite' on canvas and black-lacquered wood
50 × 63¼ in. (126.5 × 160.5 cm.)
Sold 5.12.83 in Rome for L.23,000,000 (£10,000)

JACKSON POLLOCK
American 1912 – 56
Number 12A 1948: Yellow, Gray, Black
Signed and dated 48
Enamel on gesso ground on paper
$22\frac{3}{4} \times 30\frac{1}{4}$ in. (57.5 × 78 cm.)
Sold 9.11.83 in New York for $187,000 (£124,666)
From the collection of Betty Parsons

ROBERT RAUSCHENBERG
American b. 1925
The Red Painting
Signed and dated 53 on the reverse
'Combine painting': oil, fabric and
paper on canvas
70¾ × 48 in. (179.5 × 122 cm.)
Sold 8.11.83 in New York for
$462,000 (£308,000)
Record auction price for a work by
the artist
From the collection of David
Whitney

FRANZ KLINE
American 1910 – 62
Harleman
Signed and dated 60 on the reverse
Oil on canvas
53 × 102¼ in. (134.5 × 259.5 cm.)
Sold 8.11.83 in New York for $506,000 (£337,333)
Record auction price for a work by the artist
From the collection of Pauli Hirsh

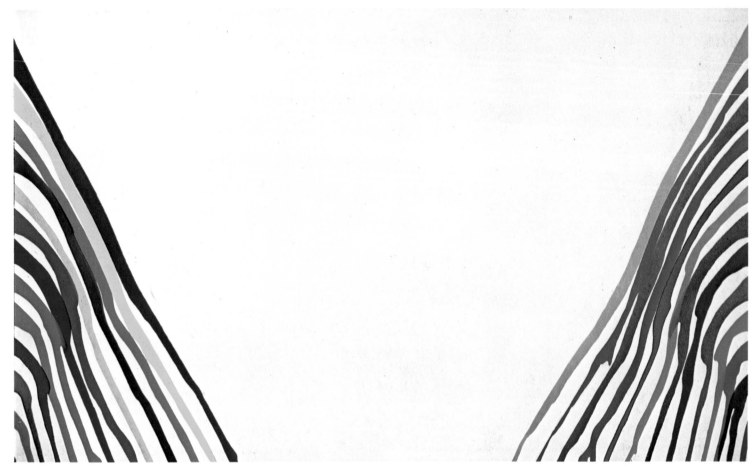

MORRIS LOUIS
American 1912 – 62
Sigma
Acrylic on canvas
Painted in 1961
103 × 170½ in. (261.6 × 433.1 cm.)
Sold 8.5.84 in New York for $473,000 (£337,857)
From the collection of Mr and Mrs Eugene M. Schwartz

ANDY WARHOL
American b. 1930
Coca-Cola
Signed and dated 62 on the reverse
Oil on canvas
82 × 57 in. (208 × 145 cm.)
Sold 8.11.83 in New York for
$143,000 (£95,333)
From the collection of Pauli Hirsh

ANDY WARHOL
American b. 1930
Self-Portrait
Signed on the reverse
Acrylic and silk screen on canvas
Painted *c.*1967
72 × 72 in. (182 × 182 cm.)
Sold 26.6.84 in London for £72,360 ($99,133)
From the estate of the late Karl Ströher, Darmstadt

RICHARD DIEBENKORN
American b. 1922
Yellow Porch
Initialled and dated 61
Oil on canvas
69 7/8 × 66 5/8 in. (177.5 × 169.2 cm.)
Sold 8.5.84 in New York for $440,000 (£314,285)

DUANE HANSON
American b. 1925
Man against Wall
Polyester resin, fibreglass, oil and
mixed media
Executed in 1974
69 in. (175 cm.) high
Sold 8.11.83 in New York for
$121,000 (£80,660)
Record auction price for a work by
the artist

Opposite
RICHARD LINDNER
German 1901 – 78
Couple
Signed and dated 1977
Oil on canvas
80 × 70 in. (203.2 × 177.8 cm.)
Sold 8.5.84 in New York for
$253,000 (£180,714)

GEORG BASELITZ
German b. 1938
Elke (schwarze Akt)
Signed and dated 76 on
the reverse
Oil on canvas
98½ × 78¾ in.
(250 × 200 cm.)
Sold 26.6.84 in London
for £86,400 ($118,368)
Record auction price for
a work by the artist

WILLIAM ROBERTS, R.A.
British 1895 – 1980
Died of Wounds
Signed and dated 1919
Watercolour, bodycolour, pen and black ink
$17\frac{1}{2} \times 20\frac{3}{4}$ in. (44.4 × 52.2 cm.)
Sold 9.3.84 in London for £18,900 ($27,972)
Record auction price for a work by the artist

PERCY WYNDHAM LEWIS
British 1882 – 1957
Red and Black Olympus
Signed and dated 1922
Watercolour, bodycolour, pen and black ink
10 × 17 in. (25.4 × 43.2 cm.)
Sold 9.3.84 in London for £30,240 ($44,755)
Record auction price for a work by the artist

DAVID BOMBERG
British 1890 – 1957
Composition: study for 'Reading from Torah' (recto and verso)
Recto only showing
Signed *c.*1914
Watercolour, bodycolour and pencil (recto), pencil (verso)
7⅞ × 8½ in. (20.2 × 21.5 cm.)
Sold 8.6.84 in London for £12,960 ($18,273)

WALTER RICHARD SICKERT, A.R.A.
British 1860 – 1942
Brighton Pierrots
Signed and dated 1915
Oil on canvas
25 × 30 in. (63.5 × 76.2 cm.)
Sold 4.11.83 in London for £64,800 ($92,200)
Record auction price for a work by the artist

SIR JOHN LAVERY, R.A., R.S.A., R.H.A.
British 1856 – 1941
The Weighing Room, Hurst Park
Signed, inscribed and dated 1924
Oil on canvas
30 × 40 in. (76.2 × 101.6 cm.)
Sold 21.11.83 in London at Christie's South Kensington for £26,000 ($39,000)

SIR ALFRED MUNNINGS, P.R.A.
British 1878 – 1959
Norwich Fair: a Stall at Bungay Races
Signed and dated 1909
Oil on canvas
20 × 24½ in. (50.8 × 61 cm.)
Sold 9.3.84 in London for £70,200 ($103,896)

SIR ALFRED MUNNINGS, P.R.A.
British 1878 – 1959
The Start at Newmarket
Signed
Oil on canvas
25 × 30 in. (67.5 × 76.2 cm.)
Sold 9.3.84 in London for £237,600 ($351,648)

LAURENCE STEPHEN LOWRY, R.A.
British 1887 – 1976
Industrial Landscape
Signed and dated 1944
Oil on panel
21½ × 24 in. (54.6 × 60.9 cm.)
Sold 4.11.83 in London for £29,160 ($43,740)
By order of the Executors of the late Dame Rebecca West, D.B.E.

Drawings, Watercolours and Prints

GIULIO PIPPI, IL ROMANO
Italian, Rome 1499 – Mantua 1546
Design for a Fruit Bowl, with Vine Branches, Leaves and Grapes
Black chalk, pen and brown ink, brown wash
12³⁄₄ × 13¹⁄₄ in.
(32.6 × 33.8 cm.)
Sold 3.7.84 in London for £172,800 ($231,552)
By order of the Trustees of the Chatsworth Settlement
Drawn for Federigo II Gonzaga, Duke of Mantua, in the 1520s

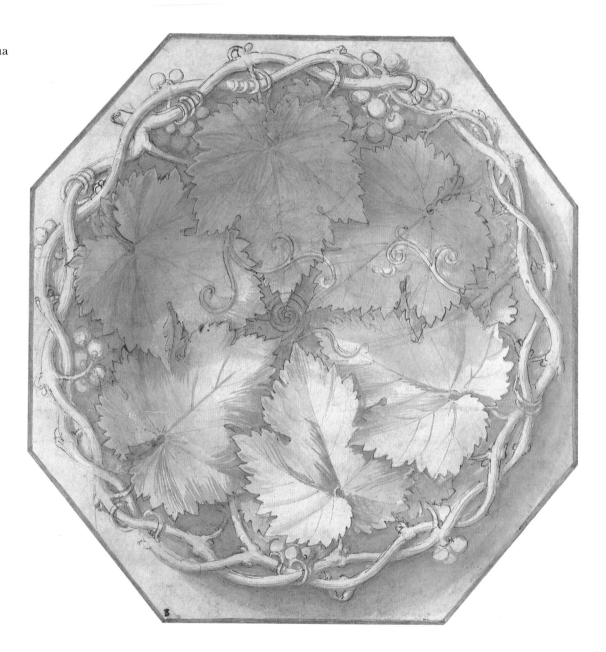

Old Master Drawings from Chatsworth

NOËL ANNESLEY

So much has already been written about this event that another article may seem superfluous, and too many sales have been described as 'the sale of the century'. Yet this has as good claims as any. Old Master drawings are, on the whole, of somewhat cerebral appeal and attract a comparatively small following of collectors, dealers and museum people. But many weeks before the evening of 3 July, and even before the appearance of the catalogue, we were besieged with requests for seats at the sale. By seven o'clock Christie's was thronged as if in the rush hour, and crowds of excited bystanders spilled down the staircase into the street, where contact with the auction was by association only. The heat generated by the television lights made everyone grateful that the spell of warm weather had been replaced by the cooler temperatures more characteristic of an English summer. From the competition for the first lot, a very fine drawing by the Florentine sculptor Baccio Bandinelli, it was clear that an unusually high proportion of those present were not mere spectators but determined to bid and to buy, and the prices for the two Baroccis that followed, four and five times their respective estimates, set a pattern for much for the sale.

The fame of the collection of drawings at Chatsworth, formed for the most part by William Cavendish, 2nd Duke of Devonshire (1672 – 1729), has been established since the beginning of the 18th century. Moreover, with just a few exceptions, notably the three Raphael 'auxiliary cartoons' for the *Transfiguration* which the 6th Duke was generous enough to give to Sir Thomas Lawrence, and the Claude *Liber Veritatis* and the Van Dyck sketchbook which had been allocated to the British Museum in part satisfaction of death duty in 1957, the collection had remained undisturbed until this group of 71 drawings, from a total of some 2,000, came on the market.

The selection had been made with the aim of expressing the character of the collection as a whole, with its particular strength in the Italian Schools and in the work of Rubens, Van Dyck and Rembrandt, while minimising the overall loss. It is, of course, not size that makes the collection so remarkable, but the high level of quality throughout. It conspicuously lacks the plethora of copies and optimistic attributions often found in old (and sometimes in newer) collections, and the Duke, who is believed to have been bidding himself at the Lely sale of 1688 when aged only 16, must have been an exceptional judge of a drawing. For this, not his rank, he certainly earned the respect of his fellow-collectors at the time, and when in 1723 he brought off his greatest coup in buying the collection of Nicolaes Flinck, Pierre Crozat, the leading French connoisseur, wrote to congratulate him. Many of the finest sheets at Chatsworth bear the Lely or Flinck marks. In the present sale 11 came from Lely, the most important being the Raphael *Saint Paul*, and no less than 24 from Flinck, the group of Rembrandt landscapes, taken from the series of 29 that mark his best known contribution to Chatsworth, three Van Dycks, and, perhaps less expectedly, many Italian sheets including a Giulio Romano that had previously belonged to Lely, and the Leonardo da Vinci caricatures.

ANDREA MANTEGNA
Italian, Padua 1431 – Mantua 1506
Saints Peter, Paul, John the Evangelist and Zeno
Pen and brown ink
$7\frac{3}{4} \times 5\frac{1}{4}$ in. (19.5 × 13.2 cm.)
Sold 3.7.84 in London for £1,188,000 ($1,591,920)
A study for the left wing of the San Zeno altarpiece in Verona, painted in 1456 – 9

The 2nd Duke was always eager to show his collection to other enthusiasts, and this hospitable attitude has been maintained by his successors. Furthermore, since the last war the drawings have been the subject of eight special exhibitions at home and abroad, two of which, in 1962 – 3 and 1969, were seen at more than a dozen museums in the United States and Canada, and selections shown in Tokyo, Jerusalem and elsewhere. In 1979 – 80 the widely travelled *Treasures from Chatsworth* exhibition also included 40 drawings, and, in addition, individual sheets continue to be lent to exhibitions all over the world.

The unique opportunity to acquire drawings with this provenance, where even the lesser masters were represented by work of exceptional quality, caused prices to reach dizzy heights, so that the phrase 'an auction record for a work by the artist', familiar to readers of Christie's annual *Review*, and perhaps in these inflationary days over-familiar, has been omitted as otiose from the captions to the drawings here illustrated. Of the 39 artists represented, only three failed that peculiar test. The earliest drawing from Chatsworth was a study by Mantegna for the left wing of his altarpiece in the Church of San Zeno, Verona, executed in 1456 – 9. The four standing saints, including Zeno himself, form a group of almost sculptural precision and are projected with a power out of all proportion to the small dimensions of the sheet. The rich brown ink is marvellously preserved. This became the first drawing to exceed a million pounds at auction and was bought by the Getty Museum. To continue this brief survey chronologically, we come to the four tiny caricatures by Leonardo da Vinci. Leonardo's caricatures are less appealing to modern taste than they were to his contemporaries, and it is perhaps for no better reason that these, completely characteristic though they are in the minute delicacy of touch lavished upon monstrous features, were questioned in some quarters before the sale, though accepted by all Leonardo scholars. The caricatures, like many more at Chatsworth and in the Royal Collection, come from the series etched by Wenceslaus Hollar in the 17th century, so popular that it 'ran' to three editions. All had previously belonged to Thomas Howard, Earl of Arundel, the contemporary of Charles I, and the 2nd Duke's only noble predecessor as a collector of drawings. The quartet aroused strong competition, and the most expensive is illustrated on the contents page. Also deriving from the end of the 15th century, but in every other way contrasted, was the two-sided album page, of imposing size, assembled by Giorgio Vasari, the 16th-century Florentine painter, architect and author of the *Lives of the Painters*, who has claims to be the first systematically to collect drawings. These he mounted in large volumes, probably as many as twelve, usually several drawings to each page, embellished by Vasari himself with the decorative borders and other motifs. Dispersal of the collection began quite soon after his death in 1574, and in course of time most of the pages were dismembered and the individual drawings sold. Of the relatively few to survive intact this one from Chatsworth is surely the most spectacular to remain in private hands. The nine drawings arranged on front and back are by Filippino Lippi and his circle. Perhaps the most remarkable in sensitivity and charm is the *Head of a Youth*, executed in metalpoint on a violet ground of a shade that eludes the art of colour reproduction. This seems to be by Raffaellino del Garbo, while the sheet mounted below it, prepared with an ochre ground, could only be by Filippino, who brought to the medium of metalpoint a unique dash and flair. Among so many arresting objects in the sale the 'Vasari Sheet' exercised a potent spell, and a very high price had been predicted. Even so the £3,240,000 ($4,341,600) paid by the New York collector Ian Woodner, outbidding the Getty Museum, confounded all expectations. It had been Raphael's turn a few minutes before. Raphael was

PAGE FROM VASARI'S *LIBRO DE'*
DISEGNI

Approximately $22\frac{1}{2} \times 18\frac{1}{4}$ in.
(57×46 cm.) overall
Sold 3.7.84 in London for
£3,240,000 ($4,341,600)

Recto
Head of a Youth, by
Filippino Lippi or Raffaellino
del Garbo
Metalpoint heightened with
white bodycolour on pale
mauve preparation
$11\frac{1}{4} \times 8\frac{1}{4}$ in.
(28.8×20.1 cm.)
Sheet of Figure Studies, by
Filippino Lippi
Metalpoint heightened with
white bodycolour on ochre
preparation
$8\frac{3}{4} \times 13$ in. (22.1×33 cm.)
Two smaller studies in
metalpoint attributed to
Filippino Lippi

Verso
A Putto with a Piece of
Drapery, by Raffaellino del
Garbo
Pen and brown ink
8 × 5 in. (20.3 × 12.3 cm.)
Design for an Altarpiece in a
Frame with Pilasters and an
Acanthus Frieze: Saint James
between Saints Anthony
Abbot and Catherine of
Alexandria, attributed to
Raffaellino del Garbo
Pen, brush and brown ink,
watercolour and bodycolour
12 × 10 in. (31.1 × 25.5 cm.)
Two pen studies of angels by
Filippino Lippi, and two
metalpoint studies attributed
to him

the last of the great Italian Renaissance masters to employ metalpoint, and the *Saint Paul rending his Garments*, a study for the tapestry cartoon now in the Royal Collection, is an exquisite example. On this occasion the Getty Museum were successful, at £1,512,000 ($2,026,080). Another drawing by Raphael, the *Head and Hand of an Apostle*, was the single most important in the sale. Executed in black chalk, this life-size auxiliary cartoon for his last masterpiece, *The Transfiguration* of 1520, dominated the viewing beforehand. Here again the Getty Museum was outbid by a private American collector, who had to pay £3,564,000 ($4,775,760), a record price for any drawing.

A feature of the Chatsworth collection is the rich holding not only of Raphael himself but of artists in his school, some of them exceptionally gifted in their own right, and here seen at their best. Giulio Romano, for instance. Shortly after Raphael's death he went to work for the Gonzagas, Dukes of Mantua. His major decorative schemes for the Palazzo del Te were represented in the sale, as was a less demanding side of his employment, with a design for a fruit bowl to be made of vine leaves in silver or gilt. This beautiful drawing, as fresh in condition as in conception, was bought by a private collector for £172,800 ($231,552).

There is no space to describe the other Italian sheets in such detail. The 2nd Duke, in common with his contemporaries, must have had a passion for the elegant draughtsmanship of Parmigianino. Of the 54 sheets he assembled, three were chosen to display different facets of this delightful artist. The intimate red chalk study of the *Virgin nursing the Child,* where she has forsaken a chair in favour of a more comfortable position on the ground, anticipates the naturalism often espoused by the Carraccis, and even that of certain French 18th-century draughtsmen. It fetched £167,400 ($224,316), while a fastidious profile study of a man, executed in pen and ink with a concentration worthy of Dürer, fetched £75,600 ($101,304). A magnificent landscape study, one of the few generally accepted as the work of Titian, and full of Giorgionesque echoes, brought £410,400 ($549,936).

The Dutch and Flemish drawings at Chatsworth are no less remarkable than the Italian. The acquisition of Nicolaes Flinck's collection has already been mentioned, and it was no surprise that the group of landscape drawings by his father Govaert's master, Rembrandt, attracted enormous interest. The earliest was the *Two Cottages*, of the late 1630s, and this shows Rembrandt's preoccupation with form and texture, and the particular relish with which he conveys the moss forming on the decaying thatch in craggy penwork of the kind that inspired Van Gogh. In the 1640s and early 1650s the artist was in the habit of walking and sketching in the immediate vicinity of Amsterdam, and he produced on a small, yet almost infinite scale, haunting evocations of this quiet, undemonstrative countryside. He would choose a modest farmhouse or ruin, a bend in the river, a view across a dyke or an estuary, a road in woodland, and convey air, atmosphere, light, with the utmost economy of means, a few pen strokes, whether delicate or firm, and (usually) light applications of washes. Sometimes, as in the view of the Castle of Kostverloren on the Amstel, he would prepare the paper with a warm brown tint. This was the most powerful drawing of the group and fetched the highest price. But others preferred the sailing-boat near a clump of reeds, or the view by the ramparts of Amsterdam, close to where Rembrandt lived for the last ten years of his life.

While Rembrandt brought a quality of apparent simplicity and directness to landscape, he was not, of course, the only great Northern artist to respond with enthusiasm to what he saw

Opposite

RAFFAELLO SANZIO, called RAPHAEL
Italian, Urbino 1483 – Rome 1520
A Man's Head and Hand
Black chalk over dotted underdrawing pounced through
14¼ × 13½ in. (36.3 × 34.6 cm.)
Sold 3.7.84 in London for £3,564,000 ($4,775,760)
The auxiliary cartoon for the head and hand of one of the
Apostles in Raphael's *Transfiguration*, commissioned by Cardinal
Giulio de'Medici and now in the Vatican. The altarpiece was
almost completed at the time of Raphael's death in 1520.

in the country. The 2nd Duke must have greatly admired
Rubens's nature studies, to judge from those at Chatsworth,
and one of the finest, *A Man threshing beside a Waggon*, was in
the sale. Drawn about 1615 – 17 in black chalk with touches
of colour and pen, this freshly observed scene fetched £756,000
($1,013,040). The waggon occurs in three paintings. Rubens's
pupil Van Dyck seems to have made his rare landscape studies
more for his own relaxation than with any painting in view.
The one in this sale, however, from the 1630s, typical in its
fluent use of watercolour which anticipates effects attempted
by English artists 200 years later, is related to the background
of an idealised portrait of Margaret Lemon, the painter's
mistress. Both artists' diverse gifts were well displayed.
Rubens's studies for a *Last Supper* show an adaptation for his
own use of earlier models in penwork at once powerful and
personal, while Van Dyck's early *Entombment* may be dependent on both Titian and Rubens, but yields to neither in pro-
fundity of expression. And his chalk portrait of the painter
Hendrick van Balen, one of several such studies from Flinck's
collection at Chatsworth, shows his powers of characterisa-
tion at their most subtle.

RAFFAELLO SANZIO, called RAPHAEL
Italian, Urbino 1483 – Rome 1520
Saint Paul rending his Garments
Metalpoint heightened with white bodycolour on lilac-grey
preparation
9 × 4¼ in. (22.9 × 10.3 cm.)
Sold 3.7.84 in London for £1,512,000 ($2,026,080)
A study for the figure of Saint Paul on the left of the tapestry
cartoon of the *Sacrifice at Lystra*, now on loan from the Royal
Collection to the Victoria & Albert Museum. The cartoons were
executed in 1514 – 15.

Chatsworth is noted for its superb series of drawings by the French print-maker Jacques Callot, and two large and important studies for prints were in the sale, the *Prince de Phalsbourg* and a *View of Florence*, the second of which was classified as Claude's until the 1920s, no doubt owing to the rich and atmospheric use of wash.

There are fewer German and Swiss drawings, but the Holbein portrait is a widely exhibited masterpiece which made a strong end to the sale. The unidentified sitter has been well described as probably 'one of the powerful and not usually overscrupulous members of the Court of Henry VIII', but whatever the defects of his character Holbein has modelled his features and the textures of skin and incipient beard with astonishing refinement. It became the fifth lot in the sale to exceed one million pounds when the Getty Museum acquired it for £1,566,000 ($2,098,440).

In the space of just under two hours these drawings from Chatsworth were sold for a total of £21,179,880 ($28,381,039), the highest yet for any single-session sale. It was an experience that no one present is likely to forget.

GIROLAMO FRANCESCO MARIA
MAZZOLA, IL PARMIGIANINO
Italian, Parma 1503 – Casal
Maggiore 1540
The Virgin nursing the Child
Red chalk heightened with white
bodycolour on pale grey paper
$9\frac{1}{2} \times 7$ in. (24.3 × 17.5 cm.)
Sold 3.7.84 in London for
£167,400 ($224,316)
Datable to 1524, when
Parmigianino was working for
Conte Gian Carlo Sanvitale
at Fontanellato. A similar chair
appears in his portrait of the
Count now at Naples.

Opposite
GIOVANNI ANTONIO LICINIO DA
PORDENONE
Italian, Pordenone *c.*1484 –
Ferrara 1539
An Allegory of Time
Pen and brown ink, brown wash
heightened with white on grey
(formerly blue?) paper, faintly
squared in black chalk
$11 \times 16\frac{1}{2}$ in. (27.5 × 41.9 cm.)
Sold 3.7.84 in London for
£388,800 ($529,992)
A *modello* for a section of the attic
story of the façade fresco of
Palazzo d'Anna, Venice, datable
to the early 1530s. The
composition was used for a
chiaroscuro woodcut by Niccolò
Vicentino.

FEDERICO BAROCCI
Italian, Urbino 1526 – 1612
The Entombment
Black chalk and oil paint on
oiled paper
18¾ × 14 in.
(47.6 × 35.5 cm.)
Sold 3.7.84 in London for
£388,800 ($529,992)
A study for the altarpiece
painted for the church of
Santa Croce at Senigallia
in 1579 – 82. This was one
of Barocci's most influential
compositions. The building
in the background is the
Ducal Palace at Urbino.

SIR PETER PAUL RUBENS

Flemish, Siegen 1577 – Antwerp 1640

Three Groups of Apostles in a Last Supper

Inscribed by the artist *Gestus magis largi longiqué – Brachijs extensis* (The gestures [should be] more expansive with arms outstretched)

Pen and brown ink

11 1/2 × 17 in. (29.5 × 43.5 cm.)

Sold 3.7.84 in London for £604,800 ($810,432)

One of two drawings with projects for a *Last Supper* composition, echoing a number of Italian prototypes including Raphael, Michelangelo and possibly Caravaggio. On the back of this sheet are three studies of Medea with her slain children.

HANS HOLBEIN THE YOUNGER
German, Augsburg 1497 –
London 1543
Portrait of a Scholar or Cleric
With initials H.H. top left
Black and red chalk, brush
and grey-black ink and wash
on pale pink preparation
8½ × 7¼ in.
(21.8 × 18.4 cm.)
Sold 3.7.84 in London for
£1,566,000 ($2,098,440)
This portrait of a cleric,
scholar or possibly a lawyer
was executed by Holbein in
his second English period,
1532 – 43. It may have
formed part of the celebrated
album of portrait studies
formerly in the Lumley and
Arundel Collections.

SIR ANTHONY VAN DYCK
Flemish, Antwerp 1599 –
London 1641
Portrait of Hendrick van Balen
Black chalk
$9\frac{1}{2} \times 7\frac{1}{2}$ in.
(24.3 × 19.7 cm.)
Sold 3.7.84 in London for
£583,200 ($781,488)
Drawn between 1627 and
1632, this portrait of the
painter under whom Van
Dyck had studied in 1610 was
made in connection with the
Iconography, for which it was
engraved by Pontius

JACQUES CALLOT
French, Nancy 1592 – 1635
Louis de Lorraine-Guise, Prince de Phalsbourg, on Horseback
Black chalk, brown wash
9³⁄₄ × 13 in. (24.7 × 33.3 cm.)
Sold 3.7.84 in London for £124,200 ($166,428)
The Prince de Phalsbourg was a bastard of Cardinal de Guise. The drawing was etched by Callot in or before 1624.

REMBRANDT HARMENSZ. VAN RIJN
Dutch, Leyden 1606 – Amsterdam 1669
View on the Amstel with the Castle of Kostverloren
Pen and brown ink, brown wash and touches of bodycolour on paper tinted brown
$5\frac{3}{4} \times 8\frac{1}{2}$ in. (14.5 × 21.2 cm.)
Sold 3.7.84 in London for £648,000 ($868,320)
One of the celebrated series of landscapes acquired by the 2nd Duke of Devonshire with the Flinck Collection in 1723, this dates from
1650 – 2 and is one of no fewer than six representations by Rembrandt of the Castle of Kostverloren, which was on the stretch of the
Amstel where he evidently walked most frequently

GIOVANNI BATTISTA TIEPOLO
Italian, Venice 1692 – Madrid 1770
The Rest on the Flight into Egypt
Black chalk, pen and brown ink, brown
wash, laid on an 18th-century Venetian
sheet
11 × 7½ in. (27.3 × 19.8 cm.)
Sold 29.11.83 in London for £34,560
($50,803)
One of over 70 drawings of the Holy
Family datable 1754 – 62 from an
album formerly in the Cheney
Collection. Another drawing from the
series was sold 4.7.84 in London for
£37,800 ($50,652).

HUBERT ROBERT
French, Paris 1733 – 1808
*View from the Southern Vestibule
of Maderna's Portico of
St. Peter's, Rome, looking West,
showing Michelangelo's Old
Sacristy*
Red chalk
$17 \times 12\frac{3}{4}$ in.
(43.2 × 32.7 cm.)
Sold 3.4.84 in London for
£25,920 ($37,325)
Record auction price for a
drawing by the artist
Drawn about 1763, early in
Robert's sojourn in Rome

JACOB JORDAENS
Flemish, Antwerp
1593 – 1678
Head of a Woman
Black and red chalk, brown
wash heightened with white
9¼ × 7¼ in.
(23.7 × 18.7 cm.)
Sold 4.7.84 in London for
£64,800 ($86,832)
Record auction price for a
drawing by the artist
This drawing, which fetched
£1,600 in 1955, is datable
*c.*1635 and was evidently
drawn from life

SIR PETER PAUL RUBENS
Flemish, Siegen 1577 – Antwerp 1640
A Man in Korean Costume
Grey-black chalk, with touches of red on
the mouth, nose, cheekbones and ear
15 × 9¼ in. (38.7 × 23.4 cm.)
Sold 29.11.83 in London for £324,000
($476,280)
Now in the J. Paul Getty Museum,
Malibu, California
First recorded in the collection of the elder
Richardson, this drawing was engraved by
Captain Baillie in 1774 when it was owned
by Ralph Willett. Datable before 1617 it is
the first of a number of studies of figures
in oriental costume; the models were
evidently Jesuits attached to the college of
that Order at Antwerp.

JAN JOSEFSZ. VAN GOYEN
Dutch, Leyden 1596 –
The Hague 1665
*A Military Encampment by a Fort
on an Estuary*
Black chalk, with touches of
light brown wash
7 × 11¼ in. (17.6 × 28.3 cm.)
Sold 15.11.83 in Amsterdam
for D.fl.79,800 (£17,733)
Dated 1651 by Dr Beck

ROELANDT SAVERY
Netherlandish, Courtrai 1576
– Utrecht 1639
*A Rocky River Landscape with a
Waterfall*
Signed
Black chalk, red-brown wash
12½ × 16 in.
(31.6 × 40.8 cm.)
Sold 15.11.83 in Amsterdam
for D.fl.228,000 (£50,666)
Record auction price for a
drawing by the artist
Now in the J. Paul Getty
Museum, Malibu, California

PIERRE JOSEPH REDOUTÉ
French, Saint Hubert 1759 –
Paris 1840
*A Spray of Pink Roses, with a
Brimstone, a Blue and another
Butterfly*
Signed and dated 1829
Pencil and watercolour on
vellum
$15 \times 11\frac{1}{4}$ in. (38.4 × 28.4 cm.)
Sold 3.4.84 in London for
£27,000 ($38,880)
Record auction price for a
drawing by the artist
Formerly in the collection of
the Duchesse de Berry

The Architect's Eye and Collector's Choice

EILEEN HARRIS

Little is known about the history of collecting architectural drawings. Giorgio Vasari evidently acquired such material in connection with his famous biographical work, *Le Vite de' più eccellenti pittori, scultori e architettori* (1550). Vincenzo Scamozzi owned all of Andrea Palladio's drawings, which he sold, together with his own drawings, in 1614 to Inigo Jones and Lord Arundel. Jones's purchase was almost certainly prompted by sheer veneration for Palladio rather than for any utilitarian purpose. William Talman and his son John were the first, at the end of the 17th century, to amass a corpus of architectural drawings with some practical end in mind. There were approximately 100,000 drawings in their possession by 1719 when William died. The antiquarian William Stukeley was awed by the sight in 1715 of John Talman's 'Nobel and Sumptuous Collection … in abt 200 volls … the Vast volumes … are Four-feet high & require two men to open & shut'.

At about the same time and on a similar scale architectural drawings were being collected in Sweden by another father and son, Nicholas Tessin the elder (d. 1681) and the younger (d. 1728). Their collection, which concentrated on French design of the second half of the 17th century and was less eclectic than the Talmans', is now in the National Museum in Stockholm.

Another distinguished collector emerged in London, Richard Boyle, 3rd Earl of Burlington, who as 'Architect Earl' collected drawings as exemplars. In 1718 he bought in Rome, through John Talman's intervention, Palladio's reconstruction of Roman antiquity. To complete this collection he then purchased all the architectural designs by Palladio, as well as those by Inigo Jones and John Webb, from John Talman in 1720 and 1721. Burlington was one of the earliest identifiable collectors, at least in England, of theatre designs, buying extensively at Talman's sales after 1727, and acquiring the famous sketchbook of masque designs by Jones and another by Filippo Juvarra. Obsessed by precedent and authority, he was perhaps one of the first, if not the first, architect to use Old Master drawings to reform and rule the taste of his time. This was to become standard Beaux-Arts practice in the later 19th century.

The two earliest public collections of architectural drawings, both formed mainly to benefit the profession, were founded in London within a year of each other: Sir John Soane's Museum in 1834 and the Institute of British Architects in 1835. Soane was undoubtedly the first to acquire designs by his contemporaries, which included the entire contents of the offices of the Adam brothers and of George Dance the younger, as well as important trophies of the works of Sir William Chambers, John Carr of York and many other British architects. Not until 1870 did the RIBA begin to collect modern drawings 'to record architects' professional exertions'.

The formation of architectural libraries as a complement to drawing collections for study and use, as well as for vanity value, was also led by Soane. The extent to which this kind of subject collecting grew in the second half of the 19th century is partly demonstrated by the great architectural sales that took place in the 1860s and 1870s: Leon de Klenze's library in 1864, the Levergne architectural library in 1879 and the tremendous Hippolyte Destailleur sales of

GIACOMO QUARENGHI
Italian 1744 – 1817
North Elevation of the Alexander Palace at Tsarskoe Selo
Pen and black and brown ink, grey wash and watercolour
18⅝ × 25⅛ in. (47.3 × 64 cm.)
Sold 30.11.83 in London for £10,260 ($15,082)

some of the finest and rarest architectural books, drawings and manuscripts in the 1870s. From these sales other important collections in the field were generated: Richard Morris Hunt's library, now in the American Institute of Architects in Washington, Giovanni Piancastelli's, whose 12,000 drawings went to form the nucleus of the Cooper Hewitt Museum in New York, and Charles Mèwes's, of the firm of Mèwes & Davis, architects of the London and Paris Ritz hotels, whose collection was sold *en bloc* to Mrs Wrightsman, and through her generosity is now partly in the Metropolitan Museum of Art, New York.

Prior to Christie's sale on 30 November 1983 of Sir Albert Richardson's collection, the most celebrated sale of architectural drawings in the present century was the Marquess of Bute's, on 23 May 1951. Then, 264 drawings, including more than 120 from Sir Christopher Wren's office, fetched a total of £1,563. The RIBA and a few discerning dealers like John Hewitt and Alan G. Thomas were almost the only buyers of architectural drawings in the 1950s. The 1960s saw Hyatt Mayor and John McKendry acquiring a wealth of material for the Metropolitan, and Phyllis Lambert starting to build her important collection recently established as the Centre Canadien d'Architecture in Montréal-Quebec. Richard Wunder's architectural collection was sold at Christie's in 1976. The 50 exhibitions put on by the RIBA Drawings Collection at the Heinz Gallery since 1972 have contributed to the rocketing revaluation of architectural drawings and as a result their own meagrely funded acquisitions have suffered. Finally, in the last months of 1983 and the first of 1984 we have had two major events involving architectural drawings: the sale of the Richardson Collection at Christie's, followed by the exhibition of *Images et Imaginaires d'Architecture* in Europe from the 19th century to the present at the Centre Georges Pompidou in Paris.

Christie's 1983 sale of architectural drawings is recorded in this *Review of the Season*. Like Lord Burlington, Sir Albert Richardson, or 'The Professor' as he was familiarly called, collected drawings both as exemplars from which to work and as commemorative trophies of architects who had greatly influenced him in his own practice.

The Professor's manner was that of the many provincial architects of the 18th century who shaped the Georgian cathedral towns he loved so much. His devotion to the Georgian style did not stop at collecting architectural books and drawings, furniture and all kinds of other objects. He transported himself physically into that period, dressing in 18th-century clothing and living in an 18th-century house without such modern conveniences as central heating and electricity. Thus, he saw his drawings just as their Georgian makers saw them.

Richardson's dependence upon the drawings he collected can be measured by the scale of his collection, which is unlikely to be matched by any private dispersal in the future. Perhaps the one item that most reveals his constant use of the material is the well-worn album by J.E. Goodchild *Reminiscences of my Twenty-six Years Association with the late Professor C.R. Cockerell, Esq.* (1887), recording virtually all his master's projects from 1833 to 1859. Richardson's great admiration for Cockerell found expression not only in his own buildings but also in his book, *Monumental Classic Architecture in Great Britain and Ireland* (c. 1915). He would doubtless have approved of the RIBA's purchase of this album for £5,184 ($7,620) to enrich their already considerable C.R. Cockerell holdings.

Sir William Chambers was another of Richardson's heroes. Chambers's design for the library ceiling at Woburn Abbey was one of the plums of the collection, unexcelled for sheer beauty and quality of design. The drawing was almost certainly coloured by G.B. Cipriani, who was paid £597 for painting the actual ceiling with Biagio Rebecca. It was drawn in 1768, exhibited at the Royal Academy in 1770 and sold in Chambers's sale in 1811 with two other Woburn ceiling designs for only five guineas. It now brought £7,560 ($11,113) on its own!

The book, *Robert Mylne, Architect and Engineer*, published by Richardson in 1956 was the direct result of his acquisition of a large volume of drawings of Mylne, a Georgian architect of Scottish origin, whose refinement and correct use of the classic vocabulary appealed to the Professor. The Mylne drawings filled 33 lots and fetched a total of £35,040 ($69,480).

Unfortunately, Richardson did not keep records of his acquisitions or investigate their provenance. Charles James Richardson, one of Soane's assistants, was the probable source of many of the items owned by his namesake. C.J. was evidently led by intense jealousy of his master and a sense of his own inferiority to take home some bundles of drawings from the office, which later in life he sold either on the open market or to the Victoria & Albert Museum. One of these bundles contained the Soane drawings, which the Professor must have been pleased, and certainly was fortunate, to obtain, and which were dispersed in 20 lots for £18,530 ($27,239). The design for Tyringham Park, Hunts., alone fetched £4,536 ($6,668).

Like the best wine, the highlight of the sale was saved for last. This was a group of drawings by Giacomo Quarenghi, architect to Catherine the Great, which was presented, almost certainly at the Empress's instigation, to Sir Charles Whitworth, Ambassador to St. Petersburg from 1789 to 1800. The prices fetched by these drawings were appropriate to their importance and aesthetic quality: £7,560 ($11,113) for the Peterhof English Palace, £10,260 ($15,082) for an elevation and plan of the Alexander Palace at Tsarskoe Selo, £10,260 ($15,082) for the saloon of the Alexander Palace and £5,400 ($7,938) for St. George's Hall in the Winter Palace at St. Petersburg. This was a triumphant finale to the Richardson sale, which formed the first and major part of a morning devoted to architecture, ornament and decoration.

The second half of the sale focused on one family and one house, the Freemans of Fawley Court just outside Henley. John Cooke (1689 – 1752) inherited Fawley from his uncle, William Freeman, whose surname he took. Upon his death the house went to his son, Sambrooke, and

SIR WILLIAM CHAMBERS, R.A.
British 1726 – 96
Design for the Library Ceiling at Woburn Abbey
Pen and grey ink and watercolour
27 3/8 × 18 1/2 in. (69.7 × 47.1 cm.)
Sold 30.11.83 in London for £7,560
($11,113)

ENGLISH SCHOOL
To the design of Sambrooke Freeman, *c.* 1760
Design for a Fountain-Pagoda, for Ralph Allen, Prior Park, Bath
Pencil, pen and grey ink and watercolour
39¼ × 13¾ in. (99.7 × 35 cm.)
Sold 30.11.83 in London for £11,880 ($17,464)

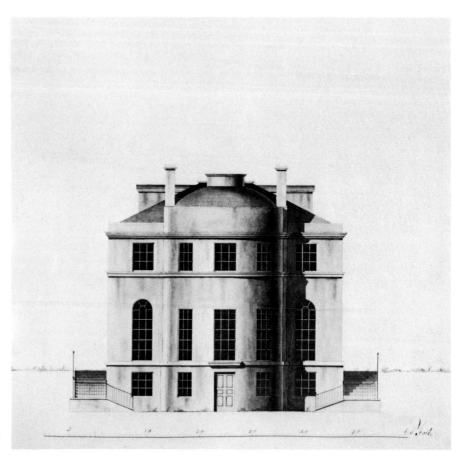

ROBERT MYLNE
British 1733 – 1811
Designs for a House: Back Elevation
Pen and grey ink, grey and ochre wash or watercolour
17¾ × 11¾ in. (45 × 29.6 cm.)
Sold 30.11.83 in London for £4,536 ($6,668)

thence to the latter's nephew, Strickland Freeman. All the members of the family were amateurs in architecture, none more so than John Cooke Freeman, who designed the family mausoleum still standing in Fawley churchyard, several architectural curiosities and follies in the gardens at Fawley and the saloon at Honington Hall, Warwickshire, for his friend Joseph Townsend. The three generations of Freeman drawings presented an exceptional picture of the participation of the owners of a great house in its design and decoration.

The most interesting designs were those by James Wyatt from the earliest period of his professional career around 1770 when Sambrooke commissioned him to redecorate Fawley. The highly coloured drawing-room ceiling as executed brought £702 ($1,031) and an especially important design for the Etruscan room in the Island Temple at Henley brought £972 ($1,428). The island with its elegant Wyatt temple is a familiar sight at the Henley Regatta, but less familiar is the interior, decorated to Wyatt's design and the very first example of Etruscan-style decoration in Europe, predating Robert Adam's famous Etruscan room at Osterley by a few years.

What undoubtedly stole the show was an astonishing design for a fountain-pagoda for Ralph Allen at Prior Park, Bath, attributed to Sambrooke but probably coloured by a professional artist. A comparison with the well-known pagoda at Kew Gardens designed by Sir William Chambers in 1759 is inevitable. The remarkable decorative quality and eccentricity of this design, which belongs to the age of the rococo and the ambiance of Vauxhall Gardens, were reflected in the £11,880 ($17,463) it fetched.

MARCELLUS LAROON
British 1679 – 1774
A Birdcatcher
Pencil, red and white chalk on buff
paper
12³⁄₈ × 8 in. (31.6 × 20.3 cm.)
Sold 10.7.84 in London for £20,520
($26,676)
From the collection of Dr Robert
Hemphill

WILLIAM BLAKE
British, London 1757 – 1827
Job and his Daughters
Pencil, brush and grey ink and watercolour
7³⁄₄ × 10 in. (19.6 × 25.4 cm.)
Sold 10.7.84 in London for £56,160 ($73,000)
Record auction price for a watercolour by the artist
From the collection of Dr Robert Hemphill
Previously sold in the W. Graham Robertson sale at Christie's, 22 July 1949, for 200 gns. Related to the artist's series of etchings,
Illustrations of the Book of Job, 1825, Plate 20.

THOMAS ROWLANDSON
British, London 1756 – 1827
Box-Lobby Loungers
Pencil, pen and grey ink and watercolour
14¾ × 22 in. (37.2 × 55.8 cm.)
Sold 10.7.84 in London for £81,000 ($105,300)
Record auction price for a watercolour by the artist
From the collection of Major Leonard Dent, D.S.O.
One of the most celebrated of the artist's works, this was exhibited at the Royal Academy in 1785. It was in the Earl of Warwick's sale at Christie's, 21 May 1894 (80 gns.), and that of Desmond Coke, 22 November 1929 (190 gns.).

THOMAS ROWLANDSON

British, London 1756 – 1827

The Coach Booking Office: Thomas Rowlandson and Henry Wigstead booking their Passage

Pencil, pen and ink and watercolour

7 × 11½ in. (17.7 × 29.2 cm.)

Sold 10.7.84 in London for £16,200 ($21,060)

From the collection of Major Leonard Dent, D.S.O.

Previously sold from the Desmond Coke collection at Christie's, 22 November 1929, for 46 gns.

Over 20 years Major Leonard Dent built up one of the most distinguished collections of the work of Thomas Rowlandson. His was a discerning eye inspired with a singular vision of Rowlandson's stature as one of the great draughtsmen of the English school. In 1935, the year in which he became Master of the Grocers' Company, he purchased his first Rowlandson, a richly coloured landscape. This choice marked the direction that his subsequent acquisitions would take, away from the prevalent view of Rowlandson as a brilliant but somewhat coarse caricaturist to the reassessment of him as the outstanding landscape and figure draughtsman of his age. Major Dent adopted from Osbert Sitwell his own motto of Rowlandson's achievement, 'the greatest master of pure line that England has had the good fortune to produce'. The extraordinary success of the sale, which brought £292,842 ($380,695) for only 35 lots, showed that the current generation of collectors share wholeheartedly Major Dent's vision.

JOSEPH MALLORD WILLIAM TURNER, R.A.
British, London 1775 – 1851
The Valley of the Washburn, Ottley Chevin in the Distance
Watercolour and bodycolour on grey paper
13 × 16 in. (33 × 40.6 cm.)
Sold 15.11.83 in London for £91,800 ($137,700)
By order of the Trustees of the W.A.H. Harding Trust
Drawn for the artist's patron Walter Fawkes of Farnley Hall and sold by his descendant W.R. Fawkes in these Rooms, 2 July 1937.
It is based on pencil sketches in the British Museum probably dating from 1817, and is one of the series of views of Farnley and the neighbourhood that remain Turner's most personal expression of his friendship with Fawkes.

PETER DE WINT
British, Stone, Staffordshire 1784 – London 1849
Matlock High Tor from the South
Inscribed on the reverse by Harriet de Wint, the artist's widow, 'Rocks at Matlock', and with the lot number 329 from the artist's sale
Pencil and watercolour
$17\frac{1}{4} \times 23\frac{3}{4}$ in. (43.6 × 60.2 cm.)
Sold 15.11.83 in London for £22,680 ($34,020)
Record auction price for a watercolour by the artist
Previously sold in the artist's sale at Christie's, 24 May 1850, for 6 gns.

WILLIAM CALLOW
British, Greenwich 1812 – Great Missenden 1908
Palazzo Pisani Moretta, Venice
Signed
Watercolour with touches of white heightening
$9\frac{5}{8} \times 12\frac{7}{8}$ in. (24.1 × 33 cm.)
Sold 10.7.84 in London for £15,120 ($19,656)
Record auction price for a watercolour by the artist

Opposite
MYLES BIRKET FOSTER
British, North Shields 1825 – Weybridge 1899
The Country Inn
Signed with monogram
Pencil, watercolour and bodycolour
$31 \times 26\frac{1}{2}$ in. (78.7 × 67.3 cm.)
Sold 15.5.84 in London for £22,680 ($31,525)
Record auction price for a watercolour by the artist

JOHN DICKSON BATTEN
British, Plymouth 1860 – 1932
The Garden of Adonis: Amoretta and Time – 'He flies about, and with his flaggy wings
Beats down both leaves and buds without regard, Nor ever pity may relent his malice hard'
Signed with monogram and dated 1887
Tempera on canvas
39½ × 49 in. (100.3 × 124.3 cm.)
Sold 5.6.84 in London for £15,120 ($21,470)
One of two works by the artist sold by his grandson

Right
EDWARD CHARLES CLIFFORD
British, London 1858 – 1910
Souvenirs
Signed
Watercolour
19 × 6⅛ in. (48.2 × 15.3 cm.)
Sold 9.5.84 in London for
£5,400 ($7,560)
From The Diploma
Collection of The Royal
Institute of Painters in
Watercolours which made a
total of £68,844 ($96,381)

Far right
HENRY RAYMOND THOMPSON
Irish n.d.
'O holy Night! from thee I learn to
    bear
What man has borne before!
Thou layest thy finger on the lips
    of Care,
And they complain no more.'
Signed, dated '1897 – 98' and
inscribed in a cartouche
Watercolour
50 × 20 in. (126.9 × 50.8 cm.)
Sold 16.2.84 in London for
£5,940 ($8,613)
From the collection of Claude
Thompson, Esq., son of the
artist

ALBERT GOODWIN
British, Maidstone 1845 –
London 1932
Westminster from a House Top
Signed, inscribed and dated
1915
Pencil, pen and grey ink and
watercolour
12½ × 20 in.
(31.7 × 50.8 cm.)
Sold 11.10.83 in London for
£10,260 ($15,698)

SIR EDWARD COLEY BURNE-
JONES, BT., A.R.A.
British, Bennett's Hill,
Birmingham 1833 – London
1898
*Chaucer in the Garden of Idleness:
Design for 'The Romance of the
Rose'*
Black chalk, lightly squared
27½ × 58 in.
(69.8 × 147.2 cm.)
Sold 15.5.84 in London for
£13,500 ($18,765)
From the collection of
Mrs Susan Robinson
In 1874 William Morris was
commissioned by Sir Lowthian
Bell to provide an
embroidered frieze for the
dining-room of Rounton
Grange. Burne-Jones
designed the figures, Morris
the briar background.

HELEN ALLINGHAM
British, near Burton-on-Trent
1848 – Haslemere 1926
Tigbourne Farm near Witley
Signed
Watercolour
$10\frac{1}{2} \times 15$ in. (26.6 × 38.1 cm.)
Sold 15.5.84 in London for
£8,640 ($12,010)

ARCHIBALD THORBURN
British, Dalkeith
1860 – Godalming 1935
A Woodcock in the Snow
Signed and dated 1924
Watercolour with touches of
white heightening
$11\frac{1}{4} \times 15$ in. (28.2 × 38.1 cm.)
Sold 11.10.83 in London for
£10,800 ($16,524)

PETER SEVERIN KROYER
Danish 1851 – 1909
The First Communion
Signed with initials and
dated St. Manet 86
Pastel
24¾ × 19¼ in.
(62.7 × 48.9 cm.)
Sold 22.3.84 in London for
£12,960 ($18,532)

GIULIO and DOMENICO
CAMPAGNOLA
Italian *c.*1482 – 1515; Italian
1484 – 1550
Shepherds in a Landscape
(Bartsch 9)
Engraving, a very fine
impression of this very rare
print
P. 5½ × 10¼ in.
(13.4 × 25.9 cm.)
Sold 27.6.84 in London for
£21,600 ($29,592)

ANDREA MANTEGNA
Italian 1431 – 1506
The Battle of the Sea Gods (left half)
(Bartsch 18)
Engraving, a very fine, early
impression
S. 11⅛ × 16 in.
(28.7 × 42.7 cm.)
Sold 1.11.83 in New York for
$35,200 (£23,624)
Formerly in the collection of
Robert Stayner Holford and
sold in these Rooms on 11
July 1893 for £50

Rembrandt and Dürer: Masters of Printmaking

DAVID LLEWELLYN

Two remarkable prints by the two greatest Old Master printmakers were sold by Christie's in the last year. The Dürer *Coat of Arms with a Skull* at £65,880 ($90,255) provided a new auction record for a print by the artist, and the Rembrandt *Saint Jerome reading in an Italian Landscape* at $181,500 (£121,812) established an auction record not only for the artist's prints but also for any print sold, Old Master or Modern.

The majority of Rembrandt's landscape etchings take the artist's own immediate surroundings as their subjects. The landscape in which Saint Jerome conducts his studies differs by having an Italianate nature, the composition being an imaginative distillation of the artist's study and appreciation of the Venetian masters such as Campagnola and Titian.

The print displays many of the painterly qualities inherent in the artist's major prints. Gradations of hatching are used to convey varying degrees of shade and light. The cross-hatching on the Saint's hat and face contrast not only with the denser mesh of cross-hatching in the darker shadows of the tree but also with the few sketchy lines that delineate the rest of his body, which seems to disappear, like the rock on which he leans, in a suffusion of bright Italianate sun. Drypoint has been used not only to suggest the furry texture of the lion's mane but also to act as an ingenious means of defining and separating the foreground from the distant landscape. Two small figures to the right of the lion's head have been picked out in drypoint and serve as visual clues to the distance and depth of the landscape. The impression sold in New York is quite exceptionally rich in burr, which suggests that it must be one of the earliest pulls taken from the plate. The use of Japanese paper helps to soften the contrast between the etched and drypoint lines and gives the composition tone and colour, painterly qualities seen at their best in only the finest impressions of the artist's prints, of which this is a magnificent example.

While Rembrandt's *Saint Jerome reading in an Italian Landscape* can be seen as an example of the artist's brilliance in the medium of etching, so the *Coat of Arms with a Skull* can be viewed as an example of Dürer's incomparable virtuosity in the medium of engraving. The print is an intriguing mixture of heraldic representation and naturalism that is imbued with the theme of Love and Death. In a very balanced, still composition Dürer demonstrates his extraordinary mastery over the technical difficulties of engraving in portraying so successfully a multiplicity of textures and surfaces that range from the soft, ordered hair of the young lady and the delicacy of her head-dress, to the unkempt locks and shaggy beard of the satyr, the smooth rounded surface of the helmet above the skull and the soft feathers of the spread wings that reach to the top of the composition. The superb, rich impression that realised an auction record for a print by the artist is one of the finest known and captures all the detail and intricacy of the line that characterises Dürer's work. The print last appeared at Christie's in 1887 in the sale of the Duke of Buccleuch's collection, noted for the excellence of its Rembrandts and Dürers. The exceptionally fine quality of this particular impression of the *Coat of Arms with a Skull* must have been appreciated even then, for at £58 it was the highest priced Dürer. This, by coincidence, was the same price that was paid for the *Saint Jerome reading in an Italian Landscape* when it appeared in the sale of the collection of Sir Francis Seymour Haden four years later, in 1891.

REMBRANDT HARMENSZ. VAN
RIJN
Dutch 1606 – 69
*Saint Jerome reading in an Italian
Landscape*
(Bartsch 104)
Etching with drypoint and
engraving, first state (of two),
a magnificent impression on
fairly thick, warm-toned
Japan
P. $10\frac{3}{16} \times 8\frac{1}{16}$ in.
(25.8 × 20.5 cm.)
Sold 1.11.83 in New York for
$181,500 (£121,812)
Record auction price for any
print

ALBRECHT DÜRER
German 1471 – 1528
Coat of Arms with a Skull
(Bartsch 101)
Engraving, a superb
impression
S. 9 × 6½ in.
(22.6 × 16.2 cm.)
Sold 27.6.84 in London for
£65,880 ($90,255)
Record auction price for a
print by the artist
Formerly in the collection of
the Duke of Buccleuch and
sold in these Rooms on 19
April 1887 for £58

REMBRANDT HARMENSZ. VAN RIJN
Dutch 1606 – 69
A Woman at the Bath with a Hat beside her
(Bartsch 199)
Etching with drypoint, second (final)
state, a very fine impression of this
extremely rare print, on Japan
P. 6¼ × 5 in. (15.9 × 12.9 cm.)
Sold 27.6.84 in London for £64,800
($88,776)
Formerly in the collection of
Edward Vernon Utterson and sold in
these Rooms on 17 February 1848 for
£2. 10s.

After PIETER BRUEGHEL THE ELDER
Flemish 1512 – 69
The Witch of Malleghem, by P. van der Heyden
(Bastelaer 193)
Engraving, the rare third state (of six)
P. 14 × 19 in. (35.7 × 48 cm.)
Sold 27.6.84 in London for £15,120 ($20,714)

GABRIEL DE SAINT-AUBIN
French 1724 – 80
Marché du Boeuf Gras
(Dacier 1)
Etching with drypoint, the extremely rare and
possibly unique first state (of two), a very fine
impression
P. 5½ × 7 in. (13.9 × 17.1 cm.)
Sold 27.6.84 in London for £20,800 ($28,496)
Record auction price for a print by the artist

PRINCE RUPERT OF THE RHINE
German 1619 – 82
The Standard Bearer, after
P. della Vecchia
(Chaloner Smith 5)
Mezzotint, second state (of
three), a fine, rich impression
S. $11 \times 7\frac{1}{2}$ in.
(27.7 × 19.7 cm.)
Sold 27.6.84 in London for
£18,360 ($25,153)

HENDRIK GOLTZIUS
Dutch 1558 – 1617
The Cave of Eternity
(Hirschmann 374)
Chiaroscuro woodcut from
three blocks, printed in black,
beige and greenish brown, a
rare proof impression
L. $13\frac{5}{8} \times 10\frac{3}{8}$ in.
(34.7 × 26.2 cm.)
Sold 1.5.84 in New York for
$15,400 (£10,921)

GIOVANNI BATTISTA TIEPOLO
Italian 1696 – 1770
A Shepherd with Two Magicians,
Plate 16 from *Scherzi*
(De Vesme 28)
Etching, first state (of two),
before the number, a brilliant
impression
P. 9 × 7 in. (22.3 × 17.5 cm.)
Sold 27.6.84 in London for
£6,480 ($8,877)

ALBRECHT DÜRER
German 1471 – 1528
Saint Jerome in his Study
(Bartsch 60)
Engraving, an
extraordinarily fine, brilliant
and silvery impression
P. $9\frac{3}{4} \times 7\frac{1}{2}$ in.
(24.6 × 18.8 cm.)
Sold 1.11.83 in New York for
$46,200 (£31,000)

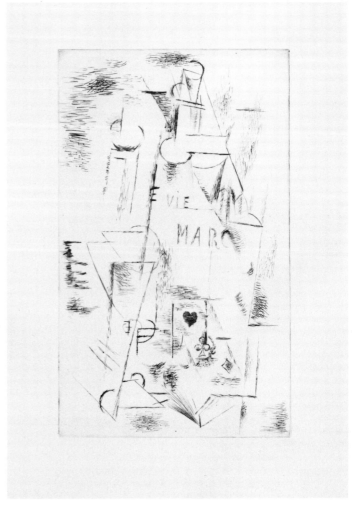

ODILON REDON
French 1840 – 1916
Araignée
(Mellerio 72)
Lithograph, 1887, a fine impression of this extremely rare
lithograph, signed in pencil upper right, from the edition of 25
L. 11 × 8½ in. (28 × 21.6 cm.)
Sold 1.11.83 in New York for $55,000 (£36,913)
Record auction price for a print by the artist

PABLO PICASSO
Spanish/French 1881 – 1974
Nature morte, Bouteille
(Bloch 24)
Drypoint, 1912, a fine impression, signed in pencil, numbered
36 from the edition of 100, printed by Delâtre for Kahnweiler
P. 19¾ × 12⅛ in. (50.2 × 30.8 cm.)
Sold 1.11.83 in New York for $33,000 (£22,148)

Opposite
HENRI DE TOULOUSE-LAUTREC
French 1864 – 1901
L'Anglais au Moulin Rouge
(Delteil 12)
Lithograph printed in colours, 1892, a very fine, fresh and
unusually brilliant impression, signed in pencil, numbered 24
from the edition of 100
S. 24¾ × 19⅟₁₆ in. (62.9 × 48.4 cm.)
Sold 1.5.84 in New York for $66,000 (£46,808)

HENRI DE TOULOUSE-LAUTREC
French 1864 – 1901
Femme au Tub, from *Elles*
(Delteil 183)
Lithograph printed in colours, 1896, second (final) state, a very fine impression, from the edition of 100
S. 16 × 20½ in. (40.5 × 52.8 cm.)
Sold 8.12.83 in London for £35,640 ($52,034)

EDVARD MUNCH
Norwegian 1863 – 1944
Madonna – Liebendes Weib
(Schiefler 33b)
Lithograph printed in black, royal blue and
pale orange-red over a buff tint, 1895 – 1902,
signed in pencil, a superb, sharply printed
impression
L. 22 × 13½ in. (55.7 × 34.3 cm.)
Sold 26.6.84 in London for £49,600
($67,952)

EDVARD MUNCH
Norwegian 1863 – 1944
Mädchenkopf am Strande
(Schiefler 129)
Woodcut, printed in
three colours (orange,
ochre and sea green),
1899, signed in pencil, a
brilliant, atmospheric
impression of this
extremely rare print
L. 18½ × 16½ in.
(46.8 × 41.5 cm.)
Sold 8.12.83 in London
for £56,160 ($81,999)

EDVARD MUNCH
Norwegian 1863 – 1944
Frauen am Meeresufer
(Schiefler 117 a2)
Woodcut printed in four colours (black, green, orange-brown and slate blue), with the promontory of the shore handcoloured to tone in with the green of the ground and a few small dots of blue pastel in the sea at the right, 1898, signed and inscribed in pencil, a superb, beautifully printed impression of this rare print
L. 18 × 20¼ in. (45.8 × 51.5 cm.)
Sold 8.12.83 in London for £70,200 ($102,492)

OTTO DIX
German 1891 – 1969
Der Krieg
(Karsch 70a – 119a)
Etchings and drypoints, 1924, the set of
50 plates, each plate signed and
numbered in pencil 2/70, superb rich
impressions
S. 13½ × 18½ in. (34.7 × 46 cm.)
Sold 26.6.84 in London for £28,080
($38,469)

KARL SCHMIDT-ROTTLUFF
German 1884 – 1976
Köpfe II
(Schapire 67)
Woodcut, 1911, signed and dated in
pencil, a very fine, black impression
L. 20 × 15½ in. (50.6 × 39.6 cm.)
Sold 26.6.84 in London for £12,960
($17,755)

ROBERT DELAUNAY
French 1885 – 1941
La Tour
(Loyer & Pérussaux 3)
Lithograph, 1925, signed and
inscribed in pencil, a superb,
rich and black impression of
this rare print
L. 24 × 17½ in.
(61.2 × 44.8 cm.)
Sold 26.6.84 in London for
£18,300 ($25,071)

WASSILY KANDINSKY
Russian 1866 – 1944
Fröhlicher Aufstieg
(Roethel 177)
Lithograph printed in
colours, 1923, an
exceptionally fine impression,
signed in pencil, from (or
apart from?) the edition of
100 published in the
*Meistermappe der Staatlichen
Bauhauses*, München, Weimar
L. 13 1/2 × 10 5/8 in.
(34.2 × 27 cm.)
Sold 1.11.83 in New York for
$22,000 (£14,765)

CONRAD FELIXMÜLLER
German 1897 – 1977
Kohlenbergarbeiter
(Söhn 211)
Lithograph printed in colours with extensive
pastel handcolouring, 1920, signed, inscribed,
numbered, titled and dated in pencil, a fine
impression of this rare print
L. 22½ × 15½ in. (57.6 × 39.1 cm.)
Sold 26.6.84 in London for £9,720 ($13,316)
Record auction price for a print by the artist

WINSLOW HOMER
American 1836 – 1910
Fly Fishing, Saranac Lake
(Goodrich 104)
Etching, 1889, a fine impression, signed and numbered in pencil
P. 14$\frac{1}{16}$ × 20$\frac{3}{8}$ in. (35.7 × 51.8 cm.)
Sold 21.9.83 in New York for $24,200 (£15,921)

Books and Manuscripts

CORNELIUS NOZEMANN,
MARTINIUS HOUTTUYN
and JAN CHRISTIAN SEPP
Nederlandsche Vogelen
250 hand-coloured
engraved plates
Sold 27.6.84 in London
for £17,280 ($24,192)
The first comprehensive
account of the avifauna
of Holland

JOHANN EMMANUEL FISCHER VON ERLACH
Anfang einiger Vorstellungen der Vornehmsten
Gebäude ... von Wien
27 plates
Oblong folio
Augsburg, Pfeffel, 1719
Sold 9.12.83 in London for £6,480
($9,460)

BLAEU
Théâtre des Etats de son Altesse Royale le
Duc de Savoye
Volume I, Le Piemont
Volume II, La Savoye
131 engraved plates
The Hague, Adrian Moetjens, 1700
Sold 9.12.83 in London for £6,264
($9,145)

LOUIS XVI
Autograph manuscript of the King's speech before the Etats-Généraux on 23 June 1789
3 pages, quarto
Sold 28.3.84 in London for £45,360 ($65,772)
A document of outstanding importance in French history, marking the Monarch's last attempt to assert his authority before the outbreak of the French Revolution

Far right
THOMAS TRAHERNE
Commentaries of Heaven
Unpublished autograph manuscript comprising 94 commentaries on religious and secular topics, given alphabetically from 'Abhorrence' to 'Bastard', including 99 poems
Probably written in 1673
Sold 18.5.84 in New York for $110,000 (£78,014)
From the collection of Mr and Mrs J.L. Wookey
Now in the British Library

Right
ALBERT EINSTEIN
Autograph manuscript of an article 'Altes und Neues zur Feld-Theorie'
12 pages
Late 1928 or early 1929
Sold 16.12.83 in New York for $55,000 (£39,000)

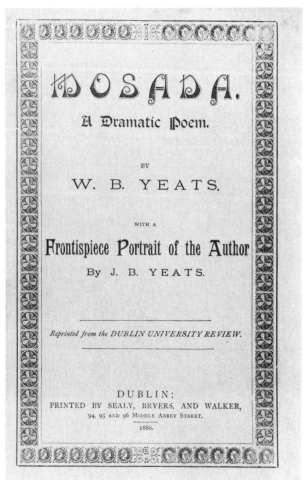

Thomas Mann

Buddenbrooks

Verfall einer Familie

Roman

Berlin 1901
S. Fischer, Verlag

Above left
BIBLE IN LOW-GERMAN
Biblia Dudesch
Two volumes, 119 large woodcut illustrations
Halberstadt, L. Stuchs, 1522
Sold 30.5.84 in London for £7,020 ($9,774)

Above
WILLIAM BUTLER YEATS
Mosada. A Dramatic Poem
First edition, original painted buff wrapper as issued
Dublin 1886
Sold 16.12.83 in New York for $33,000 (£23,404)

Left
THOMAS MANN
Buddenbrooks, Verfall einer Familie
First edition, two volumes, inscribed by the author
Sold 9.12.83 in London for £7,776 (£11,352)

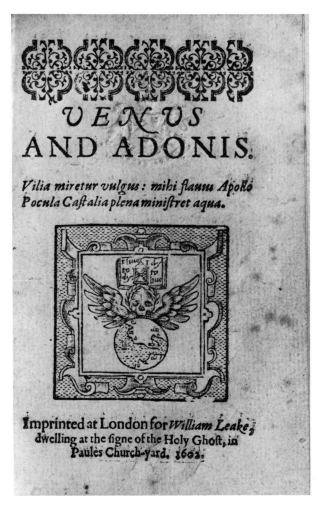

W. H. AUDEN

POEMS

S. H. S. : 1928.

W. H. AUDEN

This valuable work to
David Ayerst from
Stephen Spender, the
printer. But if he has a true
regard for the future at Christie's,
he will also get the author's
signature.

Feb 1st 1929.

To David
with love and best wishes

Wystan Auden

Above
WILLIAM SHAKESPEARE
Venus and Adonis
London 1602
Sold 30.5.84 in London for £129,600 ($180,144)
From the collection of Viscount Parker
A unique issue of the ninth edition and the only complete copy printed before 1636 in private hands

Right
W.H. AUDEN
Poems
Edition limited to about 45 copies
S.H.S. (Stephen Spender), 1928
Sold 9.11.83 in London for £6,696 ($10,044)
Presentation inscription from the publisher and the author

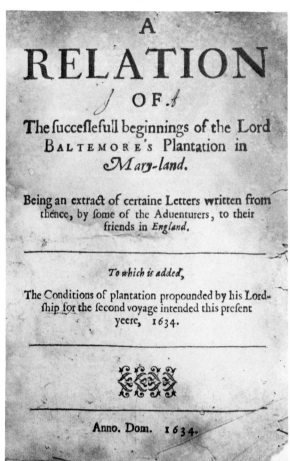

FELIX MENDELSSOHN-BARTHOLDY
Autograph manuscript album illustrating his tour of Scotland with Karl Klingemann in July and August 1829
25 leaves, each with an original fine pencil drawing, with long captions in ink, many in verse
January 1847
Sold 28.3.84 in London for £70,200 ($101,790)

JOSEPH HAYDN
Missa, sunt bona mixta malis, a 4tro voci alla cappella, del giuseppe Haydn, mpria [manu propria] [1]768
Autograph manuscript in ink, of parts for four voices and organ, the two movements, Kyrie and Gloria, of a D minor mass
Sold 28.3.84 in London for £151,200 ($219,240)
The only manuscript of the newly discovered 'lost' mass

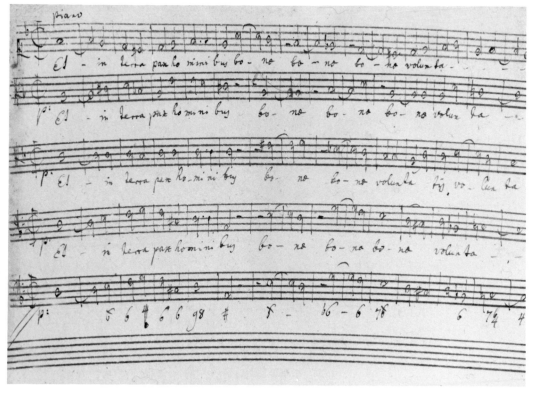

Amaryllis Formosissima   *Amaryllis Lys St. Jacques.*

PIERRE JOSEPH REDOUTÉ
Les Liliacées
Eight volumes, 486 plates after
Redouté, all except one printed in
colours and finished by hand
*Paris, chez l'auteur de l'Imprimérie de
Didot Jeune, 1802 – 16*
Sold 16.11.83 in London for
£62,640 ($93,960)

GEORGE BROOKSHAW
Pomona Britannica: or a collection of the most esteemed fruits as present cultivated in this country ... selected principally from the Royal Gardens at Hampton Court
90 coloured aquatint plates finished by hand
For the author by T. Bensley, 1812
Sold 14.3.84 in London for £33,480 ($49,215)
First edition of one of the first and most celebrated of all fruit books, described by Prideaux in *Aquatint Engraving* as 'one of the finest colour plate books in existence'

PLATE XLIV.
Painted & Published as the Act directs by the Author G.Brookshaw 1807.

LORENZ JANSCHA and JOHANN ZIEGLER

Collection de cinquante Vues du Rhin … Fünfzig malerische Ansichten des Rhein-Stromes von Speyer bis Düsseldorf nach der Natur gezeichnet

50 hand-coloured plates, ink and wash borders

Folio

Vienna, Artaria & Co., 1798

Sold 14.3.84 in London for £37,800 ($55,566)

DAVID ROBERTS
The Holy Land, Syria, Idumea, Arabia, Egypt and Nubia
Six volumes, 241 lithographed plates, finely hand-coloured and mounted on card, by L. Haghe after Roberts
Large folio
F.G. Moon, 1842 – 9
Sold 27.6.84 in London for £45,360 ($61,236)
By order of Newcastle upon Tyne City Libraries

SIGNERS OF THE DECLARATION
OF INDEPENDENCE
*Complete set of 56 autograph letters,
documents and other
items, various sizes –
46 are of Revolutionary War date
and 43 are dated 1776*
Sold 18.5.84 in New York
for $352,000 (£249,645)
From the collection of
Donald and Robert Sang

Opposite
PIERRE DE RONSARD
Florilège des Amours
Illustrated by Henri Matisse,
in an *irradiante classique*
binding of rose levant
morocco by Paul Bonet
Paris, Skira, 1948
Sold 18.5.84 in New York for
$46,200 (£32,765)

GIOVANNI BATTISTA **and** FRANCESCO
PIRANESI
Collection of 20 works
Bound in 22 volumes, with
contemporary cream boards,
parchment spines and original printed
paper labels
Large folio
Rome 1750 – 91
Sold 16.12.83 in New York for
$187,000 (£132,624)

PIRANESI
Vedute di Roma
Part of the set

Sales on the Premises

Belton House, Lincolnshire

Sales on the Premises

HUGH ROBERTS

Since James Christie founded the firm in 1766, sales on the premises have always figured large in the sale-room year. Among Christie's earliest house sales – within a carriage ride of London – were included such diverse items as a field of standing corn and a deceased owner's dog; and in the 18th and 19th centuries sales on the premises in London houses were relatively commonplace. It is difficult to imagine how our forebears in those days – or even our pre-war forebears – could have coped with this year's extraordinarily rich and varied harvest of sales: 17 in all, ranging from the Eastern seaboard of the United States to East Anglia, from Amsterdam to Dublin and from Kent to the North of Scotland.

Among the most colourful was that at Luttrellstown Castle, Mrs Aileen Plunket's extraordinary castellated grey stone extravaganza, set in a romantically picturesque park just outside Dublin. The crowds flocked in the warm September sun to see this famous house, once the home of the notorious Luttrells and for the past 40 years the setting for much enviable hospitality, dispensed with incomparable style by Mrs Plunket, granddaughter of the 1st Earl of Iveagh. The magic of the Guinness name drew buyers from far and wide – as was to be seen again at Elveden. Interest from America was noticeably strong and many of the most striking pieces of furniture and decoration – chosen for the most part by Mrs Plunket with the help of Felix Harbord, the architect and decorator who had helped her transform the house in the 1950s and 1960s – have now crossed the Atlantic. As will be seen elsewhere in this *Review*, the Luttrellstown results showed that for the exceptional – whether very rare, very decorative or very well preserved – there was really no limit to the depth of buyers' pockets. The Russian carpet in the Ballroom (IR£81,000/£64,800) demonstrated this point admirably, being remarkably decorative, rare and in very fine condition.

The spell of a great house, shuttered and barred to the world for years on end, cannot but be very powerful, and if its history combines a dash of oriental romance with the aura of money and – most potent of all – a famous name its magnetic power becomes irresistible. How far this is true was amply shown at Elveden. From the moment of the call to a private press-view of an unnamed country house – *The Times* guessed the answer but only after much research – to the last fall of the hammer, the level of interest was absolutely without precedent. As is now widely known thanks to Clive Aslet's newly researched history of the house, commissioned to accompany the six-volume catalogue, Elveden was in the 19th century the property of the Maharajah Duleep Singh, the deposed son of the Lion of the Punjab, in whom Queen Victoria took a particular motherly interest. Duleep Singh remodelled an 18th-century house, enclosing a ravishing Indian interior in solid and respectable red bricks. On Duleep's death in exile, house and estate were bought by the 1st Earl of Iveagh, who more than doubled the size of the house and built the extraordinary Indian Hall, completed in 1903. The life-span of the new house, furnished by Lord and Lady Iveagh in great style, was astonishingly short. It was closed down just before the Second World War and only partially reopened after its war-time occupation

The Ballroom, Luttrellstown
Castle, Dublin

The Ballroom, Luttrellstown
Castle, Dublin

by the R.A.F. and U.S.A.F. Since that time the house had been largely dormant, the furniture carefully laid to rest under fitted dust-sheets and covers. It was in this condition of partial mummification that the teams of cataloguers first saw the house and its remarkable contents, coming to grips on freezing January days with the gigantic piles of carpets, the rows of sinfully comfortable day-beds, the miles of brilliantly coloured tapestries, the acres of brown furniture all grouped by type, the mountainous stacks of prints and all the paraphernalia of a luxuriously appointed and well-run Edwardian country house. Eighteen thousand people came to the view, and, as at Luttrellstown, buyers flocked from all corners of the globe, vying with each other for possession of the most coveted lots. Of all the varied and unusual things in the house, perhaps the

The Marble Hall under
dust-sheets, Elveden
Hall, Norfolk

Duleep Singh's White
Drawing-Room, Elveden
Hall, Norfolk

The Marble Hall, Elveden
Hall, Norfolk

The Gatehouse of St. Osyth's Priory, Essex, by Tristram Hillier, R.A.

most surprising was the fitted cupboard in Lord Iveagh's dressing-room, discovered in the course of research for the catalogue to be the long-lost medal cabinet designed by Sir William Chambers for the 1st Earl of Charlemont in 1767. The 1st Lord Iveagh had bought the cabinet in Dublin in the late 19th century and installed it at Elveden as a wardrobe. By a singular stroke of good fortune, Chambers' drawings of the cabinet survived at Elveden too, so the purchaser will have the opportunity to recreate the original setting for this unique object.

The 1st Lord Iveagh, as is well known, formed a superb collection of pictures which he bequeathed to the nation with Kenwood House. It transpired from the Elveden sale that his eye for tapestries and textiles was equally acute. Taking advice from leading English and French dealers, he formed a wide-ranging collection, including three late Gothic panels illustrating the life of St. Bernard of Clairvaux (£64,800/$90,720), a magnificent Louis XIV Gobelins *Chancellerie* tapestry £86,400 ($120,960) and three ravishingly coloured *Enfants Jardiniers* panels in the most wonderfully fresh condition £145,800 ($204,120). With the carpets his eye was no less sure, and, interestingly, most of his purchases bore handwritten linen labels indicating origin and date of acquisition. All the carpets had been very carefully maintained – aired and mothballed every year – so that the condition was outstandingly good, accounting no doubt for the unusually fierce and competitive bidding. The textile section alone contributed £1,520,525 ($2,128,735) to the total.

Textiles, especially tapestries, were very much in evidence at the best of the Scottish house sales this year, Earlshall in Fife, remodelled in the early part of the century by the leading Scottish architect of the period, Sir Robert Lorimer. Lorimer also designed some furniture for the house, and in a relatively uncharted area of the furniture market his beautifully made and amusingly designed marquetry pieces attracted some exceptional prices – a dresser made £9,500 ($14,250) – and a flurry of interest among collectors. At the sale in July at South Lodge, Lower Beeding in Sussex, for the Executors of the late Miss C.E. Godman, the Middle Eastern textiles and carpets collected in the last two decades of the 19th century by her father, a celebrated Islamic scholar and connoisseur, also sold for remarkable prices.

At a time when the 'Heritage' is front-page news, the sale of the remaining contents of Belton House at the end of April highlighted in a constructive way the best aspects of a carefully controlled, well-planned and painstakingly thought-out hand-over of a great private house and its major contents to the National Trust, who were able, with the timely aid of the Trustees of the National Heritage Memorial Fund, to endow the house properly and purchase by private treaty nearly all the most significant items of furniture, pictures, silver, porcelain and books. Belton, the outstanding masterpiece of Restoration domestic architecture, was thus saved in all its essential aspects for future generations, and the sale disposed of mainly later accretions which had come to the family through various 19th-century inheritances. At the same time, the handsome sale catalogue provided an opportunity for publishing specially undertaken research into the history of the picture collection and recording in a lasting fashion the items that were sold. Happily, the National Trust was able to purchase, with the advent of additional funds, a few items that it had previously reluctantly let go, chiefly a spectacularly radiant 17th-century lapis lazuli cabinet (£102,600/$143,640) and a rare Japanese 17th-century lacquer coffer (£17,280/$24,192).

Every sale on the premises has a peculiar fascination and individuality; and as a means of disposing of the contents of a house – and not by any means necessarily a 'great' house – sales of this kind have few rivals for the attention of collectors, dealers or the public at large. The range this year, in terms both of celebrity and value, is enormous: from the epic heights of Elveden or Belton to the respectable solidity of The Avenue, a handsomely furnished Edinburgh town house, or The Lodge, Holyport, a comfortable, rambling establishment near Reading, remarkable for its Tiffany lamps and fine garden sculpture; from St. Osyth's Priory, characterised by the eclectic taste of Mr Somerset de Chair mingled with the historic Fitzwilliam possessions of Lady Juliet de Chair, to the Middle Eastern textiles and well made but essentially modest Victorian furnishings of South Lodge. The chart below speaks for itself.

King Street

Luttrellstown Castle, Dublin	£2,332,553	(IR£2,892,365)	26 – 8 Sept. 1983
Belton House, Lincolnshire	£1,234,323	($1,728,052)	30 Apr. – 2 May 1984
Elveden Hall, Norfolk	£6,162,719	($8,627,806)	21 – 24 May 1984
St. Osyth's Priory, Essex	£581,547	($785,088)	4 – 5 June 1984
South Lodge, Sussex	£391,932	($529,108)	16 – 17 July 1984

South Kensington

Binfield Manor, Berkshire	£74,917	($112,375)	23 Jan. 1984
Yotes Court, Kent	£172,523	($241,532)	16 Apr. 1984
The Lodge, Berkshire	£387,428	($542,399)	16 – 19 June 1984

Glasgow

Earlshall, Fife	£343,823	($515,734)	12 Sept. 1983
Finavon Castle, Angus	£99,308	($148,962)	11 Oct. 1983
Braco Castle, Perthshire	£108,056	($162,084)	24 Oct. 1983
The Avenue, Edinburgh	£221,987	($310,781)	13 Dec. 1983
Binney House, West Lothian	£117,720	($164,808)	9 Apr. 1984
Marchmont, Berwickshire	£314,280	($408,564)	5 June 1984

Amsterdam

Wit Kasteel, Brabant	£156,710	(D.fl.681,691)	7 May 1984

New York

Gallison Hall, Virginia	£295,833	($443,750)	11 Oct. 1983
Malabarra, Massachussetts	£323,383	($420,398)	24 July 1984

TOTAL	£13,319,842

Furniture

One of a pair of George II white-painted and
parcel-gilt torchères
15 in. (38 cm.) diameter; 49 in. (124.5 cm.)
high
Sold 28.6.84 in London for £20,520 ($28,112)

George II giltwood armchair
29 in. (74 cm.) wide; 39½ in. (115 cm.) high
Sold 28.6.84 in London for £41,040 ($55,404)
A chair of identical design belonged to David Garrick and is now in the Victoria & Albert Museum

One of a pair of Queen Anne
black and gold lacquer and
giltwood side-chairs
44 in. (112 cm.) high; 21¾
in. (55 cm.) wide
Sold 29.3.84 in London for
£62,640 ($91,454)
From the collection of the
Marquess of Cholmondeley,
G.C.V.O., M.C., D.L.

Above
One of a pair of George III mahogany open armchairs carved with the crest of the Connocks of Treworgey, Cornwall
23 in. (58.5 cm.) wide; 37½ in. (95 cm.) high
Sold 28.6.84 in London for £21,600 ($29,592)

Above left
One of a set of 10 George III mahogany open armchairs
23½ in. (60 cm.) wide; 39¼ in. (99.5 cm.) high
Sold 28.6.84 in London for £54,000 ($73,980)
By order of the Trustees of the late
W.W. Marsh, Esq.

Left
One of a set of 14 George III mahogany dining-chairs
In the manner of John Cobb
21½ in. (55 cm.) wide; 37½ in. (95 cm.) high
Sold 28.6.84 in London for £43,200 ($59,184)
By order of the Trustees of the J.S. Sykes
Marriage Settlement Trust

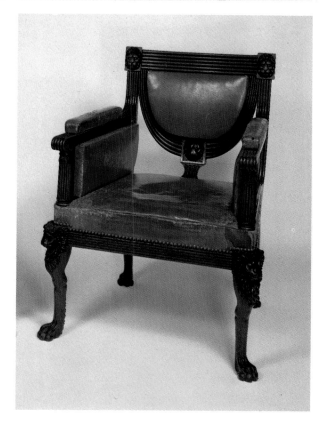

Above
One of a pair of early George III mahogany open armchairs
Sold 21.5.84 at Elveden Hall for £41,040 ($57,456)
From the collection of the Earl of Iveagh

Above right
One of a pair of early George III mahogany open armchairs
Sold 21.5.84 at Elveden Hall for £45,360 ($63,504)
From the collection of the Earl of Iveagh

Right
One of a set of 12 Regency mahogany dining-chairs
20½ in. (51 cm.) wide; 35½ in. (90 cm.) high
Sold 29.3.84 in London for £75,600 ($110,376)
Made for the 2nd Earl Talbot while Viceroy of Ireland, 1817 – 21

Above left
One of a set of 16 Irish mid-Georgian mahogany dining-chairs
37 in. (94 cm.) high; 21 in. (53.5 cm.) wide
Sold 21.5.84 at Elveden Hall for £60,480 ($84,672)
From the collection of the Earl of Iveagh

Above
One of a set of 12 early George III mahogany dining-chairs
39 in. (99 cm.) high; 27½ in. (70 cm.) wide
Sold 21.5.84 at Elveden Hall for £97,200 ($136,080)
From the collection of the Earl of Iveagh

Left
George III mahogany stool
By Thomas Chippendale
26 in. (61 cm.) wide; 18 in. (46 cm.) high; 18 in. (46 cm.) deep
Sold 29.3.84 in London for £14,580 ($21,287)
Made as part of a set of four at a cost of £7. 8s. for Sir Edward Knatchbull, Mersham-le-Hatch, Kent in 1772

Queen Anne walnut settee upholstered in contemporary St. Cyr needlework
54 in. (137 cm.) wide; 41 in. (104 cm.) high
Sold 17.11.83 in London for £66,960 ($100,440)

George II giltwood pier-glass carved with the
Wentworth crest
87 in. (221 cm.) high; 45½ in. (116 cm.) wide
Sold 4.6.84 at St. Osyth's Priory for £37,800
($53,676)
From the collection of Mr Somerset and Lady
Juliet de Chair
Formerly at Wentworth Woodhouse, Yorkshire

Queen Anne gilt-gesso side-table
37 in. (94 cm.) wide
Sold 29.3.84 in London for £30,240 ($44,150)

One of a pair of George II giltwood pier-tables
In the manner of William Kent
40½ in. (103 cm.) wide; 32½ in. (83 cm.) high; 19½ in. (49.5 cm.) deep
Sold 28.6.84 in London for £43,200 ($58,320)

George II scarlet lacquer mirror
By Giles Grendey
47 1/2 in. (121 cm.) high;
24 1/4 in. (62 cm.) wide
Sold 14.4.84 in New York for $82,500
(£58,098)
From the collection of the Rosen
Foundation
Made for the castle of the Duke of
Infantado at Lazcano, near San
Sebastian, Spain, and originally part
of a celebrated suite, including chairs,
all decorated in the same manner

Charles II ebony, ivory and marquetry centre-table
42½ in. (108 cm.) wide; 30½ in. (77 cm.) high; 27 in. (69 cm.) deep
Sold 29.3.84 in London for £36,720 ($53,611)

George III ormolu-mounted mahogany oval wine-cooler
28 in. (71 cm.) wide
Sold 21.5.84 at Elveden Hall for £24,840 ($34,776)
From the collection of the Earl of Iveagh

William and Mary walnut and seaweed marquetry cabinet-on-cabinet
Inscribed 'The property of King George I and II George Spencer Duke of Marlborough and Rich Bartholomew Esq.'
44 in. (112 cm.) wide
Sold 29.3.84 in London for £41,040 ($59,918)
From the collection of Captain H.L. Bucknall

George III satinwood and marquetry semi-elliptical commode
Attributed to Ince & Mayhew
72½ in. (184 cm.) wide; 36¾ in. (93.5 cm.) high; 29¼ in. (74 cm.) deep
Sold 29.3.84 in London for £140,400 ($204,984)
William Ince and John Mayhew, Chippendale's leading rivals in London and one of the longest lasting partnerships of the 18th-century cabinet-making world, specialised in high quality neo-classical marquetry furniture of this type. This attribution rests on the recent discovery of a fully documented commode of very similar type made to the design of Robert Adam in 1775.

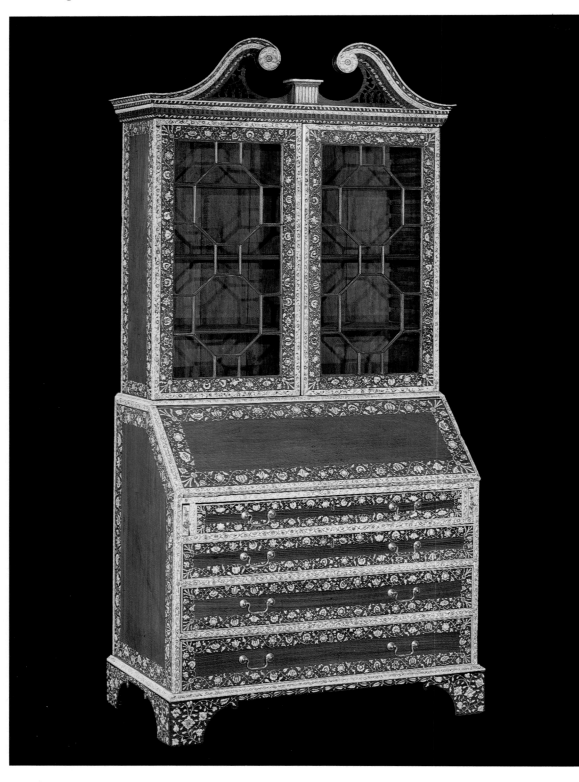

Anglo-Indian ivory-inlaid
padoukwood
bureau-cabinet
Late 18th century
44 in. (112 cm.) wide; 91 1/2
in. (232.5 cm.) high; 24 in.
(61 cm.) deep
Sold 28.6.84 in London for
£43,200 ($58,320)

One of a pair of George II white-painted side-tables, from Wardour Castle
63½ in. (161 cm.) wide; 32½ in. (80 cm.) high; 30½ in. (77.5 cm.) deep
Sold 26.9.83 at Luttrellstown Castle for IR£118,800 (£95,040)
From the collection of The Hon. Mrs Aileen Plunket
A selection of Qing Dynasty porcelain sold for a total of IR£15,120 (£12,096) is displayed on the table top

Early George III library staircase
122 in. (310 cm.) high; 49½ in. (126
cm.) wide; 67½ in. (171.5 cm.) deep
Sold 30.4.84 at Belton House for £48,600
($68,040)
From the collection of Lord Brownlow
and the Trustees of the Brownlow
Chattels Settlement

George III paktong basket-grate and fender
Attributed to Robert Adam
The grate 37½ in. (95 cm.) wide; 37 in. (94 cm.) high; the fender 56 in. (142 cm.) wide
Sold 28.6.84 in London for £25,920 ($34,992)
Paktong, a name derived from the Chinese word meaning white copper, is a rare non-tarnishing alloy of copper, nickel and tin or zinc. Its unusual qualities, especially suited to such purposes as chimney-furniture, were well recognised in 18th-century Europe, and from about 1750 a restricted number of articles including grates are known to have been made in England from this material. Adam's name has been linked with the designs for several grates of paktong, including a pair from Battle Abbey complete with fenders and fire-irons, of which the fluted supports and urn finials are identical to those on the present example. Bonnin, who wrote the standard work on paktong, characterises this grate as 'probably one of the finest specimens known'.

Pair of Louis XVI ormolu and Meissen porcelain candelabra
Modelled by J.J. Kändler
11¼ in. (28.5 cm.) high
Sold 1.12.83 in London for £51,840 ($76,205)

Louis XVI ormolu-mounted biscuit and Paris porcelain mantel clock
By Jean Nicolas Schmit
23 in. (58.5 cm.) wide; 22 in. (58 cm.) high
Sold 26.9.83 at Luttrellstown Castle for IR£19,440 (£15,805)
From the collection of The Hon. Mrs Aileen Plunket

One of a set of six Louis XV
beechwood fauteuils
By Jean Mercier
82 in. (205 cm.) wide
Sold 22.11.83 in New York
for $203,500 (£136,577)

One from a suite of Louis
XIV walnut seat furniture
Comprising six fauteuils
and a canapé
43½ in. (110 cm.) high;
26½ in. (67 cm.) wide
Sold 12.4.84 in London for
£54,000 ($78,840)

Royal Louis XVI giltwood fauteuil By François II Foliot Carving by Babel, after designs by Gondoin Sold 22.11.83 in New York for $220,000 (£147,651) Made for the *Grand Cabinet Intérieur* of Marie-Antoinette at Versailles, *c.*1779, and purchased by Gouverneur Morris in Paris, *c.*1789 – 94

Louis XV tulipwood commode
Attributed to N.-J. Marchand
38½ in. (97 cm.) wide; 33 in. (83.5 cm.) high; 23 in. (59 cm.) deep
Sold 26.9.83 at Luttrellstown Castle for IR£86,400 (£69,120)
From the collection of The Hon. Mrs Aileen Plunket
This commode bears the obliterated inventory number 2016, indicating that it was supplied in 1755 together with a matching commode with cupboards in the place of drawers, now in the Wallace Collection, for the bedroom of Louis XV at the Château of Fontainebleau

THE BUREAU PLAT OF MADAME SOPHIE FROM THE PALACE OF VERSAILLES,
Louis XVI marquetry bureau plat
By J.-H. Riesener
$52\frac{1}{2}$ in. (133 cm.) wide; $26\frac{1}{2}$ in. (67 cm.) deep; $30\frac{3}{4}$ in. (78 cm.) high
Sold 1.12.83 in London for £259,200 ($381,024)
Bought by the Musée de Versailles
This desk was delivered by Riesener to Versailles on 18 March 1779 for the use of Madame Sophie de France, sixth daughter of
Louis XV. The inventory number (2979) on the underside of the table, almost obliterated by the passage of time, was revealed with
the pioneering use of laser photography by the Forensic Laboratories of Scotland Yard, thus making possible the precise identification
of this long-lost piece of French Royal furniture.

Louis XVI marquetry table à écrire
By J.-H. Riesener
31½ in. (79.7 cm.) wide; 16¾ in. (42.5 cm.) deep; 28½ in. (72.5 cm.) high
Sold 1.12.83 in London for £259,200 ($381,024)

The Bureau Plat of the Empress Maria Feodorovna from the Palace of Pavlovsk

HUGH ROBERTS

This celebrated piece of furniture, which has now come to rest at Malibu, has had a more than usually interesting history. It was made by the distinguished *ébéniste* Martin Carlin under the direction of the leading Parisian *marchand-mercier* Dominique Daguerre, whose label it bears. Most of the Sèvres porcelain plaques are dated 1778 and were probably painted by the flower-painter Bouillar. A number of the plaques still have their original price tickets on the back, ranging from 96 *livres* for the large carved panels at the end to 30 *livres* for the small side-panels. The design of the table is very unusual and suggests that it was perhaps originally conceived for a bowed or oval room. We do not know from whom Daguerre received the original commission, but we do know that the table was back in his shop in the Rue St. Honoré in May 1784, for on the 25th of that month he was visited by the Grand Duke Paul of Russia and his wife Maria Feodorovna, son and daughter-in-law of Catherine the Great. They were in the middle of an extended tour of Europe, travelling incognito as the Comte and Comtesse du Nord, buying grand and expensive furnishings for their new palace Pavlovsk, built as a present from the Empress. On this visit they spent 35,093 *livres* at Daguerre's shop and came away with – among other things – four porcelain-mounted pieces of furniture, all by Carlin, including this table.

Some years after her return to Russia, the Grand Duchess compiled a detailed inventory of her possessions, and in the charming account of her luxuriously decorated bedroom notes this table standing by her chaise longue. There it remained until just after the Russian Revolution when, together with a number of other major pieces of furniture and tapestries, it was sold to Lord Duveen, the enormously successful and influential art dealer. Among his richest clients at that time was the widow of the pioneer motor manufacturer Mrs Horace Dodge, and it was through Duveen that Mrs Dodge acquired her fabled collection of paintings, furniture and works of art to furnish her re-created Trianon, Rose Terrace, on the shores of Lake Michigan. After her death, the table (and the choicest part of her collection) came to Christie's in London, where in June 1971 it fetched the world record price of 165,000 gns. ($415,800). On its second visit to London, after 12 years in a Continental collection, it became again one of the most expensive pieces of furniture in the world, selling to the Getty Museum for £918,000 ($1,349,460).

THE BUREAU PLAT OF THE EMPRESS MARIA FEODOROVNA FROM THE PALACE OF PAVLOVSK
Louis XVI porcelain-mounted bureau plat
By Martin Carlin
51¾ in. (131.5 cm.) wide; 24½ in. (62 cm.) deep; 30¼ in. (77 cm.) high
Sold 1.12.83 in London for £918,000 ($1,349,460)
Bought by the J. Paul Getty Museum, Malibu, California

Louis XVI parquetry
table à transformations
19¼ in. (49 cm.) wide
Sold 12.4.84 in London
for £32,400 ($47,304)

Louis XVI ormolu-mounted tulipwood and bois satiné commode
By C. Topino
Stamped C. TOPINO JME
38½ in. (98 cm.) wide; 35 in. (89 cm.) high; 19 in. (48 cm.) deep
Sold 12.4.84 in London for £20,520 ($29,959)

Louis XVI tulipwood
and kingwood armoire
By J.-F. Leleu
53½ in. (136 cm.) wide;
75 in. (191 cm.) high;
17½ in. (44.5 cm.) deep
Sold 1.12.83 in London
for £108,000 ($158, 760)

Louis XV kingwood coiffeuse
By B. Peridiez
With St. Cloud porcelain and vernis Martin fittings
31 in. (79 cm.) wide; 19 in. (48.5 cm.) deep; 36 in. (91 cm.) high
Sold 5.7.84 in London for £32,400 ($43,470)

Louis XIV ormolu-mounted ebony and tortoiseshell marquetry commode à vantaux
55¼ in. (140 cm.) wide; 32½ in. (82.5 cm.) high; 28½ in. (72.5 cm.) deep
Sold 12.4.84 in London for £486,000 ($709,560)
By order of the Trustees of the Cholmondeley Settlement, removed from Houghton Hall, Norfolk
Bought by the J. Paul Getty Museum, Malibu, California
The monumental design of this commode, which incorporates the wings and caduceus of Mercury on the front, reflects some aspects of the known work of the greatest of Louis XIV's cabinet-makers, André-Charles Boulle. Its 18th-century history remains obscure, though there is a nearly identical piece, perhaps originally a pair to this, in the Hermitage, Leningrad.

Transitional black
lacquer secretaire à
abattant
By René Dubois
19½ in. (50 cm.) wide;
50½ in. (128 cm.) high;
10 in. (25.5 cm.) deep
Sold 1.12.83 in London
for £86,400 ($127,008)

Roman trumeau
*c.*1720
102½ in. (260 cm.) high; 52¼ in.
(132 cm.) wide; 26½ in. (67 cm.) deep
Sold 29.11.83 in Rome for L.40,000,000
(£18,785)

Late 17th-century lapis lazuli
table-cabinet
42 in. (107 cm.) wide; 17¾
in. (45 cm.) deep; 67½ in.
(172.5 cm.) high
Sold 30.4.84 at Belton House
for £102,600 ($143,640)
From the collection of Lord
Brownlow and the Trustees of
the Brownlow Chattels
Settlement
Purchased by The National
Trust to remain at Belton
House

Italian pietra dura marble top of a Regency giltwood pier-table
17th – 18th century
53 in. (134.5 cm.) wide
Sold 5.6.84 at Marchmont, Berwickshire, for £60,480 ($81,648)

Set of Dutch early 18th-century floral marquetry furniture
Sold 11.5.84 in Amsterdam for a total of D.fl.522,000 (£120,000)

This is one of the most important sets of Dutch early 18th-century floral marquetry furniture of the so-called 'William and Mary' type ever to be sold. The set, comprising a cabinet, a side-table, a pair of guéridons and a mirror, sold for a record price and was bought by *Stichting tot behoud van Kasteel Amerongen.* This means that the set will now return to its original home. The furniture was the property of the late Goddard John George Charles, Count of Aldenburg Bentinck, Lord of Amerongen, and, together with another similar set of floral marquetry furniture, furnished the great hall at Amerongen Castle. It is likely that one set was originally made for Amerongen while the other originates from the Castle of Zuylesteyn, and was therefore once the property of William of Nassau Zuylesteyn, the 1st Earl of Rochford (1649 – 1708). He was a personal friend of William III and after having rendered great services to the 'Stadhouder-Koning' he retired to Zuylesteyn. In the 1830s, when the last of the male heirs of the Van Nassau of Zuylesteyn had died, Zuylesteyn was inherited by George Goddard Henry, Count of Reede, 8th Earl of Athlone. His sister, Lady Villiers, removed part of the furnishings of this castle to Amerongen, where she stayed during her visits to The Netherlands. Because of the similarity of the two sets of furniture, it is generally assumed that they were both made by the same cabinet-maker and, although none of the furniture is signed, one of the outstanding cabinet-makers of Amsterdam, Jan van Mekeren, is generally regarded as the maker. Van Mekeren (1658 – 1733) was one of the leading artists in his field and an inventory drawn up after his death in 1733 shows that he had a large and important clientele in the Amsterdam area.

Federal mahogany accordion-action dining-table
New York, 1800 – 10
29 in. (74 cm.) high; 187½ in. (476 cm.) long; 60 in. (152.5 cm.) wide
Sold 21.1.84 in New York for $187,000 (£133,571)
Record auction price for a piece of American Federal furniture
According to family tradition, the table belonged to Martin Van Buren (1782 – 1862), President of the United States from 1837 to
1841, and was used in his house, Lindenwald, in Kinderhook, N.Y. Dr John Vanderpoel, an early owner of the table, was Van
Buren's personal physician and lived in Kinderhook. Lindenwald was built in 1797 by Judge Van Ness. Van Buren purchased it in
1839 and moved in after his presidential term expired in 1841. He lived there until his death in 1862, when the house passed to his
sons, who then sold it to Leonard Jerome. It was probably during this time that the furnishings were dispersed.

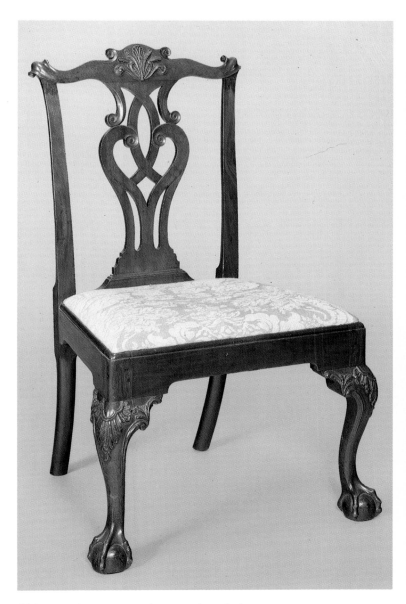

Chippendale carved mahogany side-chair
Philadelphia, 1765 – 85
Sold 14.10.83 in New York for $23,100 (£15,298)
From the collection of the Benjamin Ginsburg Antiquary

Queen Anne carved mahogany side-chair
New York, 1745 – 65
Sold 14.10.83 in New York for $275,000 (£182,119)
From the collection of the Benjamin Ginsburg Antiquary

Chippendale mahogany serpentine chest of drawers
Salem, Massachusetts, 1800
40¼ in. (102 cm.) high; 42 in. (106.6 cm.) wide; 20 in. (50.8 cm.) deep
Sold 16.6.84 in New York for $93,500 (£66,785)
From the collection of Mr and Mrs Hugh B. Cox

Queen Anne carved walnut high chest of drawers
Salem, Massachusetts, 1740 – 60
87¾ in. (220.8 cm.) high; 41⅞ in. (105.4 cm.) wide; 22 in. (55.8 cm.) deep
Sold 16.6.84 in New York for $82,500 (£58,928)

Chippendale mahogany double chair-back settee
Massachusetts, 1760 – 80
39 in. (99 cm.) high; 61 in. (154.8 cm.) wide; 27 in. (68.5 cm.) deep
Sold 16.6.84 in New York for $93,500 (£66,785)
From the collection of Mr and Mrs Hugh B. Cox

Two from a set of six Chippendale carved mahogany side-chairs
By Samuel Walton, Philadelphia, 1765 – 85
Sold 16.6.84 in New York for $110,000 (£78,571)
From the collection of Mr and Mrs Hugh B. Cox

Italian violin
By Carlo Tononi, Venice 1725
Length of back 13 15/16 in. (35.4 cm.)
Sold 20.6.84 in London for £34,560 ($47,693)

THE ELPHINSTONE
STRADIVARI
Italian violin
By Antonio
Stradivari, Cremona
1684
Length of back 14 in.
(35.5 cm.)
Sold 20.6.84 in
London for £91,800
($126,684)

Italian violoncello
By Carlo Ferdinando Landolfi, Milan 1758
Length of back 28 13/16 in. (73.4 cm.)
Sold 21.11.83 in London for £29,160 ($43,448)

Italian violoncello
By J. & A. Gagliano, Naples 1837
Length of back 29 9/16 in. (75.1 cm.)
Sold 21.11.83 in London for £27,000 ($40,230)

French violin
By Jean-Baptiste Vuillaume, Paris
*c.*1860
Length of back 14 in. (35.6 cm.)
Sold 20.6.84 in London for £19,440 ($26,827)

Italian viola
By Pietro Giovanni Mantegazza
*c.*1780
Length of back 16 in. (40.6 cm.)
Sold 21.11.83 in London for £16,200 ($24,138)

Louis XIV Gobelins tapestry depicting Spring
From the Infant Gardeners after Charles Le Brun
10 ft. 10 in. × 16 ft. 8 in. (3.3 × 5.08 m.)
Sold 22.5.84 at Elveden Hall for £59,400 ($83,160)
From the collection of the Earl of Iveagh

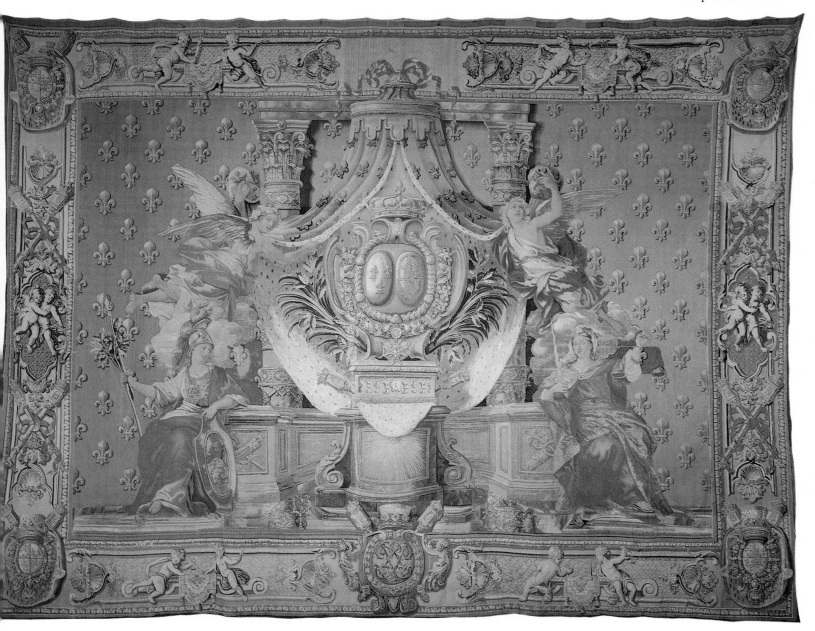

Louis XIV Gobelins Chancellerie tapestry
11 ft. 6 in. × 14 ft. 9 in. (3.5 × 4.5 m.)
Sold 22.5.84 at Elveden Hall for £91,800 ($128,520)
From the collection of the Earl of Iveagh

Nicholas I tapestry carpet
Bearing the mark of the Russian Imperial manufactory
Dated 1835
16 ft. 3 in. × 15 ft. 7 in. (4.94 × 4.74 m.)
Sold 26.9.83 at Luttrellstown Castle for IR£81,000 (£64,800)
From the collection of The Hon. Mrs Aileen Plunket

Antique Qashqai rug
Labelled *3670, Harvey Nichols,*
September 1894
9 ft. 5 in. × 5 ft. 11 in. (286 × 180 cm.)
Sold 22.5.84 at Elveden Hall for £16,200
($22,600)
From the collection of the Earl of Iveagh

Antique Tabriz carpet
Labelled *7561, Liberty,
September 1903*
14 ft. 2 in. × 10 ft. 4 in.
(431 × 314 cm.)
Sold 22.5.84 at Elveden
Hall for £20,520 ($28,728)
From the collection of the
Earl of Iveagh

Isfahan carpet
12 ft. × 9 ft.
(366 × 274 cm.)
Sold 23.3.84 in
London for £10,800
($15,768)

Antique Heriz carpet
15 ft. 6 in. × 11 ft. 5 in.
(471 × 347 cm.)
Sold 1.12.83 in London
for £12,960 ($19,051)

Shirvan Alpen rug
Dated AH 1230 – AD 1814
7 ft. 1 in. × 4 ft. 7 in. (215 × 140 cm.)
Sold 1.12.83 in London for £6,480
($9,526)

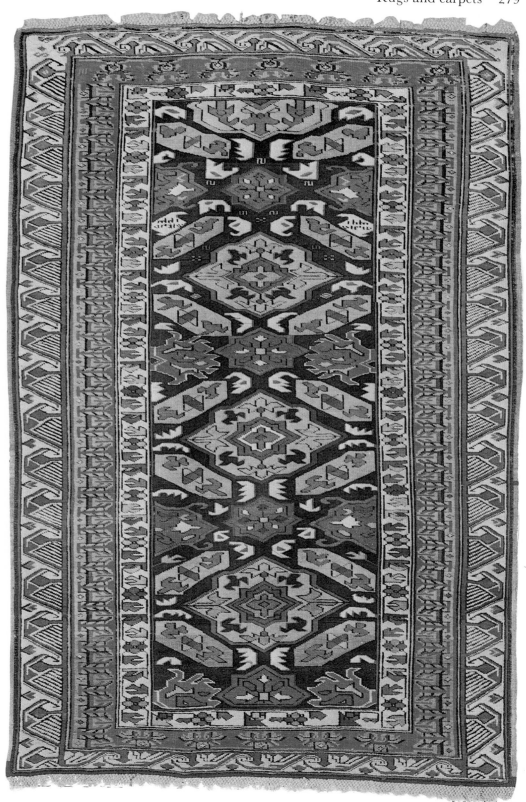

Canton embroidered
satin hanging
Late 19th century
137 × 120 in.
(347.8 × 304.7 cm.)
Sold 22.5.84 at Elveden
Hall for £3,456 ($4,838)
From the collection of the
Earl of Iveagh

Clocks and Watches

French gilt brass drum clock
Probably Blois, first half
16th century
Stamped *I.DE.P* in rectangular
punch
1¼ in. (3.4 cm.) high; 1¾ in.
(4.3 cm.) diameter
Sold 18.4.84 in New York for
$99,000 (£69,231)

English automaton musical clock
Made for the Maharajah of Hyderabad, in the manner of James Cox, with enamel plaques by *Craft*
*c.*1775
17½ in. (44 cm.) high
Sold 16.5.84 in Geneva for Sw.fr.159,500 (£50,634)

French gilt brass table clock
with minute hand, calendar
and alarm
Signed *G. Estienne À Caen*
Second quarter 17th century
12 in. (30.5 cm.) high
Sold 24.10.83 in New York
for $242,000 (£161,333)
From the collection of
The University of Rochester

Far left
Joseph Knibb, London: Charles II ebony half grande sonnerie bracket clock
*c.*1685
12 in. (30.5 cm.) high
Sold for £19,440 ($28,771)

Left
Dan. Quare, London, 138: George I walnut striking bracket clock with alarm
*c.*1715
16½ in. (42 cm.) high
Sold for £22,680 ($33,566)

Both sold 24.11.83 in London
From the collection of Melvyn H. Rollason, Esq.

Late Stuart silver-mounted tortoiseshell quarter-striking bracket clock
Signed *Wm. Davis Londoni 16 Fecit 86*
Probably *c.*1715
24 in. (61 cm.) high
Sold 23.5.84 in London for £19,440 ($27,216)

English gilt metal pair-cased
musical coach watch
Unsigned and numbered
1363
*c.*1780
6¼ in. (16 cm.) diameter
Sold 16.5.84 in Geneva for
Sw.fr.66,000 (£20,952)

Swiss gold, enamel and pearl-set watch with musical automaton
Attributed to Piguet et Meylan
*c.*1810
2¼ in. (5.5 cm.) diameter
Sold 15.11.83 in Geneva for Sw.fr.55,000 (£17,190)

Swiss gold, enamel and pearl-set watch with musical automaton
Stamped *PM* for Piguet et Meylan
*c.*1810
1 ³⁄₄ in. (4.7 cm.) diameter
Sold 15.11.83 in Geneva for Sw.fr.85,800 (£26,800)

Above
Swiss gold and enamel automaton musical watch
In the manner of Piguet et Meylan
c. 1810
2¼ in. (5.5 cm.) diameter
Sold 16.5.84 in Geneva for Sw.fr.50,600 (£16,063)

Above right
Swiss gold and enamel quarter-repeating Jaquemart
automaton watch
Attributed to Piguet et Meylan
c. 1810
2¼ in. (5.5 cm.) diameter
Sold 16.5.84 in Geneva for Sw.fr.49,500 (£15,714)

Right
Swiss gold and enamel bras-en-l'air automaton watch
Signed *Guillarmod Frères*
c. 1800
2¼ in. (5.5 cm.) diameter
Sold 15.11.83 in Geneva for Sw.fr.39,600 (£12,375)

Above
English gold keyless lever tourbillion watch
Signed *Dent, watchmaker to the King, 61 Strand & 4 Royal Exchange London No. 56423*
London 1906
2¼ in. (5.5 cm.) diameter
Sold 23.5.84 in London for £22,680 ($31,752)

Above right
English enamel and pearl-set cylinder watch
Signed *William Anthony, London, No. 1849*
*c.*1790
2½ in. (6.3 cm.) diameter
Sold 15.11.83 in Geneva for Sw.fr.41,800 (£13,060)

Right
Swiss gold minute-repeating split-second chronograph with perpetual calendar and moon phase
Signed *Patek Phillippe and Co., Geneva, No. 97782,* retailed by *Bailey, Banks and Biddle Co., Philadelphia*
2¼ in. (5.5 cm.) diameter
Sold 18.4.84 in New York for $55,000 (£38,461)

Germanic brass astronomical compendium
Signed *C.H. SCHINDLER, IUN, PRAG FECIT*
Probably first quarter 18th century
4 in. (11.5 cm.) long
Sold 18.4.84 in New York for $24,200 (£16,923)

Polish gilt metal surveyor's quadrant and geometric square
Signed *Pragae Fecit Erasmus Habermelius*
Late 16th century
Sold 23.5.84 in London for £16,500 ($22,680)

Germanic gilt brass and silver geared universal equatorial dial
The chapter ring signed *P:IP:SI*
Early 18th century
4 ¾ in. (12 cm.) long
Sold 18.4.84 in New York for $28,600 (£20,000)

French chased silver astronomical clock watch
Signed *N. Vollant à Paris*
First half 17th century
2¼ in. (5.5 cm.) diameter
Sold 18.4.84 in New York for $37,400 (£26,154)

Jewellery

THE MAHJAL DIAMOND
Unmounted fancy yellow
cushion-shaped diamond
Weighing 139.385 carats
Sold 26.11.83 in Geneva for
Sw.fr.1,320,000 (£412,500)
The diamond is said to have
been part of the collection of
the Maharajah of
Kapurthala, who wore it as a
turban piece

The Magnificent Jewels of Florence J. Gould

NEIL LETSON

The romance, legend, fact and fiction surrounding the sale of important jewels have as long and interesting a history as that of auctions themselves. In 1795 all of London flocked to Mr Christie's Great Rooms in Pall Mall to see Madame Dubarry's jewels come under the hammer. In 1927 the sale of some of the Russian Crown Jewels attracted the same attention. During the last two decades Geneva saw the dispersal of the jewels of Nina Dyer and Lady Deterding and all previous sales records broken. On 11 April 1984, the attention of the jewellery world focused on New York for the sale of the magnificent jewels of Florence J. Gould, which in less than one and a half hours of lively bidding, brought $8.1 million (£5.6 million) and set a new record for the sale of a one-owner jewellery collection.

Mrs Florence J. Gould

Once Christie's had been selected by the executors of Mrs Gould's estate, New York was chosen for the site of the sale because the gilded and impetuous destinies of the Gould family have been of compelling interest to Americans since Jay Gould founded the family fortune in the 19th century by becoming a railway magnate. The magnitude of the Gould holdings may be gathered from the fact that at the time of his death in 1892 it was said that one in every 10 miles of railroad in America was under Jay Gould's control, with the Western Union Telegraph Company providing a minor source of additional revenue. One social historian has said that the Goulds never considered it necessary to inform other family members of financial transactions involving less that $50 million.

Frank Gould was Jay Gould's youngest son. A sportsman, turf enthusiast, amateur archaeologist, Francophile, proprietor of the Palais de la Méditerranée (the superb gambling establishment at Cannes), he built the Provençal Hotel and developed Juan-les-Pins as a resort for international society.

Florence was the daughter of Maximilien Lacaze, a French publisher, and was born in San Francisco in 1895. She was an aspiring opera singer, but after two unsuccessful marriages gave up this plan when she married Frank Gould in 1923, and they moved permanently to the South of France.

It was at the spacious villa, El Patio, a few miles from Cannes and at their Paris residence in the Avenue Malakoff that the volume and degree of the Gould hospitality became legendary and where Florence began a 40-year tradition of encouraging the arts. She led a life remarkable in its diversity and dedicated to beauty in every form, whether it was painting, jewellery, furniture, literature or music.

She inherited a literary salon from her close friend Marie-Louise Bousquet, then in charge of French *Vogue*, which counted such brilliant names as Marcel Jouhandeau and Jean Paulhan as members. Florence presided over her salon on Thursdays in the Avenue Malakoff, and her *déjeuners littéraires* became a magnet for the academic and artistic world. To an already heady mix, she added her own secret ingredient: the knowledge that writers like meeting society people and a salon frequented only by intellectuals lacks elegance.

Sapphire and diamond
necklace
Centring upon three oval-cut
sapphires weighing
approximately 24.09, 40.87
and 26.95 carats, suspending
an oval-cut sapphire weighing
approximately 114.3 carats
known as *The Blue Princess*
Sold 11.4.84 in New York for
$1,320,000 (£916,666)
From the collection of
Florence J. Gould

Artists Marie Laurençin and Jean Dubuffet, musician George Auric and writers Paul
Leautaud, François Mauriac and Jean Cocteau added to the stimulating company and assisted
Florence in her influential role as an encouraging force to young, creative talent after the war.
In 1955 she took over responsibility for the *Prix des Critiques* and founded both the *Prix Max
Jacob* and the *Prix Roger Nimier*. For her contributions to fine arts and literature she was made
an *Officier de la Légion d'Honneur* and became one of the few women to hold the rank of *Correspon-
dant Étranger de l'Académie des Beaux-Arts* in Paris.

The years between 1950 and 1970 were the years of serious if eclectic jewellery collecting
for Florence Gould. She patronised the leading houses – Van Cleef & Arpels, Cartier, Tiffany,

Bulgari, Chaumet, M. Gerard, André Col and Fred – as well as commissioning work from private master craftsmen. Perhaps half the jewels in the collection were inspired by her own designs or executed under her well-informed supervision. *Art & Auction* (April 1984) points out that her jewels '*reflected tastes* rather than taste itself, which is a denominator as difficult to define in jewellery as in any branch of the decorative arts'.

Mrs Gould was seldom seen without an array of precious gems. These ranged from casual day jewellery, represented in the sale by a charming set of carved ivory dolphins set with diamonds and emeralds by M. Gerard, which fetched $12,100 (£8,402), to the larger and more important items which appeared as the day wore on. One friend recalls seeing her depart by pedicab into the steaming Cambodian jungle to explore the ruins of Angkor Wat shimmering in diamonds. Somehow she managed to do this without creating an impression of excess, and her imposing and bejewelled silhouette became her trademark.

Sapphire and diamond ring
The sapphire weighing
approximately 65.53 carats
Sold 11.4.84 in New York for
$440,000 (£305,555)
From the collection of
Florence J. Gould

In 1978 she was the victim of a robbery that took almost half her collection. 'Thank goodness they took only my everyday things,' Mrs Gould remarked as she set about refurbishing her jewel case and looking into such gloomy matters as steel shutters, ferocious guard dogs and night-watchmen. Thieves made another attempt on the Gould collection in January 1984, when masked gunmen burst into Christie's London sale-rooms during an exhibition of the jewels, smashing vitrines and forcing staff and visitors to the floor. If it had not been for adroit and quick-witted actions on the part of a young Christie's jewellery expert much more would have been taken. As it was, only two items were stolen, neither of them major Gould pieces.

Prior to the sale, the 86-item collection was shown not only in London but also in San Francisco, Los Angeles, Dallas, Houston, Chicago and Philadelphia. In New York a series of glittering social events was arranged to promote the sale and give as many prospective buyers as possible an opportunity to examine jewels the Shah of Iran once compared favourably to his own treasures and which certainly ranked in the top 10 private jewel collections in the world. In reviewing plans and prospects for the sale, Christie's Senior Vice-President, Francois Curiel, himself an authority of international reputation in the area of fine jewellery and rare gemstones, said, 'Perhaps no comparable collection will come up for auction again since its overall consistency in calibre, quality and workmanship contribute to make this one of the truly great jewellery collections of the century.'

The sale-room of Christie's Park Avenue literally crackled with excitement and expectancy as Chairman John Floyd began the sale, before an international audience almost as dazzling as the jewels themselves. Dealers from 47th Street, social celebrities, world-renowned jewellers, major collectors and film stars waved their tickets and jostled each other for seats as they settled in for the 'sale of the century'. Spontaneous applause rippled across the packed rooms as one sales record after another was broken, and buyers glanced nervously around for encouragement from fellow collectors. The bank of red telephones buzzed steadily as bidders around the world helped to establish record prices which may well mark the long-awaited turning-point in a jewellery market on the decline, shaken by economic and political uncertainties in the last few years.

Because pearls were Mrs Gould's favourite jewel this review of specific items in the sale begins with what many consider to be the most aesthetically pleasing piece in the collection, a beautifully cultured pearl and diamond fringe necklace made for her by Alexandre Reza of Paris, a close friend and adviser whose large and distinguished workshop in the Place Vendôme produces some of the finest jewellery in France today. The necklace, designed as a circular and marquise-cut diamond floral vine, is enhanced with six pear-shaped, round and marquise-cut diamond blossoms

THE VICTORY DIAMOND
Rectangular-cut diamond of 31.35 carats mounted as a ring
With gemological certificate number 6015074 stating that the diamond is D colour (colourless) and VS1, and the original working diagram indicating that the diamond may be potentially flawless
Sold 11.4.84 in New York for $880,000 (£611,111)
From the collection of Florence J. Gould
In 1945 a 770 carat rough diamond was discovered in the Woyie River in Sierra Leone. The stone was the third largest rough diamond found in Africa. Although its fine colour and clarity were immediately recognised, the diamond was not cut until eight years later, by the firm of Briefel & Limer of London. Thirty gems were produced. The largest diamond, an exceptionally fine gem of 31.35 carats, was named *The Victory Diamond* in honour of the Allied victory, which coincided with the gem's discovery.

mounted *en tremblant*, fringed with baguette-cut diamond stems suspending pear-shaped cultured pearls and a floral clasp suspending diamond and cultured pearl pendants. Total weight of the 371 diamonds is 123.55 carats. The necklace brought $990,000 (£687,500).

Mrs Gould's exceedingly fine cultured pearl and diamond choker with a 5.13 carat diamond clasp fetched $220,000 (£152,778) and her cultured pearl and diamond earrings with detachable pearl drops brought $121,000 (£84,028). A two-strand cultured pearl and diamond necklace made $198,000 ($137,500).

Historically, the most important item in the sale was the Victory Diamond, named to mark the end of World War II a few months after its discovery. The rectangular-cut 31.35 carat D-VS1 potentially flawless stone, mounted as a ring, is the largest of the 30 diamonds fashioned from a 770 carat rough recovered in the swampy morasses of the Woyie River in Sierra Leone. At the time of its discovery, the spectacular rough was the third largest diamond ever found in Africa and the largest from alluvial sources – a record held for almost three decades. The stone remained uncut for eight years during which it was part of an exhibition of diamonds shown to Queen Mary in 1949. The cutting was undertaken by the London firm of Briefel & Limer after a careful study of its crystaleographic characteristics and the design of a special machine for the sawing operation, made necessary by the large number of inclusions. Because of these internal impurities, it was not possible to cut a single enormous gem, but rather many stones of exceptionally fine colour, representing 36.67 per cent of the rough, an extremely high yield for a heavily included stone and a testament to the skill of the cutters.

It is uncertain whether Florence Gould knew the full history of this diamond. She wore it infrequently during her last years and left no written provenance. It was identified by Christie's New York gemologist Mary M. Murphy during her meticulous research of the collection, and through her efforts this important diamond has now been accurately documented. Coming up near the end of the sale, the Victory Diamond was sold to a private Saudi Arabian collector for $880,000 (£611,111).

Other diamonds included: a platinum necklace by Alexandre Reza, of graduated baguette-cut diamonds with a detachable pendant set with a 48.92 carat pear-shaped diamond, which sold for $660,000 (£458,333); a rectangular-cut 36.66 carat fancy yellow diamond ring mounted in platinum with baguette-cut and trapeze-cut diamonds, knocked down at $418,000 (£290,200); and a single earring (the mate having been taken during the London robbery) from Harry Winston, with diamonds totalling 32.1 carats, which brought $209,000 (£145,140).

It was Florence Gould's emeralds that dazzled San Francisco when she paid the only visit she made to her native city after her marriage, to attend the 50th anniversary of the founding of the Palace of the Legion of Honour. Her most spectacular piece was an emerald bead necklace by Alexandre Reza. This stupendous necklace, which had to be restrung every few months to support its weight, comprises 31 graduated fluted emerald beads from the collection of an Eastern potentate, weighing 890.88 carats, with a clasp set with a marquise-cut light yellow diamond weighing 7.46 carats. It sold for $495,000 (£343,750), compared with the high estimate of $220,000.

Six important lots of ruby jewellery included a ruby and diamond bead sautoir by M. Gerard, a ruby and diamond brooch, a ruby and diamond bracelet and a pair of invisibly set ruby and diamond earrings, all by Van Cleef & Arpels, as well as an important ruby and diamond cocktail ring. Together the rubies brought $638,000 (£443,050), a figure well above the highest estimate.

The last lot to be sold, a jewel which captured the imagination of press and public alike, was an unsigned sapphire and diamond necklace containing *The Blue Princess*, an oval-cut 114.3 carat stone acquired by Claude Arpels in India in 1955, when many Maharajas were disposing of their treasures. Van Cleef & Arpels set the splendid sapphire as the central pendant in a necklace of great elegance and restraint, incorporating gently curving S-scrolls in circular-cut diamonds. Later, Mrs Gould gave the piece importance by the addition of three sapphires of 24.09, 40.87 and 26.95 carats and substituting two strands of platinum mounted baguette-cut sapphires while retaining and extending the S-curve motif in circular-cut diamonds. The necklace brought $1,320,000 (£916,666) from a private collector bidding by telephone.

The necklace and a complimentary cushion-cut sapphire ring of 65.53 carats, which sold for $440,000 (£305,555), are unique on today's market, and the prices realised will aid substantially in pushing sapphires into the range formerly reserved for rubies and emeralds.

Florence Gould enjoyed her jewels and the attention they received. She wore them as jewels *should* be worn – with modest nonchalance, but with complete awareness of their history, value and the pleasure they afford both the wearer and the observer. She always intended them to be sold at auction and often said she regretted it would not be possible for her to attend the sale. It would no doubt give her great satisfaction to know they are now giving pleasure to others in many parts of the world, far removed from her beloved Côte d'Azur.

As her literary salon helped elevate and expand the questing spirit of French intellectualism, so will the sale of her jewels, which benefits the Florence Gould Foundation, further the cause of Franco-American amity and friendship, something Mrs Gould did so admirably during her lifetime.

Centre
Pair of cultured pearl
and diamond earrings
Sold for $121,000
(£84,028)

Cultured pearl and
diamond choker
Of 31 slightly
graduated pearls
measuring
approximately 13.35
to 15.3 mm.
Sold for $220,000
(£152,778)

Both sold 11.4.84 in
New York
From the collection of
Florence J. Gould

Natural pearl necklace
Of 32 graduated pearls measuring approximately 10.2 to 15.2 mm. With gemological certificate number 191764 stating that the pearls are natural
Sold 25.10.83 in New York for $374,000 (£244,444)
This necklace was originally sold by Bulgari in the 1920s, and over the next 50 years the owner embellished it by replacing individual pearls. In its present composition, the necklace compares in importance with one of the two pearl strands from the Prussian Crown Jewels sold in Holland in 1923. Weighing 1,765.32 grains, this necklace is the largest to appear on the jewellery auction market since World War II.

Cultured pearl and
diamond fringe
necklace
By Alexandre Reza,
Paris
Sold 11.4.84 in New
York for $990,000
(£687,500)
From the collection of
Florence J. Gould

Above
Pair of natural pearl and diamond ear-pendants
With an expertise by Gübelin stating that the pearls are natural
Sold 26.11.83 in Geneva for Sw.fr.132,000 (£42,581)

Above right
Natural black pearl and diamond brooch
Sold for $82,500 (£57,292)

Right
Pair of natural black and white pearl ear-pendants
Sold for $88,000 (£61,111)

Both sold 11.4.84 in New York
From the collection of Florence J. Gould

Diamond necklace
Suspending a detachable
pear-shaped diamond
weighing approximately
48.92 carats
By Alexandre Reza, Paris
Sold 11.4.84 in New York for
$660,000 (£458,333)
From the collection of
Florence J. Gould

Diamond necklace
Suspending five pear-
shaped diamond
pendants weighing
approximately 3.56,
3.57, 5.48, 5.72 and
10.25 carats
Sold 25.10.83 in New
York for $539,000
(£352,287)
From the estate of
Eleanor C. de Guigne

Sapphire and diamond
necklace
Sold 7.12.83 in
London for £54,000
($78,840)

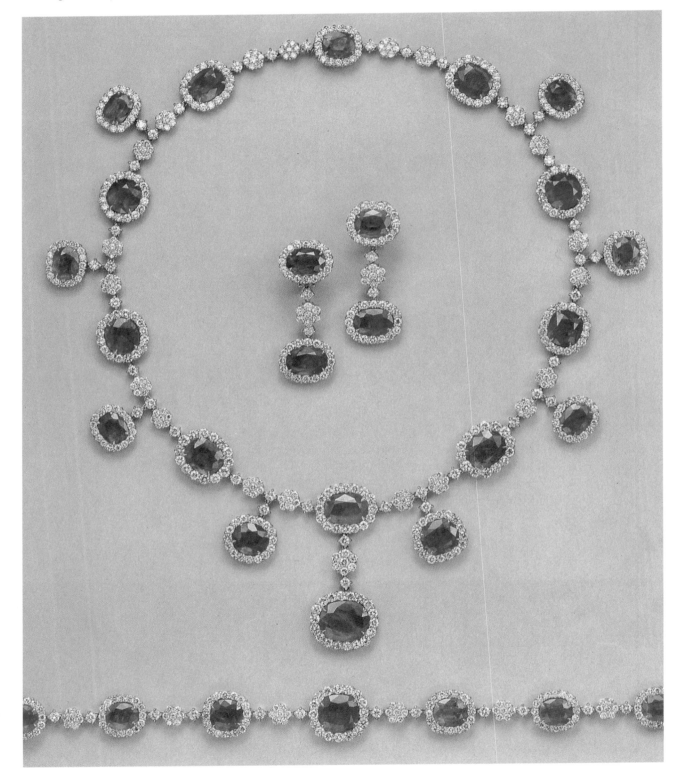

Pair of invisibly-set ruby
and diamond ear-clips
Signed by Van Cleef &
Arpels
Sold for Sw.fr.143,000
(£46,129)

Invisibly-set ruby and
diamond bracelet
Although not signed, this
bracelet was probably made
by Van Cleef & Arpels
Sold for Sw.fr.198,000
(£63,871)

Invisibly-set ruby and
diamond flower brooch
Signed by Van Cleef &
Arpels
Sold for Sw.fr.363,000
(£117,097)

All sold 16.11.83 in Geneva

Opposite
Ruby and diamond
necklace, bracelet and pair
of ear-pendants
All sold 17.5.84 in Geneva
for Sw.fr.198,000 (£62,857)

Emerald and diamond ring
The emerald weighing approximately 22.23 carats
Sold for $154,000 (£106,944)

Emerald and diamond bracelet
Signed by Van Cleef & Arpels
Sold for $264,000 (£183,333)

Single-stone diamond ring
The diamond weighing approximately 22.12 carats
With gemological certificate number 6015726 stating that the diamond is D colour (colourless) and SI2
Sold for $198,000 (£137,500)

All sold 11.4.84 in New York
From the collection of Florence J. Gould

Opposite
Carved emerald bead necklace
Of 31 graduated beads measuring approximately 10.9 to 20.9 mm.
By Alexandre Reza, Paris
Sold 11.4.84 in New York for $495,000 (£343,750)
From the collection of Florence J. Gould

Necklace of 36 graduated brilliant-cut diamond collets mounted in silver and gold
Sold for £172,800 ($226,368)

Antique diamond brooch pendant
Sold for £9,720 ($12,733)

Both sold 25.7.84 in London

Pair of art deco emerald,
diamond and ruby clips
By Cartier
Sold 7.12.84 in London for
£16,200 ($23,652)

Emerald and diamond
pendant brooch
Sold 7.12.83 in London for
£70,200 ($102,492)

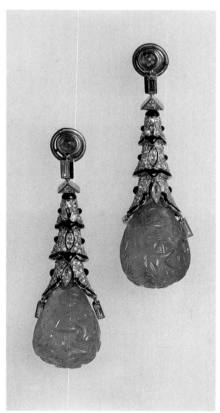

Pair of art deco emerald,
diamond and black onyx pendant
earrings
By Cartier
Sold 7.12.83 in London for
£38,880 ($56,765)

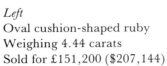

Far left
Unmounted pear-shaped fancy blue diamond
Weighing 2.83 carats
The diamond has been tested at the London
gem testing laboratory, report number
GB 2365, which states natural colour
VS1. The stone is potentially flawless
Sold for £79,920 ($109,490)

Left
Oval cushion-shaped ruby
Weighing 4.44 carats
Sold for £151,200 ($207,144)

Both sold 20.6.84 in London

Far left
Pair of fancy intense yellow and white
diamond ear-clips
The yellow diamond weighing 9.14 carats
and the white diamond 8.68 carats
Signed by Cartier
Sold 16.11.83 in Geneva for Sw.fr.330,000
(£106,452)

Left
Faint blue diamond ring
The diamond weighing approximately
10.25 carats
Sold 25.10.83 in New York for $253,000
(£165,359)

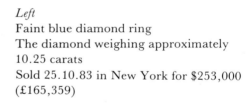

Far left
Sapphire and diamond ring
The sapphire weighing approximately
9.41 carats
Sold 7.12.83 in London for £91,800
($134,028)

Left
Ruby and diamond three-stone ring
The ruby weighing 7.49 carats
With an expertise by Gübelin stating that
the ruby is of Burmese origin
Sold 16.11.83 in Geneva for Sw.fr.715,000
(£223,437)

Far right
Single-stone diamond ring
The diamond weighing
approximately 26.23 carats
Signed by Van Cleef &
Arpels
With gemological certificate
number 6018720 stating that
the diamond is D colour
(colourless) and internally
flawless
Sold 11.4.84 in New York for
$1,375,000 (£954,861)

Right
Single-stone marquise-cut
diamond ring
The diamond weighing
approximately 21.83 carats
Signed by Harry Winston
With gemological certificate
number 6018524 stating that
the diamond is D colour
(colourless) and VVS1, and
the original working diagram
indicating that the diamond
may be potentially flawless
Sold 11.4.84 in New York for
$77,000 (£53,472)

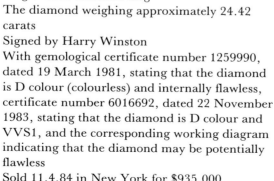

Single-stone diamond ring
The diamond weighing approximately 24.42
carats
Signed by Harry Winston
With gemological certificate number 1259990,
dated 19 March 1981, stating that the diamond
is D colour (colourless) and internally flawless,
certificate number 6016692, dated 22 November
1983, stating that the diamond is D colour and
VVS1, and the corresponding working diagram
indicating that the diamond may be potentially
flawless
Sold 11.4.84 in New York for $935,000
(£649,305)

Diamond ring
The diamond weighing approximately 10.45
carats
With gemological certificate number 6008592
stating that the diamond is F colour (colourless)
and VS2
Sold 25.10.83 in New York for $176,000
(£115,033)

Art deco coral, nephrite, opal and diamond brooch
Sold for Sw.fr.7,700 (£2,484)

Art deco onyx, multi-coloured hardstone and diamond bracelet
Sold for Sw.fr.41,800 (£13,484)

Both sold 16.11.83 in Geneva

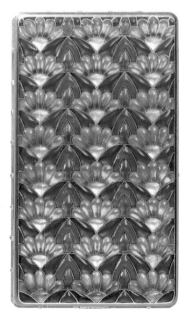

Art deco plique-à-jour enamel and diamond card case
By Van Cleef & Arpels
Sold 11.4.84 in New York for $9,350 (£6,493)
From the collection of Florence J. Gould

Three star sapphire and diamond
fish brooches
Signed by Van Cleef & Arpels
All sold 11.4.84 in New York for
$16,500 (£11,458)
From the collection of Florence J.
Gould

Pair of amethyst, sapphire and pearl
ear-pendants
Signed J.A.R.
With gemological certificate number
1922525 stating that the pearls are
natural
Sold 11.4.84 in New York for
$16,500 (£11,458)
J.A.R. stands for Joel A. Rosenthal,
a young American designer, who
established his Paris workshop on
the Place Vendôme with Pierre
Jeannet in 1978

Jewelled gold and enamel
necklace and pair of pendant
earrings in the Renaissance
style
By Ernesto Rinzi
(1836 – 1909)
Signed with initials on the
cross
15 in. (38 cm.) long
Sold 20.6.84 in London for
£8,640 ($11,923)

Silver

Pair of silver-gilt dishes
By George Wickes, 1739
12½ in. (31.1 cm.) diameter
Sold 11.7.84 in London for £75,600 ($98,280)
From a set of 12 made for the Earl of Scarbrough and engraved with the arms of Frederick, Prince of Wales. Lord Scarbrough was treasurer to the Prince.

Silver-gilt altar-service made for the Duchesse de Berry
By E. Gelez, Paris, 1819 – 38; two pieces, 1809 – 18
Sold 16.5.84 in Geneva for Sw.fr.99,000 (£31,428)

French silver-gilt tea-urn
Paris, 1819 – 38
20¼ in. (51.5 cm.) high
Sold 11.7.84 in London for £8,640
($11,232)

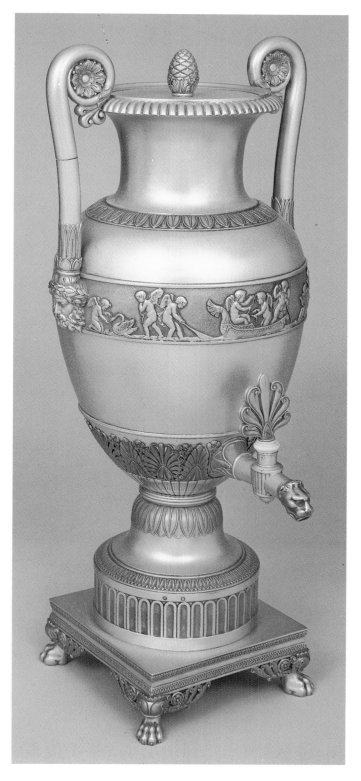

One of a pair of jardinières
By Luigi Valadier, Rome, *c.*1780
Marked on base with maker's mark and stamped 'Valadier, Roma'
12¾ in. (32 cm.) long
Sold 17.11.84 in Geneva for Sw.fr.242,000 (£75,625)

Set of eight candlesticks
Six by Salomon Dreyer, Augsberg, 1743 – 9; two by Andreas-Friedrich
Stemmler, Augsberg, 1743 – 5
Also struck with the housemark of the House of Saxony
9¾ in. (24.4 cm.) high
Sold 17.11.83 in Geneva for Sw.fr.242,000 (£75,625)

Spanish parcel-gilt custodia
*c.*1600
31¼ in. (79 cm.) high
Sold 11.7.84 in London for
£21,600 ($28,080)

Opposite right
Renaissance silver-gilt
standing-cup and cover
Cologne, *c.*1580
13 in. (33 cm.) high
Sold 17.11.83 in Geneva for
Sw.fr.110,000 (£34,375)

Opposite far right
Flemish silver-gilt mounted
façon-de-Venise
'sturzenbecher'
*c.*1600
10 in. (25 cm.) high
Sold 17.11.83 in Geneva for
Sw.fr.41,800 (£13,062)

Pair of Victorian large seven-light candelabra
By J. Hunt and R. Roskell, 1872
32¾ in. (83.2 cm.) high
Sold 24.5.84 at Elveden Hall for £32,400 ($45,360)
From the collection of the Earl of Iveagh

Pair of George IV two-handled wine-coolers
By Paul Storr, 1823
11½ in. (29.3 cm.) high
Sold 28.3.84 in London for £27,000 ($39,150)

Set of four Regency oval sauceboats
By Paul Storr, 1818
Sold 12.12.83 in London for £45,360 ($65,772)
In aid of the Ironbridge Gorge Museum
Development Trust

Opposite
Regency two-handled vase and plinth in the form of the
Warwick vase
By Paul Storr, 1812
20½ in. (52 cm.) high
Sold 12.12.83 in London for £21,600 ($31,320)
From the collection of The Rt. Hon. The Viscount
Exmouth
Presented in 1814 to Admiral Baron Exmouth,
Commander-in-Chief of the British Naval Forces in the
Mediterranean from 1811, by the Officers who served
under his command

Two identical pairs of George II candlesticks
By Paul de Lamerie, 1741 and 1744
8½ in. (21.7 cm.) high
Sold 28.3.84 in London for £51,840 ($75,168)

George II coffee-pot
By Paul de Lamerie, London,
1738
Marked on body and cover
11 in. (28 cm.) high
Sold 5.10.83 in New York for
$275,000 (£187,075)
Record auction price for a piece
of silver by the silversmith

Set of four George I table-candlesticks, candle-snuffers, stand and matching taperstick
By Thomas Merry I, London, 1715
The candlesticks 6⅞ in. (17.5 cm.) high
Sold 14.3.84 in New York for $132,000 (£88,000)

George I two-handled cup and cover
By Paul de Lamerie, London, 1718
10½ in. (26.8 cm.) high
Sold 5.10.83 in New York for $64,900 (£44,150)

George II plain
tapering cylindrical
tankard
By Paul de Lamerie,
1727
9¼ in. (23.5 cm.)
high
Sold 12.12.83 in
London for £41,040
($59,508)

Queen Anne plain tapering
cylindrical chocolate-pot
By Thomas Parr I, 1706
The swizzle-stick fully marked
9½ in. (24.2 cm.) high
Sold 28.3.84 in London for
£28,080 ($40,716)

Three from a set of four George II candlesticks
By George Wickes, 1733
14½ in. (36.8 cm.) high
Sold 5.6.84 at St. Osyth's Priory for £105,840 ($147,117)
From the collection of Mr Somerset and Lady Juliet de Chair

James II circular monteith
Engraved on the underneath with initials IMT to MT, 1687
Maker's mark B in script
10⅝ in. (27 cm.) high
Sold 12.12.83 in London for £56,160 ($81,432)

Pair of James I silver-gilt flagons
Maker's mark IM, 1610
11 in. (27.9 cm.) high
Sold for £151,200 ($196,560)

Charles I silver-gilt flagon
Maker's mark WM, 1637
13½ in. (34.6 cm.) high
Sold for £21,600 ($28,080)

Both sold 11.7.84 in London

Objects of Art and Vertu

Charles I gold tobacco-box
*c.*1640
3¼ in. (8.3 cm.) high
Sold 12.12.83 in London for
£43,200 ($62,640)

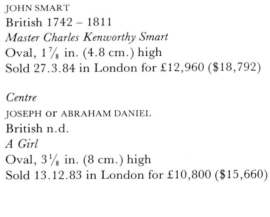

Top right and bottom left
JOHN SMART
British 1742 – 1811
Pair of miniatures of Sir Charles and Lady Helena Oakeley
Ovals, 2¼ in. (5.7 cm.) and 2⅜ in. (6.2 cm.) high
Sold 27.3.84 in London for £49,680 ($72,036)

Top left
JOHN SMART
British 1742 – 1811
Master Charles Kenworthy Smart
Oval, 1⅞ in. (4.8 cm.) high
Sold 27.3.84 in London for £12,960 ($18,792)

Centre
JOSEPH or ABRAHAM DANIEL
British n.d.
A Girl
Oval, 3⅛ in. (8 cm.) high
Sold 13.12.83 in London for £10,800 ($15,660)

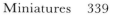

Top right
SAMUEL COOPER
British 1609 – 72
James II as Duke of York
Signed with monogram
Oval, 3 in. (7.5 cm.) high
Sold for £9,720 ($14,385)

Centre
JOHN HOSKINS
British d. 1664 – 5
A Gentleman
Signed with initials and dated 1654
Oval, 2⅜ in. (6 cm.) high
Sold for £17,280 ($25,574)

Both sold 27.3.84 in London

Top left
JOHN HOSKINS
British d. 1664 – 5
A Lady
Signed with initials and dated 1649
Oval, 2½ in. (6.5 cm.) high
Sold for £17,280 ($25,574)

Bottom right
SAMUEL COOPER
British 1609 – 72
A Lady called Mrs John Lewis (nèe Sarah Foote)
Signed with initials and dated 1647
Oval, 2⅛ in. (5.5 cm.) high
Sold for £14,040 ($20,779)

Both sold 27.3.84 in London

Above left
JOHN HOSKINS
British d. 1664 – 5
Henry, Lord Capell of
Tewkesbury
Signed with initials
Oval, 1⅛ in.
(2.8 cm.) high
Sold for £14,040 ($20,358)

Above centre
LEVINA TEERLINC
British 1510/20 – 76
A Married Lady at the Tudor
Court
1⅜ in. (4 cm.) diameter
Sold for £29,160 ($42,282)

Above right
LEVINA TEERLINC
British 1510/20 – 76
A Lady at the Tudor Court
1 in. (2.5 cm.) diameter
Sold for £5,184 ($7,517)

All sold 13.12.83 in London
From the collection of the
Duke of Beaufort, K.G.,
G.C.V.O., P.C., M.F.H.

Left
NICHOLAS HILLIARD
British 1547 – 1619
A Lady aged 16
Oval, 2¼ in. (5.6 cm.) high
Sold 13.12.83 in London for
£32,400 ($46,980)
From the collection of the
Duke of Beaufort, K.G.,
G.C.V.O., P.C., M.F.H.

Above left
SAMUEL SHELLEY
British 1750/6 – 1808
Miss P. Davis
Oval, 3½ in. (9 cm.) high
Sold for £6,696 ($8,838)

Above centre
JEREMIAH MEYER
British 1735 – 89
A Gentleman
Oval, 2⅝ in. (6.7 cm.) high
Sold for £7,560 ($9,903)

Above right
PETER EDWARD STRÖEHLING
Russian 1768 – 1826
A Lady
Oval, 3¼ in. (8.2 cm.) high
Sold for £8,100 ($10,611)

All sold 10.7.84 in London

Left
JOSEPH SAUNDERS
British n.d.
A Lady
Oval, 2⅜ in. (6 cm.) high
Sold 10.7.84 in London for
£10,260 ($13,440)

Jewelled and enamelled gold
dagger and scabbard
c. 1750
Possibly French for the
Turkish market
13¼ in. (33.7 cm.) long
Sold 5.10.83 in New York for
$35,200 (£23,945)

Swiss gold and enamel
quarter-repeating Jacquemart
automaton snuff-box
By Georges Rémond &
Cie, Geneva
c. 1810
3¾ in. (9.8 cm.) long
Sold 5.11.83 in Geneva for
Sw.fr.99,000 (£30,900)

Group of porcelain
snuff-boxes
c. 1770
Sold 18.10.83 in London for
a total of £11,016 ($16,634)

Louis XV gold box
With painted miniatures by
Van Blarenberghe
Signed and dated 1767
3¼ in. (7.8 cm.) long
Sold 15.11.83 in Geneva for
Sw.fr.363,000 (£113,437)

Louis XV gold-mounted
mother-of-pearl chinoiserie
snuff-box
Paris 1849 – 50
3½ in. (8 cm.) long
Sold 15.11.83 in Geneva for
Sw.fr.374,000 (£116,875)

Swiss gold and enamel
musical automaton box
Probably Geneva *c.* 1810
3¾ in. (9.3 cm.) long
Sold 16.5.84 in Geneva for
Sw.fr.121,000 (£38,412)

Enamelled gold snuff-box
By Georges Rémond, Geneva
c. 1815
3½ in. (8.7 cm.) long
Sold 16.5.84 in Geneva for
Sw.fr.28,600 (£9,079)

Group of gold snuff-boxes
Sold 11.7.84 in London for a
total of £9,504 ($12,830)

Louis XV mother-of-pearl
and gold carnet-de-bal
Paris 1754 – 5
3¾ in. (9.4 cm.) high
Sold 15.11.83 in Geneva for
Sw.fr.104,500 (£32,650)

Louis XV mother-of-pearl
and gold Royal snuff-box
Probably by Claude de Serre,
Paris
1728 – 9
3 in. (7.7 cm.) long
Sold 15.11.83 in Geneva for
Sw.fr.165,000 (£51,560)

Enamelled gold and
hardstone flower study of a
wild pansy
Stamped Fabergé
Signed, workmaster Henrik
Wigström, St. Petersburg
1899 – 1908
5 in. (12.5 cm.) high
Sold 15.5.84 in Geneva for
Sw.fr.132,000 (£41,250)

Agate figure of a rabbit
By Fabergé
2¼ in. (5.8 cm.) long
Sold 17.11.83 in Geneva for
Sw.fr.44,000 (£13,750)

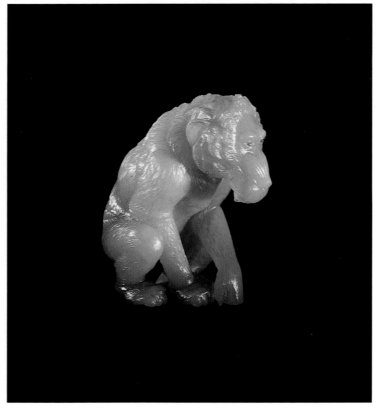

Agate figure of a mandrill
By Fabergé
2½ in. (6 cm.) high
Sold 15.5.84 in Geneva for
Sw.fr.66,000 (£20,625)

Silver and gold-mounted
guilloche enamel and seed-
pearl desk clock
By Fabergé
Workmaster Henrik
Wigström, St. Petersburg
c.1907
5 in. (12.7 cm.) diameter
Sold 14.3.84 in New York for
$16,500 (£11,000)

Guilloche enamelled
diamond-set and silver-gilt
mounted desk clock
By Fabergé
Workmaster Michael
Perchin, St. Petersburg
1896 – 1903
5 in. (12.7 cm.) diameter
Sold 5.10.83 in New York for
$17,600 (£11,973)

Silver model of a veteran motor car
Stamped Fabergé
Workmaster Henrik Wigström, St. Petersburg
1899 – 1908
10½ in. (26 cm.) long
Sold 17.11.83 in Geneva for Sw.fr.93,500 (£29,219)

Silver figure of a capercailzie hen
Signed, workmaster Julius Rappoport, St. Petersburg
15½ in. (39.5 cm.) high
Sold 15.5.84 in Geneva for Sw.fr.44,000 (£13,750)

St. George slaying the Dragon
Northern Russian School, possibly Karelia, *c*.1600
39 in. (99 cm.) high
Sold 30.3.84 in London for £16,200 ($23,490)

Dutch silver Sabbath hanging lamp
By Hendrik Griste I, Amsterdam
1755
30½ in. (77.5 cm.) high
Sold 26.6.84 in New York for $41,800 (£30,510)

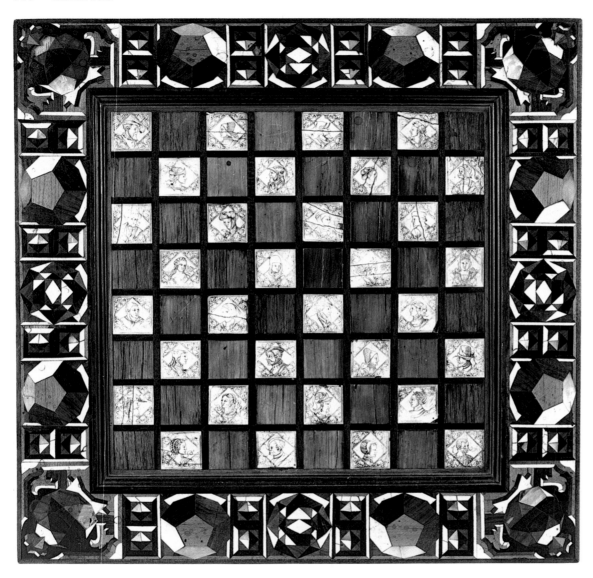

German parquetry and ivory inlaid games board, including 29 wooden pieces with engraved silver and gold centres containing Roman Emperor portrait busts
*c.*1600
18 in. (45.7 cm.) wide
Sold 12.9.83 at Earlshall, Fife, for £17,280 ($26,266)
By order of the Executors of the late Mrs R.E. Purvis, C.B.E.

Works of Art

Turquoise and dark-blue glazed
composition statuette of Isis and
Harpocrates
Ptolemaic, *c.* 3rd – 2nd century BC
5 ½ in. (14 cm.) high
Sold 11.7.84 in London for
£8,640 ($11,318)

Late 15th- or early 16th-century north Italian marble relief portrait of a
noblewoman
Attributed to Gian Cristoforo Romano
16½ × 14½ in. (42 × 36 cm.)
Sold 30.11.83 in London for £14,040 ($20,639)

15th-century Tuscan marble bust of the infant St. John the Baptist
By the Master of the Marble Madonnas
14 in. (35.5 cm.) high
Sold 30.11.83 in London for £18,360 ($26,989)

16th-century Upper Swabian polychrome
limewood statue of St. Sebastian tied to a tree
Attributed to the Meister der Biberacher Sippe
27½ in. (70 cm.) high
Sold 30.11.83 in London for £41,040 ($60,329)

19th-century French marble
statue of Arthur St. Clair
Anstruther Thomson
(1872 – 1904) as a child
By Amié Jules Dalou
Signed and dated DALOU
1877
45 in. (114 cm.) high
Sold 20.3.84 in London for
£81,000 ($116,640)
Record auction price for a
work by the artist
From the collection of Baron
Bonde

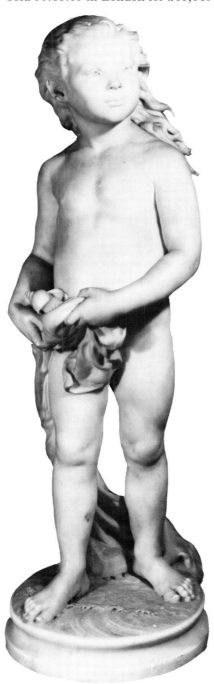

Late 16th-century Paduan
bronze statuette of Hercules
Attributed to Francesco
Segala
26 in. (66 cm.) high
Sold 15.5.84 in London for
£28,080 ($39,031)

Late 16th-century Venetian
bronze oil-lamp
Attributed to Tiziano Aspetti
19 in. (48 cm.) high
Sold 15.5.84 in London for
£16,200 ($22,518)

Late 19th-century French marble bust of Manon Lescaut
By Auguste Rodin
Inscribed on the front and signed on the side
23½ in. (59 cm.) high; 16¾ in. (42.5 cm.) wide
Sold 17.7.84 in London for £70,200 ($92,664)

HIRAM POWERS
Greek Slave
White marble allegorical female figure
Inscribed *H POWERS sculp.*
45¼ in. (115 cm.) high
Sold 9.12.83 in New York for $264,000
(£183,333)
Record auction price for a work by the artist

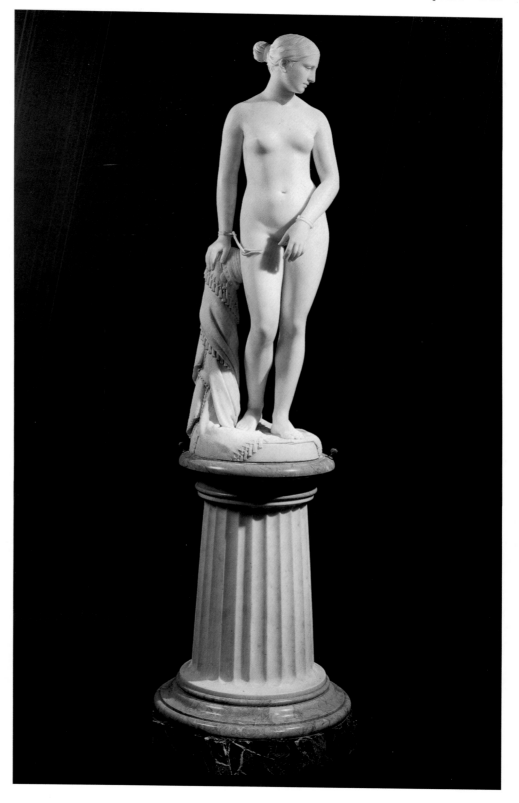

AUGUSTUS SAINT-GAUDENS
Diana of the Tower
Bronze
Inscribed *Aubry-Bros-Co. Founders.*
N.Y.
38⅞ in. (98.2 cm.) high
Sold 1.6.84 in New York for
$132,000 (£95,652)

FREDERIC SACKRIDER
REMINGTON
The Bronco Buster
Bronze
Inscribed *Copyright by
Frederic Remington* and
ROMAN BRONZE WORKS N.Y.,
the underside inscribed
No 1, the separate bronze
plaque inscribed *TO
GEORGE SEMLER ON HIS
ACCESSION TO THE
PRESIDENCY OF GEORGE
BORGFELDT & CO AS A TOKEN
OF HIGH ESTEEM AND
APPRECIATION BY THE
EMPLOYEES NEW YORK,
MARCH 22ND 1910*
32¼ in. (82 cm.) high
Sold 1.6.84 in New York
for $693,000 (£491,489)

Colourless glass 'snake-
thread' flask
Early 3rd century AD
7½ in. (19.1 cm.) high
Sold 11.7.84 in London for
£17,280 ($22,636)

Bronze figure of a hunchback slave crouching
Graeco-Roman, from Alexandria, 1st century BC/AD
3 ¼ in. (8.4 cm.) high
Sold 11.7.84 in London for £8,100 ($10,611)

Western Anatolian reddish limestone figure of a male idol
4th millennium BC
4 ¾ in. (11.3 cm.) high
Sold 11.7.84 in London for £5,400 ($7,074)

Roman bronze and silver inlaid fulcrum finial in the form of the head of a wild ass
Late 1st century BC
9¼ in. (23 cm.) high
Sold 11.7.84 in London for £12,960 ($16,977)
From the collection of Francis Moffat of that Ilk

Original Greek marble relief head of a female
Mid-4th century BC
10¼ in. (26 cm.) high
Sold 14.12.83 in London for £15,120 ($21,773)

Marble cult statue of the Goddess Cybele
Greek, Hellenistic
15 in. (38 cm.) high
Sold 11.7.84 in London for £14,040 ($18,392)

Group of three Nsaponsapo wood maternity figures
Each approximately 13½ in. (34 cm.) high
Sold 25.6.84 in London for £32,400 ($42,120)

Far right
Jokwe wood figure of a chief,
mwanangana
Muzamba region, 19th
century
19 in. (48 cm.) high
Sold 25.6.84 in London for
£25,920 ($33,696)

Right
Nootka whalebone club
18th century
23½ in. (59.5 cm.) long
Sold for £4,860 ($6,318)

Northern Plains quilled
skin-pouch
Cree or Chippewayan, *c.*1820
Sold for £6,480 ($8,424)

Both sold 25.6.84 in London

Maori wood mouthpiece, *tuki*
c.1800
7 in. (18 cm.) wide
Sold 25.6.84 in London for
£14,040 ($18,252)

Owo ivory armlet
18th century or earlier
4 3/4 in. (12.5 cm.) diameter
Sold 25.6.84 in London for
£5,940 ($7,722)

Ceramics and Glass

Tuscan two-handled albarello with
rope twist handles
3rd quarter of the 15th century
8½ in. (21.5 cm.) high
Sold 3.10.83 in London for £16,200
($24,462)

Faenza (Casa Pirota) Berrettino dish
c. 1525
9½ in. (24 cm.) diameter
Sold 3.10.83 in London for £14,040 ($21,200)

Documentary Castelli Tondo
Painted by Dr Francesco Antonio Saverio Grue
*c.*1720
12½ in. (31 cm.) diameter
Sold 26.3.84 in London for £7,020 ($10,319)
From the collection of D.J. Smethurst, Esq.
Previously sold at Christie's 18 February 1867 from
the Joseph Marryat Collection for £3. 18s.

Urbino plate representing
Orpheus at the Gates of Hell
*c.*1540
14½ in. (36.5 cm.) diameter
Sold 29.11.83 in Rome for
L.24,000,000 (£10,434)

Two Strasbourg faience
rococo appliqués
*c.*1750
18 in. (45 cm.) high
Sold 3.10.83 in London
for £18,360 ($27,724)
Now in the Musée de
Beaux-Arts, Strasbourg

Ansbach faience famille verte two-handled tureen and domed cover
*c.*1730
12 in. (30 cm.) wide
Sold 3.10.83 in London for £17,280 ($26,093)

Far left
One of a pair of Dutch
Delft polychrome duck-
tureens and covers
*c.*1760
12½ in. (31 cm.) long
Sold 2.7.84 in London
for £12,420 ($16,270)

Left
Dutch Delft blue-and-
white ewer
*c.*1690
27 in. (68 cm.) high
Sold 27.10.83 in
Amsterdam for
D.fl.34,250 (£7,953)

Capodimonte baluster coffee-pot and low domed cover
Painted by Giuseppe della Torre
*c.*1744
10¹⁄₂ in. (26.5 cm.) high
Sold 5.12.83 in London for £13,500 ($19,845)

Böttger red stoneware pear-shaped jug with silver
mounts
*c.*1715
8 in. (20 cm.) high
Sold 27.4.84 in New York for $24,200 (£17,042)

Le Nove rococo two-handled écuelle, cover and stand
*c.*1765
The stand 9 in. (22 cm.) diameter
Sold 5.12.83 in London for £4,860 ($7,144)

Meissen figure of Hanswurst
*c.*1740
7¼ in. (18.5 cm.) high
Sold for $30,800 (£21,690)

Both sold 27.4.84 in New York

Meissen figure of Pulchinella
*c.*1745
6¼ in. (16 cm.) high
Sold for $28,600 (£20,140)

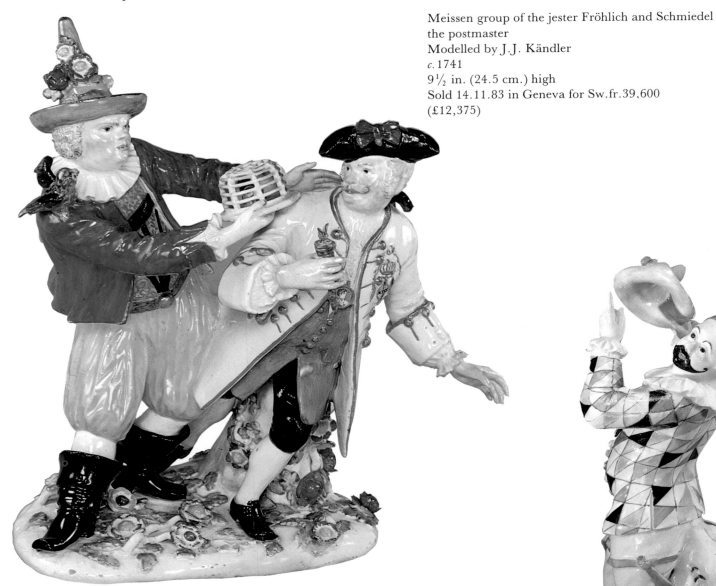

Meissen group of the jester Fröhlich and Schmiedel
the postmaster
Modelled by J.J. Kändler
*c.*1741
9½ in. (24.5 cm.) high
Sold 14.11.83 in Geneva for Sw.fr.39,600
(£12,375)

Höchst figure of a dancing Harlequin
*c.*1755
5½ in. (13.5 cm.) high
Sold 14.11.83 in Geneva for Sw.fr.39,600
(£12,375)

Meissen circular bowl with
North American fur-trapping
subject
c.1725
6 in. (15.5 cm.) diameter
Sold 14.11.83 in Geneva for
Sw.fr.44,000 (£13,750)
Now in the George R. Gardiner
Museum for Ceramics, Toronto
The drawing for this J.G.
Höroldt decoration is in his
sketchbook

Fürstenberg gold-mounted
rococo rectangular snuff-box
c.1765
3½ in. (9 cm.) wide
Sold 14.11.83 in Geneva for
Sw.fr.44,000 (£13,750)

One of a pair of Meissen ormolu-mounted figures of
golden orioles
Modelled by J.J. Kändler and P. Reinicke
*c.*1740
11¼ in. (28.5 cm.) high
Sold 27.4.84 in New York for $33,000 (£23,239)

One of a pair of Meissen figures of woodpeckers
Modelled by J.J. Kändler
1735 – 40
10¾ in. (27.5 cm.)
Sold 5.12.83 in London for £11,880 ($17,464)

Chantilly white figure of a nodding Chinaman
1725 – 35, horn mark in relief
11 in. (28 cm.) high
Sold 2.7.84 in London for £19,440 ($25,466)

Vincennes bleu celeste taper-stick
Dated 1754
2½ in. (6 cm.) high
Sold 26.3.84 in London for £3,240
($4,763)

Vincennes white group emblematic
of France
c.1752
8½ in. (21 cm.) high
Sold 2.7.84 in London for £8,640
($11,318)
Now united with its companion
figure in the Victoria & Albert
Museum

London Delft
polychrome octagonal
pill-slab with the arms
of the Worshipful
Society of
Apothecaries
1660 – 70
11 in. (27.5 cm.) high
Sold 10.10.83 in
London for £19,440
($29,354)

Far left
Cockpit Hill creamware
Royalist globular teapot
and cover
c. 1761
5¼ in. (13 cm.) high
Sold 18.6.84 in London
for £2,052 ($2,893)

Left
Saltglazed stoneware
silver-mounted armorial
tankard
c. 1710
8½ in. (21.5 cm.) high
Sold 18.6.84. in London
for £6,480 ($9,136)

Delft blue-and-white cylindrical tankard
1630
10 in. (25 cm.) high
Sold 9.4.84 in London for £6,264 ($9,020)
From the collection of P. Brooks, Esq.

London Delft blue-and-white broad cylindrical
mug
c. 1698
5½ in. (14 cm.) high
Sold 18.6.84 in London for £1,728 ($2,436)

Wedgwood creamware trial dessert-plate for The Catherine the Great Service, the centre painted in soft colours with Westcowes Castle in the Isle of Wight

*c.*1773

9 in. (22.5 cm.) diameter

Sold 10.10.83 in London for £8,640 ($13,046)

This plate was bought earlier in the year in an Isle of Wight junk shop for £15 and had been a gift to the vendor by her son and daughter-in-law on their return from their honeymoon. The plate is one of the few known prototypes for the 952-piece service made for Catherine the Great between 1773 and 1774 and now in the Hermitage Museum, Leningrad.

'Girl in a Swing' cream-jug
*c.*1750
3½ in. (8 cm.) high
Sold 13.2.84 in London for £12,960 ($18,403)

Worcester baluster vase and domed cover
Painted in the manner of James Rogers
*c.*1758
8 in. (20 cm.) high
Sold 10.10.83 in London for £7,560 ($11,416)

Above left
Chelsea small stand
*c.*1752
5½ in. (14 cm.) diameter
Sold 18.6.84 in London for
£3,456 ($4,872)

Above right
Chelsea small stand
*c.*1752
5½ in. (14 cm.) diameter
Sold 18.6.84 in London for
£2,808 ($3,959)

Right
Derby chinoiserie group
emblematic of Sight from a set of
the Senses
Modelled by Andrew Planché
*c.*1750 – 2
7¼ in. (18.5 cm.) high
Sold 10.10.83 in London for
£7,020 ($10,600)
By order of the Trustees of the
W.A.H. Harding Trust

Pair of Bow figures of an actor and actress
By the Muses Modeller
Both with incised sign for Mercury
*c.*1750
7 ½ in. and 8 ½ in. (19.5 cm. and 21.5 cm.) high
Sold 13.2.84 in London for £8,100 ($11,502)

Pair of Mintons
polychrome pâte-sur-
pâte two-handled
oviform vases
By Louis Marc Solon
Signed L. Solon
*c.*1890
21½ in.
(54.5 cm.) high
Sold 13.2.84 in
London for £20,520
($29,138)

Kurfursten humpen
Dated 1678
Central Germany
7¼ in. (18.5 cm.) high
Sold 19.6.84 in London for £4,104 ($5,704)

Fichtelgebirge 'stagenglas'
Dated 1717
10¼ in. (26 cm.) high
Sold 19.6.84 in London for £2,376 ($3,303)

Leiden diamond-engraved
wine bottle
Decorated by François
Crama
Dated 1687
9½ in. (24 cm.) high
Sold 19.6.84 in London for
£15,120 ($21,017)

Far left
Irish gilded and crested
plate
Attributed to John Grahl of
Dublin
c. 1786
9¼ in. (23.5 cm.) diameter
Sold 22.11.83 in London for
£1,404 ($2,078)

Left
Jeroboam armorial decanter
c. 1777
16 in. (40 cm.) high
Sold 22.11.83 in London for
£4,752 ($7,033)

Left
Dutch-engraved armorial
baluster goblet
The glass *c.* 1700, the
engraving mid-18th century
8½ in. (21 cm.) high
Sold for £1,296 ($1,919)

Centre
Newcastle Dutch-engraved
armorial goblet
c. 1750
7¼ in. (18.5 cm.) high
Sold for £518.40 ($767)

Right
Newcastle Dutch-engraved
Alliance goblet
c. 1745
8½ in. (21 cm.) high
Sold for £1,296 ($1,918)

All sold 22.11.83 in London

Above left
Clichy quince weight
2½ in. (6.5 cm.) diameter
Sold for £3,024 ($4,203)

Above right
Clichy flat bouquet weight
3 in. (7.8 cm.) diameter
Sold for £3,780 ($5,254)

Centre left
St. Louis red geranium
weight
2⅞ in. (7.5 cm.) diameter
Sold for £1,944 ($2,702)

Centre right
St. Louis crown weight
3⅛ in. (8 cm.) diameter
Sold for £2,160 ($3,002)

Below left
Clichy close concentric
millefiori weight
3⅛ in. (8 cm.) diameter
Sold for £2,808 ($3,903)

Below right
Clichy turquoise double-
overlay faceted mushroom
weight
3¼ in. (8.3 cm.) diameter
Sold for £4,536 ($6,305)

All sold 19.6.84 in London

One of a pair of Irish
George III glass chandelier
mirrors
34 × 21 in. (86 × 63 cm.)
Sold 28.6.84 in London for
£41,040 ($55,404)

Art Nouveau and Art Deco

Stoneware vase
By Bernard Leach
Impressed *BL* and *St. Ives*
seals
*c.*1970
14¾ in. (37.5 cm.) high
Sold 23.7.84 in London for
£3,780 ($4,951)

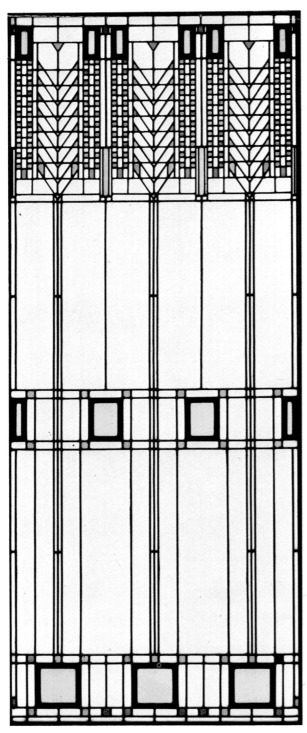

Leaded glass 'Tree of Life' door
Designed by Frank Lloyd Wright,
executed by Linden Glass Co. for the
Darwin D. Martin House, Buffalo, N.Y.
*c.*1903 – 5
Sold 16.12.83 in New York for $104,500
(£74,113)
By order of the Estate of Mrs Darwin R.
Martin

Honduras mahogany hall bench
Designed by Charles and Henry Greene, executed in the workshop of Peter Hall
for the Robert R. Blacker House, Pasadena, California
*c.*1907 – 9
Sold 16.12.83 in New York for $93,500 (£66,312)

129-piece silver flatware service
Designed by Joseph Hoffmann for the Wiener Werkstätte
c. 1921
Sold 24.5.84 in New York for a total of $73,700 (£52,642)

Silver-plated and glass table
lamp
Designed by Joseph
Hoffmann, executed by the
Wiener Werkstätte
c. 1905
Sold 16.12.83 in New York
for $38,500 (£27,305)

Mahogany, burr-walnut and ormolu guéridon
By Louis Majorelle
c. 1900
29½ in. (74.8 cm.) diameter
Sold 17.4.84 in London for £9,180 ($13,127)

Dropped head dragonfly
lampshade on a bronze,
turtle-back tile and mosaic
base
By Tiffany Studios
28½ in. (72.5 cm.) high
Sold 31.3.84 in New York for
$121,000 (£85,816)

Oriental poppy leaded-glass
and bronze floor lamp
By Tiffany Studios
76 in. (193 cm.) high
Sold 31.3.84 in New York for
$209,000 (£145,139)

Blue wisteria leaded-glass and bronze table lamp
By Tiffany Studios
27½ in. (70 cm.) high
Sold 31.3.84 in New York for $165,000
(£114,583)

Ébène de Macassar, marquetry, giltwood and marble commode
By Süe et Mare, incorporating doors decorated to a design by Mathurin
Méheut
c. 1925
33½ in. (84.5 cm.) high; 68 in. (173 cm.) wide; 26 in. (66 cm.) deep
Sold 25.5.84 in New York for $165,000 (£117,857)

Black lacquer, gilt and mother-of-pearl king-size bed
By Jean Dunand for Mme Berthelot
1930
75¼ in. (191 cm.) wide; 87 in. (221 cm.) long; 59¾ in. (152 cm.) high
Sold 1.10.83 in New York for $82,500 (£55,369)

Black lacquered wood screen
By Eileen Gray
*c.*1923
77 × 73½ in.
(195.5 × 186.7 cm.)
Sold 16.12.83 in New York
for $66,000 (£46,808)

La Tunique Rose
By Tamara de Lempicka
Oil on canvas
1927
28¾ × 46 in. (73 × 117 cm.)
Sold 1.10.83 in New York for $82,500 (£55,369)

Il Grande Pavone
By Paolo De Poli
Enamelled copper sculpture
Signed and dated 1962
61¼ in. (155.7 cm.) high
Sold 16.4.84 in London for £7,020 ($10,039)

Black Leather Suit
Bronze and ivory figure
Cast and carved from a
model by Bruno Zach
28½ in. (72 cm.) high
Sold 17.4.84 in London
for £17,280 ($24,710)

Lacquered wood panel
By Jean Dunand for Mme Jacoubovitch, Paris
*c.*1929
97 × 95 in. (246.5 × 241.5 cm.)
Sold 31.3.84 in New York for $66,000 (£45,833)

Rabelais's *Pantagruel*
Illustrated with woodcuts by André Derain
Bound in dark green Morocco by Paul Bonet
1956
Sold 13.5.84 in Geneva for Sw.fr.55,000 (£17,187)

Rémy de Gourmont's *Couleurs*
Engraved by J.-E. Laboureur
Bound in dark grey Morocco by Paul Bonet
1930
Sold 13.5.84 in Geneva for Sw.fr.44,000 (£13,750)

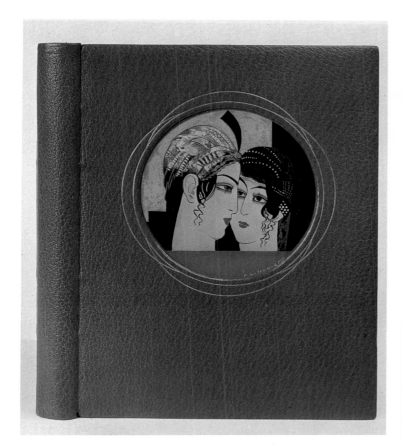

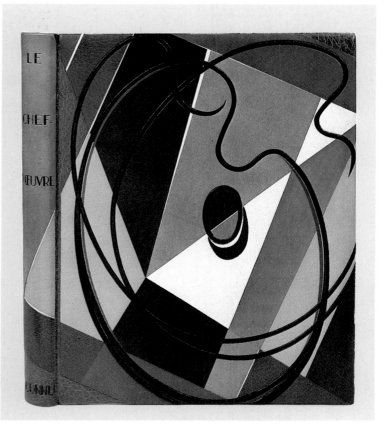

Mardrus's *Histoire charmant de l'adolescente sucre d'amour*
Illustrated by François-Louis Schmied
Bound in red Morocco, the cover bearing a lacquer medallion
by Jean Dunand
Sold 13.5.84 in Geneva for Sw.fr.99,000 (£30,937)

Balzac's *Le Chef-d'oeuvre inconnu*
Illustrated with 13 watercolours and 67 woodcuts by
Pablo Picasso
Bound in dark grey Morocco with a mosaic design by
Creuzebault
Sold 13.5.84 in Geneva for Sw.fr.49,500 (£15,468)

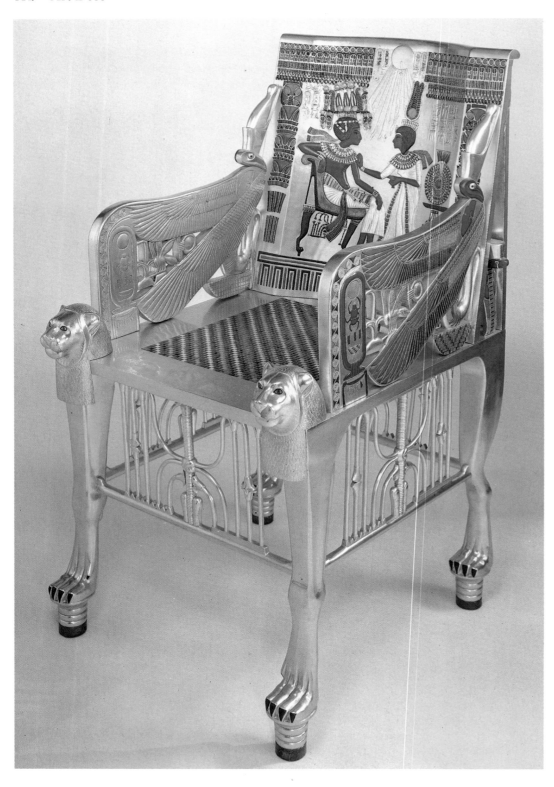

A replica of the State Throne of
Tutankhamun
41 in. (104.3 cm.) high
Sold 17.4.84 in London for £9,180
($13,127)
The influence of Egyptian art on
Europe has surfaced many times over
the centuries. Much ancient Greek
architecture was influenced by
Egyptian temples and during the
medieval period the Egyptian *ankh* or
looped cross was often incorporated
into Christian iconography.
Napoleon's campaign in Egypt during
the late 18th century rekindled an
interest that has continued until the
present day. Probably the greatest
vogue of this century was in the
1920s, after the discovery of the
Tutankhamun tomb in 1922.

Oriental Ceramics
and Works of Art

Ivory netsuke of a rat
Signed Masatsugu (Kaigyokusai
Masatsugu of Osaka, 1813 – 29) and
inscribed *Junishi Kedamono no uchi*, or
'One of the Animals of the Zodiac'
1st half of the 19th century
1 ¾ in. (4.5 cm.)
Sold 13.4.84 in London for £16,200
($23,652)

Archaic grey pottery amphora
Transitional Zhou/Han Dynasty
8 in. (20 cm.) high
Sold 30.11.83 in New York for $28,600 (£19,724)
From the estate of Rafi Y. Mottahedeh

Archaic bronze cauldron
Shang Dynasty
8¼ in. (21 cm.) high; 7 in. (17.5 cm.) wide
Sold 14.12.83 in London for £51,840 ($74,131)

Sancai and blue-glazed wine ewer
Tang Dynasty
10 in. (25.5 cm.) high
Sold 30.11.83 in New York for $209,000
(£144,138)
From the collection of Georges de Batz

Sancai glazed pottery
figure of a mounted official
Tang Dynasty
16 in. (40.5 cm.) high
Sold 30.11.83 in New
York for $72,500
(£50,000)

Far left
FU BAO-SHI
*Scholars gathering for a
Literary Meeting in the
Mountains*
Signed
Hanging scroll, ink and
light colour on paper
71½ × 24 in.
(181.5 × 60.5 cm.)
Sold 30.11.83 in New
York for $132,000
(£91,034)

Left
Polychrome terracotta
'Fat Lady'
Tang Dynasty
18 in. (46 cm.) high
Sold 30.11.83 in New
York for $46,200
(£31,862)

Underglaze-copper-red pear-shaped vase
2nd half of the 14th century
12¾ in. (32.6 cm.) high; 8½ in. (21 cm.)
diameter
Sold 10.4.84 in London for £421,200
($606,528)
When a Scottish couple visited the recently
opened Burrell Collection in Glasgow last
summer, they were surprised to see on
display a vase which appeared to resemble
one forming the base of a lamp at their home.
Christie's Glasgow office examined the lamp
for them, confirming their hope that the vase
was a very rare type dating from the 14th
century. The owners had been disappointed
to draw it in a family division several years
earlier. Luckily the vase had not been drilled
or scratched when it was made into a lamp
base, and when it was sent to London for sale
it fetched the highest price ever paid at
Christie's for a Far Eastern work of art.

Jade carving of a young
water-buffalo
Ming Dynasty
About 15 in. (38 cm.) long
Sold 30.11.83 in New York for
$132,000 (£91,034)

'Yellow jade' cup
Han Dynasty
4⅛ in. (10.5 cm.) long
Sold 30.11.83 in New York for
$33,000 (£22,759)
From the collection of Georges
de Batz

A blue-glazed buff pottery pony
Tang Dynasty
11½ in. (29 cm.) high
Sold 30.11.83 in New York for $154,000 (£106,207)
From the collection of Georges de Batz

A Cargo of Shipwrecked Porcelain

HETTI JONGSMA and COLIN SHEAF

It is unusual for an auction sale of Chinese porcelain to offer academics, ceramic historians and collectors the chance to explore a relatively unknown era of porcelain production. The successful recovery of tens of thousands of pieces of mid-17th-century porcelain from an Asian ship sunk in the South China Sea was therefore a unique occasion. It had the atmosphere of an East India Company bulk disposal sale of porcelain, which has not happened since the great days of the China trade. It also made known to scholars new kinds of early export Chinese ceramics, remarkable in their variety of shape and decoration; some pieces had not hitherto been recorded as products of the major late Ming porcelain kilns at Jingdezhen and throughout Fujian Province.

The wreck was discovered recently in the South China Sea by Captain Michael Hatcher, a salvage expert specialising in recovering cargoes of Asian tin sunk over the last two centuries. Despite his diving team's inexperience in excavating anything as fragile as porcelain, over several months they brought up in good condition some 25,000 pieces of porcelain. Many were found still packed in the freight barrels and chests, padded with rice husks, where they had survived the luckily gentle disintegration of the holed vessel. This enormous quantity of porcelain varied greatly in quality and in intrinsic interest, from the exceptional and rare, to the very mundane available in large amounts and ultimately auctioned off in lots of over 100 pieces – small teabowls, sets of saucers, pill-boxes.

It was a considerable risk to the worldwide market for Chinese porcelain to offer so much for sale, even spread over eight sessions, divided into two parts in March and June. In the event, every single lot in both sales was sold, generally at well over the high estimate and frequently at several times the amount. The enormous international interest generated by the mystique of the shipwreck, and the whole concept of what was virtually a 17th-century auction sale, contributed to a success unprecedented at Christie's Amsterdam. Commission bids and enquiries came from all over the world. Museums, collectors and dealers from everywhere between Taiwan and Brazil vied for examples of this mainly standard blue-and-white porcelain, immediately recognisable by the limpid glaze softened in tone by centuries of sea-water immersion.

Among the porcelain were, luckily, two dated pieces, domed covers for jars each painted with a cylindrical date corresponding to AD 1643. This provided one firm terminus; on stylistic grounds, and by associating recovered wares with other precisely dated examples of the same kind, the latest terminus must be about 1650. The porcelain thus dated from an era of considerable obscurity in Chinese ceramic studies. It was an era when civil war precipitated the overthrow of the native Ming Dynasty, trade and porcelain production were interrupted, and the ultimate victory of usurping northern (Manchu) families introduced new artistic tastes and stimulated new technologies.

Those who saw our large Amsterdam sale-room packed with cabinets and tables full of porcelain will not forget the spectacle. It was in the tradition of the East India House auction of 8 March 1721, when the company advertised 'Blue-and-white cups: 32,500 more or less in 32 lots, to be taken as they rise from the Pile.' The final sold total, some £1,541,465 (D.fl.6,743,554) against pre-sale estimates of one-quarter that figure, was the clearest proof of the enormous enthusiasm that this fascinating shipwreck dispersal generated.

Group of late Ming and transitional blue-and-white porcelain
In the warehouse of Christie's Amsterdam
Sold 14.4.84 and 12/13.6.84 in Amsterdam for a total of
D.fl.6,743,554 (£1,541,465)
From the Hatcher Collection
Recently recovered from an Asian vessel in the South China Sea

Gouache of Shanghai, the Bund
c.1860
39 × 19½ in.
(99 × 49.5 cm.)
Sold 23.2.84 in New York for $35,200
(£23,945)

Gouache of Tingqua's studio, Canton
Early 19th century
11 × 7¼ in.
(27 × 18 cm.)
Sold 8.3.84 in London for £3,240 ($4,828)

Early Ming red lacquer square tray
Carved and gilt with a Xuande and six-character mark, 1st half of the 15th century
15½ in. (39.5 cm.) square
Sold 14.12.83 in London for £70,200 ($100,386)
From the collection of Sir John and Lady Figgess

Famille rose standing figure of a Dutch
Merchant
Qianlong
17 ½ in. (44.5 cm.) high
Sold 6.7.84 in London for
£38,880 ($50,933)

Group of famille verte
porcelain
Kangxi
Sold individually 10.11.83 in
London for a total of
£35,208 ($52,812)

HIROSHIGE
Kakemono-e: Koyo Saruhashi no zu (The Monkey
Bridge in Koshu Province)
Signed *Hiroshige hitsu*, sealed *Ichiryusai* and
published by Tsutaya Kichizo
Sold 22.9.83 in New York for $60,500 (£39,803)

HOKUSAI
Chuban yoko-e: Soshu choshi (Choshi in Shimosa Province)
Signed *Zen Hokusai aratame Iitsu hitsu* and published by Moriya Jihei
Sold 22.9.83 in New York for $60,500 (£39,803)

Top
One of a pair of six-leaf screens in sumi, colour and
gofun on gold paper
Signed *Edokoro azukari ju-yoni-jo Tosa no kami
Fujiwara Mitsusada*
2nd half of the 18th century
Each leaf approximately 61 × 24 in. (155 × 60 cm.)
Sold 25.4.84 in London for £10,260 ($14,569)

Above
Six-leaf screen in sumi
Unsigned
A red seal late 18th – 19th century
Each leaf approximately 60½ × 24 in.
(153 × 60 cm.)
Sold 8.11.83 in London for £9,180 ($13,770)

One of a pair of Japanese
lacquer cabinets
Meiji period
65½ in. (166.5 cm.) high;
38½ in. (98 cm.) wide; 18 in.
(45.7 cm.) deep
Sold 21.5.84 at Elveden Hall
for £86,400 ($122,688)
From the collection of the
Earl of Iveagh

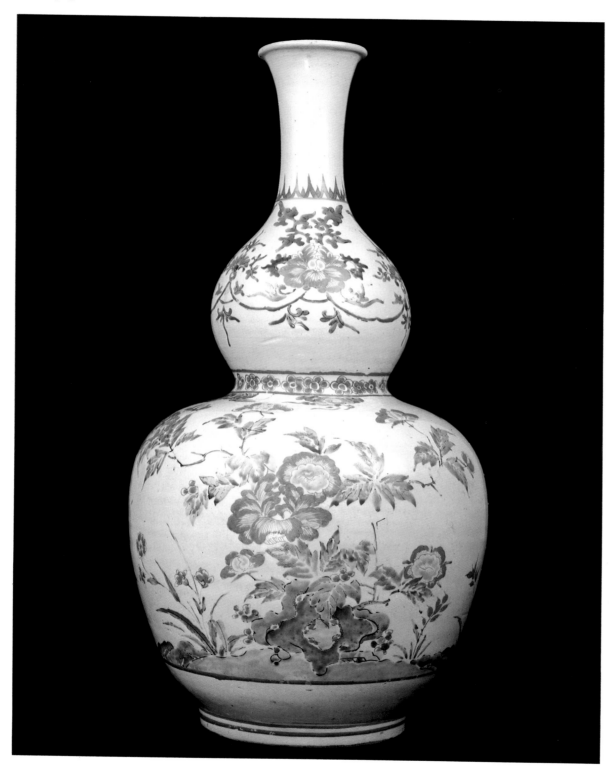

Kakiemon gourd-shaped
vase
Probably Kanbun-Enpo
period (1661 – 81)
17 in. (43 cm.) high; 8 in.
(20 cm.) maximum
diameter
Sold 22.11.83 in London
for £45,360 ($67,133)

Kakiemon model of an elephant
Probably Tenwa-Genroku period (1681 – 1703)
12¾ in. (32 cm.) long; 9¼ in. (23.8 cm.) high
Sold 22.11.83 in London for £15,120 ($22,378)

Lacquered giltwood model of the Yomei Gate of the Toshogu shrine at Nikko
27½ × 25½ × 21 in. (69 × 65 × 53 cm.)
Sold 22.11.83 in London for £4,428 ($6,553)

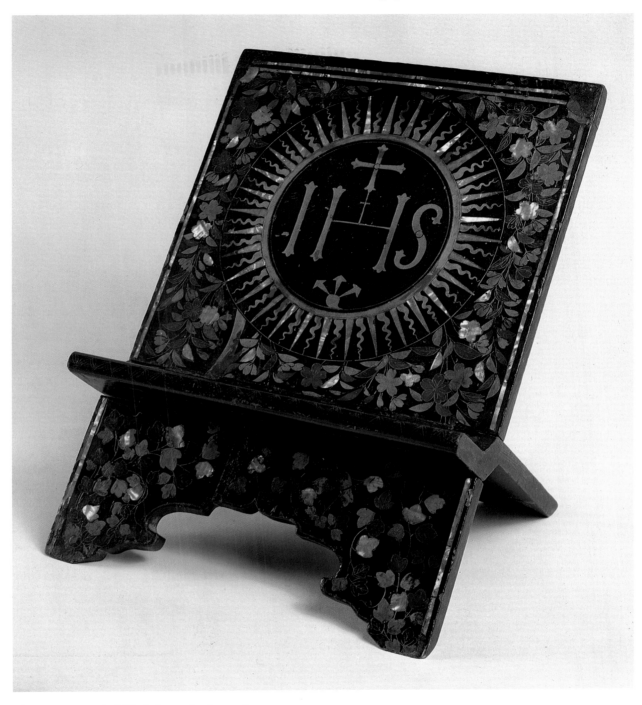

Momoyama period Christian missal stand
*c.*1600
16½ × 11¼ in. (42 × 28.7 cm.)
Sold 22.11.83 in London for £32,400 ($47,952)

Iro-Nabeshima dish
Late 17th – early 18th century
5¾ in. (14.9 cm.) diameter
Sold for $12,650 (£8,322)

Arita Namban Tokkuri
Early 18th century
8½ in. (21.5 cm.) high
Sold for $8,800 (£5,789)

Both sold 22.9.83 in New York

A group of wooden
netsuke
Sold individually
23.11.83 in London
for a total of £14,061
($20,810)

Chola bronze figure of
Balakrishna
12th century
24 in. (61 cm.) high
Sold 11.6.84 in London for
£16,200 ($22,842)

Kashmir blackstone Stele of the Brahminical Triad
9th century
5¾ in. (14.5 cm.) high
Sold 11.6.84 in London for £7,020 ($9,898)

Above
Conical bowl
Nishapur, 10th century
12 1/4 in.
(31 cm.) diameter
Sold for £3,780 ($5,330)

Below
Sgraffiato conical bowl
Nishapur, 10th century
17 in. (43 cm.) diameter
Sold for £3,780 ($5,330)

Both sold 12.6.84 in
London

Egyptian Kursi
9th century
32 in. (81 cm.) high,
17½ in.
(44 cm.) diameter
Sold 22.5.84 at Elveden
Hall for £11,880
($16,632)
From the collection of the
Earl of Iveagh

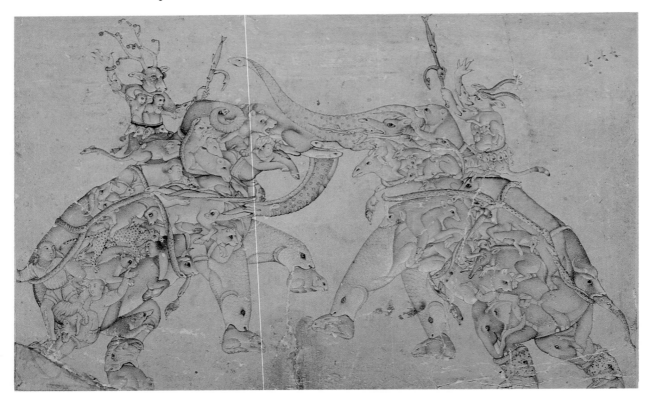

Elephants in combat
Drawing laid down on an album leaf
Inscribed in *devnagari*
Mughal, *c.*1600 – 80
4³⁄₄ × 7¹⁄₂ in. (11.8 × 18.8 cm.)
Sold 28.11.83 in London for £7,560 ($11,037)

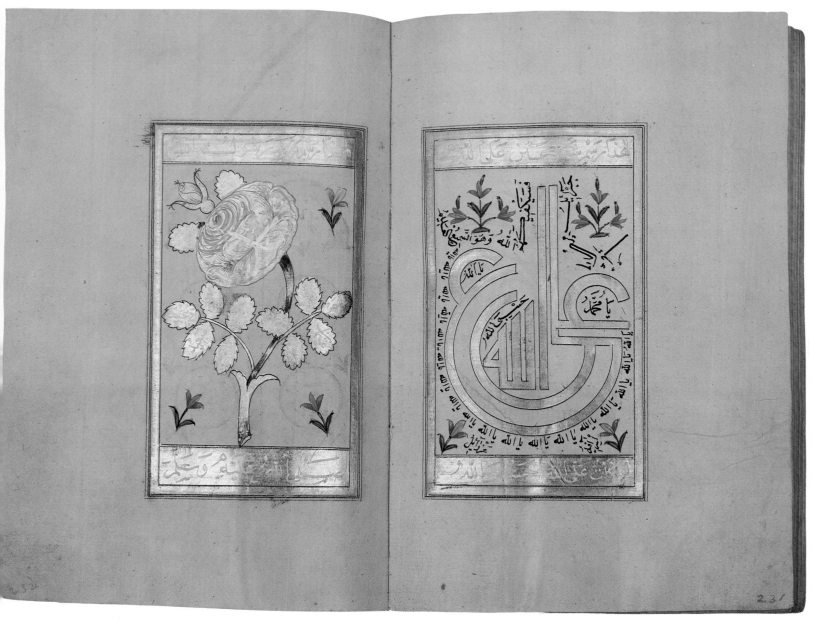

Prayer Book
Selected Quranic suras, and Arabic and Ottoman prayers
Istanbul, AH 1213 – AD 1798/9
Folio 6½ × 4¼ in. (16.5 × 10.8 cm.)
Sold 11.6.84 in London for £37,800 ($52,920)

Illustration to the Baburnama
Mughal, *c.* 1590
Folio 12 × 7¾ in. (30.2 × 19.2 cm.)
Sold 11.6.84 in London for £9,720 ($13,608)

Sporting Guns
and Arms and Armour

Self-opening sidelock ejector 12-bore (2¾ in.) d.b. gun
By J. Purdey, London
Built in 1979 and little used
Sold 14.12.83 in London for £8,640 ($12,441)

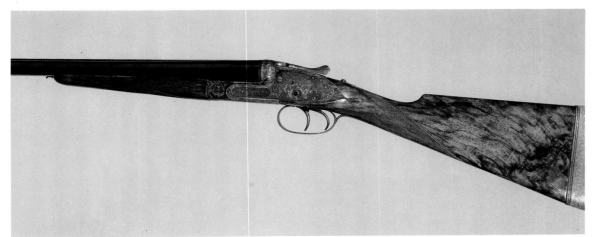

Self-opening sidelock ejector 20-bore (2¾ in.) d.b. gun, engraved with game-scenes and acanthus scrolls
By J. Purdey, London; engraved by G. Casbard
Built in 1969 and little used
Sold 21.3.84 in London for £15,660 ($22,628)

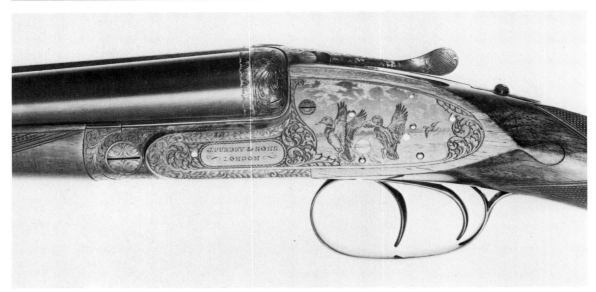

Geoffrey Casbard trained under Harry Kell and was on Purdey's staff before becoming an independent 'out-worker'. The importance of decoration on a gun is subjective, but it probably receives more public attention now than ever before. Though this may not please the purists, it seems to have raised the average standard of pictorial engraving. In the past, Kell, Sumner and other masters did not, as a rule, sign their work and their names were little known outside the trade. Today, when ordering a best gun with special embellishment, the buyer may well wish to specify not only the subject-matter but also a particular engraver.

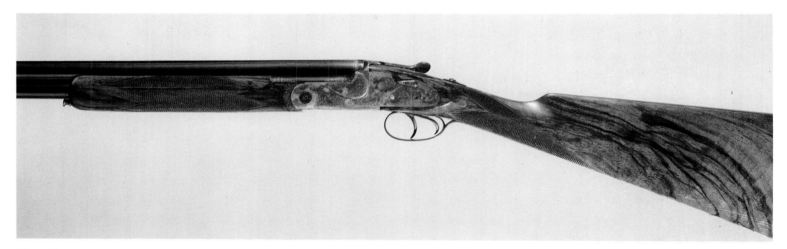

'Royal' over-and-under
sidelock ejector 20-bore
(2¾ in.) d.b. gun
(with extra barrels)
By Holland & Holland,
London
Built in 1954
Sold 21.9.83 in London for
£16,200 ($24,583)

Mounting the barrels one above the other creates design problems that do not arise in the side-by-side barrelled gun, so British over-and-unders have always been relatively rare and expensive. Nevertheless, most leading makers had their own design and produced some guns on it. The gun above is an example of Holland's second design, which was in production *c.*1950 – 8. About 25 guns of this pattern were built and this is the only known 20-bore. However, it was its qualities as a most attractive example of a scarce type, rather than its specific rarity, that excited interest. The light engraving and colour-hardened finish of its action might not suggest this maker, but a distinguishing feature is the hand-pin of its detachable lockplates. A similar pin can be seen in the detail below, which also shows Holland's characteristic 'best finish' of deeply-engraved foliate scrollwork.

'Royal Brevis Self-Opener'
sidelock ejector 12-bore
(2½ in.) d.b. gun
By Holland & Holland,
London
Built in 1936
Sold 18.7.84 in London for
£7,344 ($9,730)

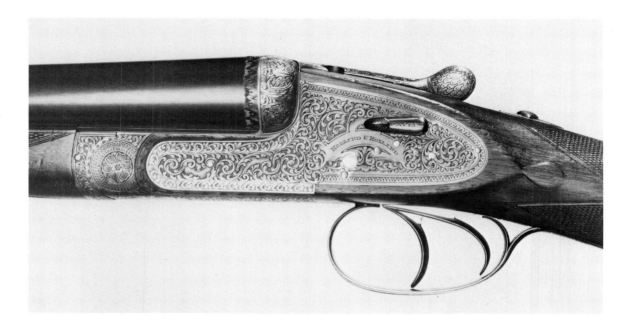

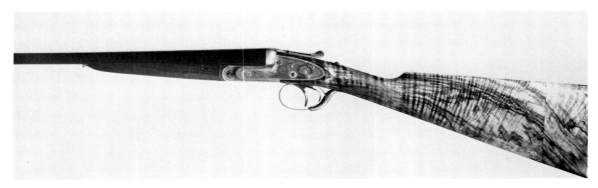

Self-opening sidelock ejector
28-bore (2½ in.) d.b. gun
By J. Purdey, London
Built in 1899
Sold 21.9.83 in London for
£8,640 ($13,930)

Pair of single-trigger sidelock
ejector 12-bore (2½ in.)
d.b. guns
By J. Lang, London
Built in 1909, when the pair
cost £136. 10s.
Sold 21.3.84 in London for
£7,020 ($10,143)

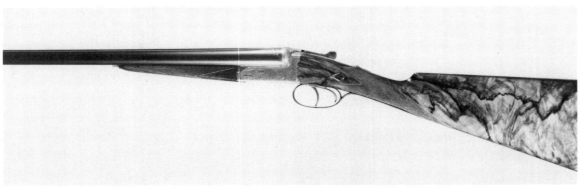

'Hercules XXV Easy-
Opening' boxlock ejector
12-bore (2½ in.) d.b. gun
By E.J. Churchill, London
Built in 1938
Sold 21.3.84 in London for
£3,024 ($4,369)

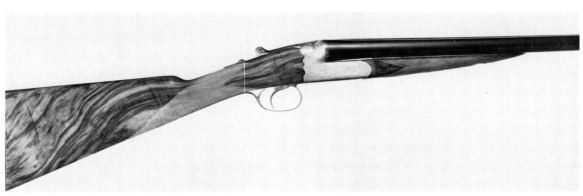

Westley Richards Patent
'One-Trigger' detachable-
boxlock ejector 12-bore
(2½ in.) d.b. gun
By Westley Richards,
Birmingham
Built in 1908
Sold 14.12.83 in London for
£2,376 ($3,421)

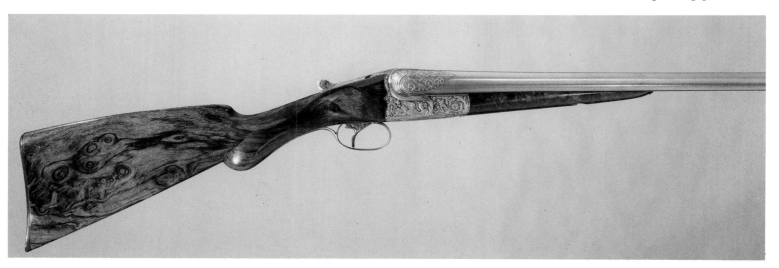

The Greener 'St George' boxlock ejector
12-bore (2$\frac{1}{2}$ in.) d.b. gun, with damascus
barrels
By W.W. Greener, Birmingham
Completed c.1903 (now out of proof and
unsuitable for use)
Sold 18.7.84 in London for £10,800 ($14,310)
From the collection of the late H. Leyton
Greener, Esq.

H. Leyton Greener (1903 – 83) described himself as 'the last of the gun-making Greeners'. He
was the grandson of William Wellington Greener, who founded the firm c.1864, and the son
of Harry Greener, who was closely involved in the design, manufacture and use of the 'St George'
gun. The gun was conceived c.1890 as a show-piece of Greener ingenuity and skills, a blend
of practical and decorative excellence in a gun that would be immediately recognisable as a
Greener. Nearly all its mechanisms are distinctive Greener patents, and the curving profiles
of its stock and action-body proclaim its origin at a distance. The overall effect is elegant, and
it is not surprising that W.W. Greener described the gun, in 1910, as 'the best advertisement
so far tried'.

For the history of the gun's design and manufacture, we are indebted to Leyton Greener,
who recorded the oral traditions passed down to him. From his account, we know that the
embellishment was designed by his father and executed by Harry Tomlinson, 'a first-class gun
engraver and in-layer'. Because of the difficulty and importance of the task, Tomlinson was
told to work on the gun only when he felt inclined, but on two occasions the strain led to his
becoming 'overtaxed ... until served with alcohol'. As each 'cure' took several days, there appears to have been more latitude for creative temperament in industrial Birmingham at the
turn of the century than one might suppose.

Sidelock non-ejector .450
(3¼ in. Black Powder)
d.b. rifle
By J. Purdey, London
Built in 1883
Sold 21.9.83 in London for
£3,672 ($5,572)

Winchester 'Special Order'
Model 1876 repeating rifle in
.45-75 calibre, 'sighted, shot
and regulated by Holland &
Holland'
By Winchester Arms Co.,
New Haven
Built in 1883
Sold 21.9.83 in London for
£3,888 ($5,900)

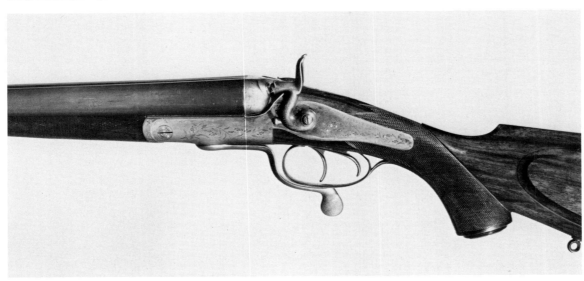

Snap-action rotary-
underlever backlock hammer
.577 (2¾ in. Black Powder)
d.b. rifle
By J. Purdey, London
('C Quality')
Built in 1882
Sold 18.7.84 in London for
£3,240 ($4,293)

Above
Smith & Wesson Model No. 3
(New Model) single-action
.450 (Eley) target revolver,
inscribed 'W.W/.450'and
'Military 20/1892'
By Smith & Wesson,
Springfield
Made specially for Walter
Winans, the celebrated pistol
and rifle shot, in 1892
Sold 18.7.84 in London for
£1,296 ($1,717)

Above right
Jarre 1871 Patent
'harmonica' 7 mm. (pin-fire)
10-shot repeating pistol, with
combined magazine and
barrel-assembly
By A. Jarre, Paris
Built *c*.1873
Sold 21.3.84 in London for
£1,350 ($1,950)

Borchardt 1893 Patent self-loading 7.65 mm. pistol with accessories (and case)
By Waffenfabrik Loewe, Berlin
Built *c*.1895
Sold 21.9.83 in London for £5,184 ($7,866)

Cased silver-mounted over-and-under single-trigger flintlock pocket pistol
By Tatham & Egg,
No. 1265
London silver hallmarks for 1812
7½ in. (19 cm.)
Sold 2.5.84 in London for £5,400 ($7,560)
Removed from Belton House, Lincolnshire

Back of 'Hungarian' shield of leather-covered wood
Mid-16th century, probably South German
36¾ in. (92.8 cm.)
Sold 2.11.83 in London for £10,800 ($16,308)
A type used in the Hussar tournaments that became popular at the Habsburg Court in the middle of the 16th century

German close helmet c.1550, probably Brunswick
11½ in. (29.2 cm.) high
Sold 2.11.83 in London for £9,720 ($14,677)

German half-armour
Early 17th century
Sold for $15,400 (£10,921)

Composite Italian half-armour
*c.*1580
Sold for $7,260 (£5,148)

Both sold 9.6.84 in New York

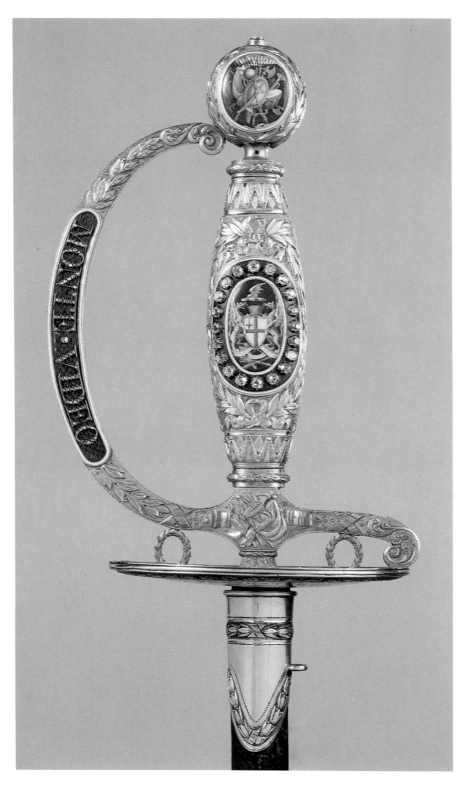

City of London gold and enamel presentation small-sword
London hallmarks for 18 carat gold for 1807
Makers' mark of John Ray and James Montague
$33\frac{3}{8}$ in. (85.8 cm.)
Sold 2.5.84 in London for £17,280 ($24,192)
The inscription reads: 'Presented By the Corporation Of The City of London Pursuant To A Vote Of The Common Council Passed The 25th September 1807. The Right Honble. Sir Wm. Leighton Kt, Mayor To Brigadier Genl. Sr. Saml. Auchmuty For His Gallant And Meritorious Conduct So Gloriously Displayed In The Attack And Capture Of The Fortress Of Monte Video In South America On The Third Day Of Feby. Last. Thereby Affording To The World At Large An Additional Proof Of British Valour.'

Sir Samuel Auchmuty, G.C.B. (1756 – 1822) is described in the *Dictionary of National Biography* as 'a distinguished general who attained his rank by merit alone'. He was the son of the Rev. Richard Auchmuty, rector of New York, where he was born. His family supported King George during the Revolutionary War, and he was present as a volunteer with the 45th Regiment at the battles of Brooklyn and Whiteplains. As a reward for his services he was awarded a commission and eventually came back to England with the regiment. He subsequently gave distinguished service in India (especially in the campaigns against Tippoo Sultan), Egypt, South America and Java. The event commemorated by this sword resulted from his command of a force sent out in October 1806 to reinforce General William Beresford after his capture of Buenos Aires from the Spaniards. On arrival he found that the Spaniards had recaptured the city, and Beresford also, but was unable to retake it. He therefore proceeded to capture the city of Monte Video, against strong opposition that cost him an eighth of his army. This was one of the few successes of an otherwise disastrous campaign, for which the commander-in-chief, General Whitelock, was cashiered. Auchmuty, however, received a vote of thanks from Parliament, and the freedom of the City of London with this sword of 200 guineas value. He died when commander-in-chief in Ireland in 1822.

Pair of French percussion pistols
By Alfred Gauvain of Paris
17 in. (43.2 cm.)
Sold 17.11.83 in New York at Christie's East for $44,000 (£29,333)
Made for the great exhibition at Crystal Palace in 1851

English riding sword
*c.*1600
Blade 37 in. (93.4 cm.)
Sold 2.5.84 in London
for £2,916 ($4,082)

Dutch silver-mounted knife and sheath
Dated 1610
The knife 9½ in. (24.1 cm.),
the sheath 9½ in. (24.1 cm.)
Sold 2.11.83 in London for £9,180
($13,862)
From the collection of R.N. Page, Esq.

Medieval sword
15th century, probably English
Blade 27¾ in. (69.9 cm.)
Sold 14.12.83 in London for £7,560 ($10,886)
From the Thames near Bull Wharf

Stamps

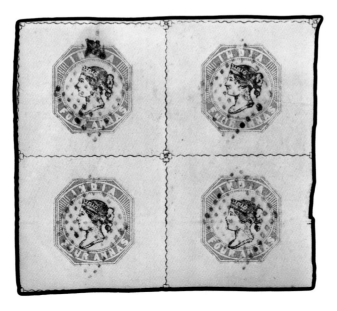

India 1854 4 annas – the 'Gibson block'
Sold 9.7.84 in London for £9,180 ($12,852)

Postage Stamps and Postal History

ROBSON LOWE

THE MARKET

During the past season, many prices have continued to improve owing to increased collector interest. Some 'investor' prices recorded in 1979 will not recover in the foreseeable future as these items are not often wanted by collectors. The latter are taking much greater interest in both handstamps and adhesive stamps used on the original letters and in cancellations. Fashions change and the science of the hobby, philately, and the unmounted mint fetish are losing ground to the humanity, postal history.

The less-rare stamps, and rarities in poor condition, have proved difficult to sell, but prices have been strong for collections comprising large quantities of common stamps.

LONDON

The most unusual auction of Great Britain held this season came from the duplicate archives of the National Postal Museum, many stamps being overprinted CANCELLED or SPECIMEN for official purposes. The imperforate imprimatur stamps were also popular.

In the other Great Britain sales there was keen competition for classics, both on and off cover, when there was anything unusual that gave the item character. A fine used penny black fetches £40 to £50 today, but a wrapper bearing a strip of five used with an 1841 1d. red-brown brought £1,512 ($2,117). An attractive example of the 1854 6d. used on a letter to Malta fetched £1,025 ($1,435).

The 20th-century errors were strongly supported. The 1935 2½d. Prussian blue, of which three sheets were sold at the Edmonton post office, realised £2,376 ($3,326). Stamps of the present reign with missing colours continued to be popular, and the 1965 Post Office Tower 3d. without the yellow fetched £351 ($491).

Great Britain 1936 King George VI 10s. imprimatur Sold 26.4.84 in London for £1,300 ($1,820)

New Zealand 1865 envelope from New Plymouth
Sold 22.2.84 in London for £1,836 ($2,570)
From the Charles McKeown Collection

The popularity of postal history was well shown when 20 letters written by a member of the Melanesian Missionary Society from Norfolk Island in the Pacific to his sister in Lincolnshire brought £7,650 ($10,710). Another correspondence from Tristan da Cunha, 'the lonely island' in the South Atlantic, addressed to a D.M. Game, who had visited the island in 1885, made £778 ($1,089) for 10 envelopes dated 1932 – 8. Then there was an 1851 letter written by a missionary in Kandy, Ceylon, to a canon at Southwark Cathedral. Finding the postage expensive he arranged with a private in the 37th Regiment to endorse the address 'soldier's letter' so that it went for a penny instead of several shillings. The rarity of a 'soldier's letter' combined with the abuse of privilege realised £184 ($258).

One of the Franklin Relief Expeditions planned to drop messages from balloons released over the Arctic. To rehearse the scheme, George Shepperd released three balloons with a dummy message in St. James's Park in 1850. Three examples of these leaflets are known and one realised £1,242 ($1,739).

The late Steuart Palmer had a consuming interest in the development of the airmail services within the United Kingdom and the British Empire. His collection filled two large cars, and though individual items were of no great worth, the airmail covers realised over £46,000 ($64,400).

The one-owner Postal History sale on 9 May comprised the collection of 'Crowned Circles' formed by Senator, The Hon. Henry D. Hicks of Ottawa. These handstamps were issued by the G.P.O. London to overseas postal administrations within the Empire and consular offices in foreign ports. The top lots were: Ireland Isle, Bermuda, £3,240 ($4,536); St. Georges, Bermuda, £4,104 ($5,746); St. Jago de Cuba, £4,644 ($6,502); Zante, £2,268 ($3,175); St. Margaret's Bay, Nova Scotia, £2,484 ($3,478); and Tenerife, £1,620 ($2,268).

Some 30 years ago, we suggested in the African volume of our *Encyclopedia* that there was great scope for the student to research the postal history of St. Helena. An Oxford solicitor, Edward Hibbert, was fired to explore. After 20 years, we published a volume on his researches. When he could do no more, he gave us the collection for sale. The auction was held on

8 February and realised £40,140 ($56,196). One of the letters from an army surgeon in 1819, where the writer mentioned 'Napoleon making many frivolous complaints', made £918 ($1,285). An 1865 letter bearing an imperforate 4d. and two perforated 1d. brought £1,404 ($1,966).

Eleven other specialised British Empire sales were held during the season, including Alfred Branston's Bahamas, Colonel David Eley's Prince Edward Island, Colonel E.E. French's Levant and Cyprus, the 'Hailsham' India, A. Leslie Leon's Lagos, L.M.W. Marshall's Antigua, Charles McKeown's New Zealand, Mark Strutt's Solomon Islands, E.V. Toeg's Montserrat, Commander Malcolm Burnett's Papua, further portions of the collections of New South Wales belonging to Dr Robert Wiggins, and Victoria, formed by the late J.R.W. Purves of Victoria.

On 13 September one of the world's rarities came up for sale: the East India Company's 1854 4 annas with the head of Queen Victoria *inverted*. Less than 20 copies are known, and when this rather poor example was last sold, in 1910, it realised £32. This time our clients from India fought and £12,000 ($16,800) was paid. A used block of four of the normal 4 annas realised £9,180 ($12,852) on 24 July.

There was keen competition in February for the New Zealand collection formed by the late Charles McKeown. An 1865 envelope from New Plymouth to Wales bearing the 4d. deep rose and 6d. red-brown brought £1,836 ($2,570) and an 1864 envelope from Invercargill to Massachusetts bearing three 6d. stamps, the back of the envelope printed with Cobb & Co.'s Royal Mail Coach advertisement, fetched £1,512 ($2,117). Two 1896 2½d. overprinted O.S.P.O. and underprinted with advertisements for sewing machines and table jelly went for £1,458 ($2,041). The highest price in the sale was £11,880 ($16,520) paid for a set of 11 rejected hand-painted essays for the 1898 pictorial issue. Collections of Stamp Duty issues at £5,828 ($8,159), revenue stamps at £4,374 ($6,124) and railway stamps at £1,588 ($2,223) demonstrate how the interest in peripheral philately has grown.

China 1923 inverted '2 Cts' on 3 cents
Sold 19.10.83 in Zurich for
Sw.fr.14,625 (£4,570)
From the Paul Hock Collection

BOURNEMOUTH

The monthly general auctions account for over 40 per cent of the home turnover and maintain their international appeal, usually close on half of each sale going in direct export. Some 3,000 lots of Great Britain are offered annually and are studied by many specialists. The Collection and Mixed Lots invariably prove to be the most popular section. The quarterly offering of sections of locals, railway and revenue stamps, forgeries and reprints arouses wide interest.

ZURICH

Eight auctions spread over three weeks during the season provided a record turnover. In October, the remarkable collection of China formed by the late Paul Hock of Vienna brought Sw.fr.1,104,266 (£345,083) with many record prices. Hock had specialised in the first issue, the Large Dragons, and this study realised Sw.fr.319,714 (£101,496), an outstanding cover from Tientsin to Germany bearing a 3 and 5 candarins together with a French 35 centimes cancelled in transit at Shanghai realised Sw.fr.18,000 (£5,625). A mint sheet of 20 of the fifth setting of the 1 candarin fetched Sw.fr.42,750 (£13,571) and a sheet of twenty-five 5 candarins brought Sw.fr.18,000 (£5,625). The top price in the sale was Sw.fr.140,625 (£43,945), paid for the rare 1897 $1 small surcharge on the 3 cents revenue stamp. There were 117 buyers competing from 18 different countries.

On the next day, another Far East sale included collections of Formosa, which brought

Russian Post Office in Peking 1881 to
St. Petersburg
Sold 12.4.84 in Zurich for
Sw.fr.28,125 (£8,929)
From the Alfred H. Wortman Collection

Sw.fr.28,670 (£8,960), Japanese Post Offices in China, Sw.fr.26,589 (£8,309), and the collection of the local posts of the Chinese Treaty Ports formed by Charles W. Dugan of Vancouver, which made Sw.fr.109,513 (£34,222). A cover from Wei-hai-Wei bearing the 1898 2 cents, a pair of the China 5 cents and the Hong Kong 10 cents brought Sw.fr.10,125 (£3,164). A further portion of the 'Hailsham' India saw Sw.fr.10,687 (£3,340) paid for a scarlet Scinde Dawk, a single of the white on cover and a strip of three both fetching Sw.fr.9,562 (£2,988). A fine used block of six of the India 1854 1 anna die III went for Sw.fr.10,250 (£3,203).

The April auctions included the collections of Disinfected Mail and Serbia formed by the late Dr Cecil Teall, the former realising Sw.fr.29,240 (£9,282) and the latter Sw.fr.130,815 (£41,529). The best single item was a bisected 40 paras ultramarine used on an 1869 entire letter, which brought Sw.fr.18,000 (£5,714). The same auction included the T.V. Roberts collection of French maritime mails, the Teall Lombardy-Venetia, part of the Dr A.H. Wortman collection of Russia and the rural Zemstovs formed by Boris Shishkin.

The Near and Far East sale that came on the following day was again very popular, with the exception of the Persia. The collection of the British Post Office in Bangkok, Siam, formed by the late Alfred J. Ostheimer realised Sw.fr.110,087 (£34,948), the best cover used in 1880 and bearing Straits Settlements 4 cents and 6 cents cancelled at the British Consulate made Sw.fr.18,000 (£5,714). The fine collection of Hong Kong formed by Everett Erle of California, and the late Dr A.H. Wortman's collection of the Russian post offices in China and Mongolia, filled the day with some surprising results: an 1861 envelope from Peking to Tientsin bearing a Russian 7 kopecs fetched Sw.fr.28,125 (£8,929) and a 1900 registered envelope from Peking to Hong Kong went for Sw.fr.21,375 (£6,786).

Serbia 1869 40 paras bisected on envelope
from Napoleon to Karanovac
Sold 11.4.84 in Zurich for Sw.fr.18,000
(£5,714)
From the Cecil Teall Collection

The June sales coincided with the National Exhibition, and the first of the two auctions featured a valuable section of Switzerland, which realised Sw.fr.162,900 (£50,123), the collection of the general issues for French Colonies formed by the late Commander C.E.D. Enoch of Pretoria at Sw.fr.34,188 (£10,520) and an attractive section of Japan at Sw.fr.140,951 (£44,746). The second day was filled with the collection of Siam formed by the late Charles Stewart of Bangkok. This was easily the finest collection of the country ever formed, the section dealing with the British Post Office in Bangkok realising Sw.fr.174,560 (£53,711); Sw.fr.28,125 (£8,654) being paid for an 1884 envelope to Tokyo bearing a Hong Kong 5 cents blue cancelled *Bangkok*. The definitive issues with the wealth of essays, proofs, varieties, covers and cancellations including the Cambodian, Laos and Malay provinces attracted enormous competition, resulting in a total of Sw.fr.748,755 (£237,700) for the first part of the collection.

NEW YORK

The 1983/84 auction season in New York showed its strength in the postal history area with the sale of two important American collections, both of which concentrated on the usage of stamps and postal markings, rather than the stamps themselves.

The first collection was a highly specialised study of early United States registered mail formed by Barbara R. Mueller in conjunction with her research of the American postal system. The collection was presented along with information from Ms Mueller's research studies, creating a new appreciation of the subject. Bidders, alerted to the rarity and significance of each item from the detailed descriptions, competed furiously. For example, a complete envelope addressed to Mexico with the rare Laredo, Texas, exchange office registry label went for $990 (£707). Without the Laredo label the cover would be worth less than £50.

Siam 1885 envelope to William Lincoln, London, stamp dealer and publisher, 1 sio and Straits Settlements 'B' on 2 cents and 8 cents cancelled Bangkok Sold 27.6.84 in Zurich for Sw.fr.20,250 (£6,429) From the Charles Stewart Collection

The Mueller collection contained items important to specialists in quite different fields. For example, there were two covers bearing stamps from the special 1876 Centennial Exposition. These attracted bids from stamp collectors, specialists in registered mail, and collectors of early American covers. The aftermath of the cross-fire was startling. The first of these covers was estimated to bring $5,000 (£3,571) and sold for $8,800 (£6,286), the other, estimated to fetch $4,000 (£2,857), caused a bidding war that established a record price of $17,600 (£12,571).

At about the time this envelope was mailed, the distinguished collector Henry C. Gibson, Sen. was born. Beginning as a child, Henry Gibson established himself as one of the first major American collectors before 1914. During the first half of this century, Henry Gibson was a dominating force in philately and acquired many of the greatest pieces known. After his collections were sold during the 1940s, Gibson's philatelic activities slowed. However, he still continued to build his collection of early American covers, and this group formed the basis of the New York auction in June. Henry Gibson now lives in Florida, and so, once more in his nearly 90 years as a collector, his prized possessions have made philatelic history.

In 1926, at the International Philatelic Exhibition in New York, Henry Gibson's exhibit of the first United States issue of 1847 earned a gold award. Therefore, it is fitting that the highest price in the sale of his collection was attained by an 1847 10 cents black on cover, unusually cancelled in green; estimated at $4,000 (£2,857), the cover soared to $14,300 (£10,214). Another classic United States cover in the Gibson collection was carried by the legendary Pony Express in 1860. Because the Pony Express operated for only 19 months, surviving examples of Pony Express mail are rare. The Gibson example showed the identifying handstamps clearly, which helped raise the price to $7,700 (£5,700).

United States Pony Express cover from San Francisco to New York
Sold 20.6.84 in New York for $7,700 (£5,700)
From the Henry C. Gibson Collection

Reviewing the philatelic activity in the New York sale-room this season, it is obvious that covers with character make the greatest appeal to collectors. Furthermore, the best prices are achieved when such lots are presented with technical information that highlights all the individual characteristics.

MILAN
There have been five auctions held during the season and the turnover was nearly double that of the previous season. Although there has been considerable variety, the major part of the sales have been the Italian States and Italy. In the March auction, there were three specialised collections, one of the cancellations of Umbria, one of the Papal States, and the other of Tristan da Cunha, the last proving to be as popular in Milan as it was in London. In June there were two sales, one being a specialised study of the cancellations of Sardinia, showing their use in other Italian States after the annexation which resulted in the formation of the Kingdom of Italy.

TORONTO
The first of our stamp auctions in Canada was held in November and brought $C297,500 (£163,625). A specialised study of the first decimal issue of 1859 made $C121,121 (£66,917), a used block of thirteen 17 cents bringing $C4,730 (£2,613). Among the covers, the top price of $C3,520 (£1,945) was paid for each of two entires, three 1c. + 5c. + 10c. pairs used to Australia, and a 12½ cents block of four and a single used to London. The collection of numeral cancellations on the 5 cents beaver made $C13,200 (£7,300).

Among the later issues, a mint block of 18, divided into 10 and 8, of the 1868 2 cents with the complete watermark, sold for $C20,900 (£11,547). The imperforate pairs of the 1908 Quebec Tercentenary made $C3,850 (£2,127) and a collection of Tobacco Tax stamps went for $C5,500 (£3,039). A collection of Newfoundland brought $C31,421 (£17,360).

The next sale in Toronto is scheduled for May 1985.

Coins and Medals

Trumpet Major Andrew Morris of the Life Guards sounding 'The Charge' on the trumpet used at the Battle of Omdurman (2 September 1898)

The trumpet and the three medals awarded to Sergeant Trumpeter Frederick Knight, 21st Lancers, were sold on 24 July 1984 for £4,200 ($5,628). Sergeant Knight enlisted in the Dragoon Guards at the age of 13 in 1878, was appointed Trumpeter in 1884 and was honourably discharged after 23 years service. On his discharge papers under 'Special qualifications for employment in civil life', it states, 'Store Keeper or position of trust. Very Good Trumpeter.'

The brass trumpet was made by Henry Potter and Co. and it retained its cords, tassles and original mouthpiece. An old label attached to the instrument stated, 'The cavalry trumpet which blew the charge of the 21st Lancers in the Sudan which broke the power of the Mahdi and ended the war.' In fact, the Mahdi himself had died earlier in 1898 and Colonel Martin, Commanding Officer of the 21st Lancers, faced the Khalifa Abdallahi and about 4,000 Dervishes with a force of less than 400. Winston Churchill himself rode in the charge and wrote a comprehensive account of the action in his book *The River War*.

Coins – a Mirror of History

ELIZABETH NORFOLK

The study and appreciation of coins and medals may appear at first to be a somewhat obscure hobby, with little to interest the non-collector, but, with the aid of some of the pieces we have been fortunate enough to sell over the past year, I hope to illustrate that this is not the case.

A coin can teach us so much about the period in which it was struck that it is almost like holding a small piece of history in your hand. The earliest coins, which date from shortly before 600 BC, were really just countermarked lumps of metal, but they soon developed into highly individual pieces that can truly be said to be works of art in themselves.

Many intriguing stories surround the personages portrayed. For example, an Aureus – or Roman gold coin – illustrated opposite (3) shows Domitia, who was implicated in the assassination of her husband, the Emperor Domitian, in AD 96. The child on the globe is said to be the couple's nameless son, who apparently died at an early age. An Aureus of Domitian himself (5) commemorates Roman victories during the first year of his reign. The female figure seated mourning represents Germany, and the broken spear below her is the symbol of defeat.

Roman coins were often used as propaganda in this way, as can be seen from the Aureus of Hadrian (AD 117 – 38) (1), on which he is shown proclaiming his visit to Italy. He spent much of his reign touring the four corners of his vast empire, and so it was important to let his subjects know that their own country was not left out of the itinerary.

Naturally enough, commemorative medals are also a great source of information about the events of the day, particularly those concerning heads of state. The gold medal issued on the death of Oliver Cromwell in 1658 (6) was struck in Holland to supply collectors unable to procure a more valuable one by Thomas Simon, who engraved the dies for many of the English coins of the period.

Two hundred years after Simon, another name becomes prominent in the world of coin and medal design, that of Wyon. Two members of that illustrious family executed a most attractive Indian Chief Medal (9), which was struck in the latter part of the 19th century. These pieces were given as a reward for loyalty to the British cause or to mark the signing of a treaty, although this particular piece, being undated and unnumbered, was evidently never awarded.

The Indian Chief Medal is illustrative of the European colonial period, which had begun some 200 years before. The era is also reflected in the coinage of the time, such as this Mexican gold 8-Escudos (8) dating from the sovereignty of Philip V of Spain, or the gold 12,800-Reis of Brazil (4) issued in 1732, when the country was under Portuguese rule.

From the design of coins through the ages we are able to appreciate the expertise and creative genius of the men who were responsible for them. This Groat of Elizabeth I (7) and the Crown of James I (2) are not only pieces of great artistic merit but are also particularly scarce because of their condition. Hammered coins are so called because they were produced by placing a coin-blank between two dies and striking it with a hammer. Owing to this manufacturing method, the coins invariably had uneven edges and were therefore very easy for villains to clip. A hammered Crown such as this is not usually found on a full round flan and in such good condition. Similarly the Groat, having originally been issued in small numbers, usually turns up in poor condition, although at least unclipped, since the beaded border was specifically introduced to prevent this illegal practice.

These two coins, as well as the others I have discussed, are a great tribute to the achievements and artistry of the past. They are perhaps a fitting conclusion to our brief trip through 2,000 years of history.

1. Hadrian, Aureus
£1,200 ($1,620)

2. James I, Crown
£2,200 ($2,970)

3. Domitia, Aureus
£4,200 ($5,670)

8. Mexico, 8-Escudos
£1,700 ($2,295)

9. Indian Chief Medal
£1,200 ($1,620)

4. Brazil, 12,800-Reis
£1,200 ($1,620)

7. Elizabeth I, Groat
£820 ($1,107)

6. Oliver Cromwell, gold medal
£1,000 ($1,350)

5. Domitian, Aureus
£3,000 ($4,050)

All sold in Geneva

Peter I, commemorative medal in silver, 1713, by Otfrid Koenig, Sw.fr.2,600 (£812)

Elizabeth,
10-Roubles, 1756
Sw.fr.4,000 (£1,250)

Peter III,
10-Roubles, 1762
Sw.fr.5,000 (£1,562)

Nicholas II,
25-Roubles, 1908
Sw.fr.10,000 (£3,125)

Alexander II,
25-Roubles, 1876
Sw.fr.4,000 (£1,250)

Nicholas I, Platinum 12-Roubles, 1830
Sw.fr.8,500 (£2,656)

Nicholas I, Platinum 6-Roubles, 1838
Sw.fr.12,000 (£3,750)

Sicily, Syracuse,
15-Litrae
$7,040 (£5,028)

Domitian, Aureus
$8,920 (£6,371)

Pertinax, Aureus
$13,200 (£9,428)

Septimius Severus,
Aureus
$11,050 (£8,214)

Paraguay,
4-Pesos, 1867
$16,500 (£11,785)

U.S.A., 4-Dollar
'Stella', 1879
$37,400 (£26,714)

U.S.A., Matte
Proof 10-Dollars, 1908
$14,300 (£10,214)

U.S.A.,
Proof 20-Dollars, 1904
$16,500 (£11,785)

U.S.A.,
5-Dollars, 1795
$15,400 (£11,000)

U.S.A.,
10-Dollars, 1795
$14,300 (£10,214)

Korea, 20-Won, 1906
$46,200 (£33,000)

U.S.A., Panama Pacific 20-Dollars, 1915
$24,200 (£17,285)

U.S.A., High Relief 20-Dollars, 1907
$18,150 (£12,964)

All sold in New York

Top row, left to right
Grand Master's Badge presented to Field Marshal, Earl French of Ypres in 1921, £6,000 ($8,400)
The Order of the Garter, a rare Chancellor's Badge, 1838, £5,200 ($7,280)

Bottom row, left to right
The Imperial Order of the Crown of India, Badge, £7,500 ($10,500)
Russia, Nicholas I, Imperial Household Decoration, £3,800 ($5,320)
The Order of St. Patrick, Badge, *c.*1860, £8,000 ($11,200)

Photographs

ANTOINE CLAUDET
Family Portraits
Two from a group of four stereoscopic daguerreotypes
c. 1851
Sold 28.6.84 in London at Christie's South Kensington for £12,000 ($16,320)

GEORGE REID
A Tour of the Cities of London and Westminster
Collection of over 1,000 photographs and glass
negatives
Late 1920s
Sold 28.6.84 in London at Christie's
South Kensington for £7,000 ($9,520)

An apparatus used by George Reid for taking
photographs was sold as part of the lot

Album of 234 photographs, mainly of English architecture by Alfred Capel-Cure
Late 1880s
Sold 27.10.83 in London at Christie's South Kensington for £13,000 ($19,890)

Right
FREDERICK H. EVANS
Wells Cathedral: A Sea of Steps
*c.*1903
Sold 27.10.83 in London at Christie's South Kensington for £9,000 ($13,770)

Far right
D.O. HILL and ROBERT ADAMSON
The Fore Tower of the Castle, St. Andrews
Mid-1840s
Sold 29.3.84 in London at Christie's South Kensington for £3,800 ($5,548)

GUSTAVE LE GRAY
Brig upon the Water
1856
Sold 29.3.84 in London at Christie's South Kensington for
£4,200 ($6,132)

ALFRED STIEGLITZ
Equivalent
Gelatin silver print
1924
Sold 7.5.84 in New York at Christie's East for $8,800 (£6,285)
From the estate of Paul Outerbridge, Jun.

D.O. HILL and ROBERT ADAMSON
One from a series of calotype views of St. Andrews
Sold 29.3.84 in London at Christie's South Kensington for
£5,800 ($8,468)

PAUL STRAND
The Beach, Percé, Gaspé, Quebec
Gelatin silver print
1924 or 1936
Sold 7.5.84 in New York at Christie's East for $7,700 (£5,500)
From the estate of Paul Outerbridge, Jun.

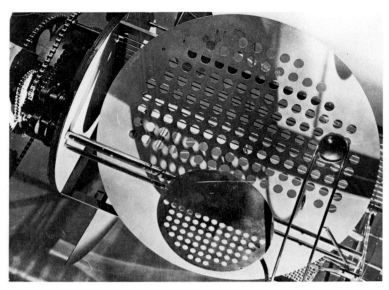

Above
LASZLO MOHOLY-NAGY
Das Lichtrequisit
Late 1920s
Sold 28.6.84 in London at Christie's South Kensington for
£4,800 ($6,528)

Above right
EDWARD WESTON
Maguey Cactus, Mexico
Platinum print
1926
Sold 8.11.83 in New York at Christie's East for $11,000 (£7,333)

Right
MAN RAY
Chez Man Ray
Gelatin silver print
1935 – 6
Sold 7.5.84 in New York at Christie's East for $8,580 (£5,720)

EDWARD STEICHEN
Dixie Ray
Gelatin silver print
1935
Sold 8.11.83 in New York at Christie's East for $5,500
(£3,666)

TOILET PAPER ADVERTISEMENT
Carbo-colour print
*c.*1938
Sold 7.5.84 in New York at Christie's East for $11,000 (£7,857)
From the estate of Paul Outerbridge, Jun.

Collectors' Sales

Turned and carved painted
wooden doll wearing original
clothes
*c.*1760
16 in. (40.6 cm.) high
Sold 21.6.84 at Christie's
Glasgow for £5,940 ($8,197)

Mechanical Music

CHRISTOPHER PROUDFOOT

It is difficult to find an all-embracing term for a department which handles barrel-organs, carpenters' planes, musical boxes, telescopes, old gramophones, sewing machines, typewriters and even foot-operated dentists' drills, but all are more-or-less mechanical, even if an all-too-small proportion are truly musical.

The appeal of these categories to the layman varies from the relatively obvious to the obscure. A truly specialised tool such as a sash dowelling box (a jig used in drilling dowel-holes in early 19th-century glazing bars) might have limited attraction to most people beyond the fact that it is a well-made artefact of some obvious age, and yet in a tool sale such a one, without a maker's signature, brought £420 ($630). The Baird Televisor could likewise be said to have little going for it visually – a piece of factory-made machinery of the early 1930s, painted a dull brown colour – but there was enough demand for this one to bring £2,400 ($3,480) when it came up for sale as part of the Ritman Collection of Wireless Equipment on 1 March 1984. This was the first sale we had ever devoted entirely to this subject, which normally forms a short opening to the Mechanical Music sales, leading into the gramophone and phonograph section. The latter was short of any outstanding items, although the trend continued for considerable preference to be given to items in first-class original condition. Mention can be made, perhaps in spite of the last comment, of a collection of nine very early phonograph cylinders, made in about 1890, of such notable speakers as Gladstone, Mrs Robert Browning and Florence Nightingale. Divided into four lots, these cylinders, which were all worn to the extent that the speakers' words were largely indistinguishable, brought a total of £2,495 ($3,542).

The 19th-century monkey automaton which brought £1,800 ($2,610), however, had a more obvious and timeless appeal; but who outside the remote world of typewriter collecting would value a typewriter at £1,300 ($1,885) instead of £100 just because it was painted red rather than black?

Baird Televisor
*c.*1930
Sold 1.3.84 in London at
Christie's South Kensington
for £2,400 ($3,480)
From the Ritman Collection
of Wireless Equipment

Atwater-Kent 4-valve
receiver ('Breadboard
model')
Sold 1.3.84 in London at
Christie's South Kensington
for £450 ($652)
From the Ritman Collection
of Wireless Equipment

A 'Most Improved' microscope by
W. & S. Jones, London, with a compass
microscope and Jones sales leaflet, in fitted
case
Sold 1.12.83 in London at Christie's South
Kensington for £1,700 ($2,550)

Monkey artist musical automaton
24 in. (60.9 cm.) high
Sold 5.4.84 in London at Christie's South
Kensington for £1,800 ($2,610)

1934 Hispano-Suiza K6
Sedanca de Ville
Coachwork by Fernandez et
Darrin
Sold 16.7.84 at Beaulieu for
£86,400 ($112,320)

1956 Ferrari 508-128B-250
Tour de France two-seater
Berlinetta
Coachwork by Scaglietti,
Modena
Sold 27.10.83 in London for
£59,400 ($87,912)

1914 Rolls-Royce 40/50 h.p.
Alpine Eagle Sporting
Torpedo
Coachwork by Portholme,
Huntingdon
Sold 22.10.83 in London for
£91,800 ($135,864)
From the collection of Stanley
Sears

1912 Rolls-Royce 40/50 h.p.
Silver Ghost semi-open drive
limousine
Coachwork by Hooper,
London
Sold 22.10.83 in London for
£91,800 ($135,864)
From the collection of Stanley
Sears

7¼ in. guage model of the London and North Western Railway Crampton (2-2)-2-2-0 locomotive and tender *Liverpool*, as built by Bury, Curtis & Kennedy, Liverpool 1848
Modelled by F.R. Wilkinson, Bexley Heath
20½ × 73 in. (52 × 185.5 cm.)
Sold 16.4.84 at the British Engineerium, Brighton, for £4,200 ($5,880)

Far left
Painted tin plate model of a 1911 Mercedes Voyager Limousine
By Bing
*c.*1911
16¼ in. (41 cm.) long
Sold 31.5.84 in London at Christie's South Kensington for £8,500 ($12.325)

Above
Victoria, a finely detailed model of a vintage battleship with grey painted hull
By Marklin
*c.*1902
29½ in. (74.9 cm.) long
Sold 31.5.84 in London at Christie's South Kensington for £8,000 ($11,600)

Left
Model of a Marshall-type cross compound jet condensing mill engine
Built by H. Wall, Southampton
10¾ × 21 in. (27.5 × 53.5 cm.)
Sold 5.12.83 at the British Engineerium, Brighton, for £1,300 ($1,950)

Right
IB Compur Leica 35 mm.
camera
No. 50587 with Elmar
50 mm. f. 3.5 lens in rim-set
Compur shutter
Sold 1.12.83 in London at
Christie's South Kensington
for £1,900 ($2,850)

Far right
V.P. Limit focal-plane
miniature plate camera
By Thornton-Pickard
Sold 3.5.84 in London at
Christie's South Kensington
for £700 ($1,015)

Right
10 × 8 box form view camera
by E. & H.T. Anthony &
Co., New York
Sold 6.10.83 in London at
Christie's South Kensington
for £1,500 ($2,250)

Far right
Stereo Photo Binocle
combined stereoscopic
detective camera and field
glasses
By C.P. Goerz, Berlin
Sold 21.6.84 in London at
Christie's South Kensington
for £1,000 ($1,350)

Right
Quarter-plate Dallmeyer's
naturalist long-focus reflex
camera
Sold 1.12.83 in London at
Christie's South Kensington
for £380 ($570)

THEATRE.

Edinburgh, January 12. 1767.

The Managers and Performers humbly hope, that, from the dangerous fituation both They and the Theatre were in on Saturday night, after the farce was over, from a party who ftaid behind the reft of the audience, in behalf of Mr *Stayley*, and by throwing ftones, pieces of fticks, halfpence, and lighted candles, COMPELLED a promife of his being engaged, as the ONLY MEANS left to *preferve the Theatre from fire and deftruction*, they fhall ftand juftified to the public in fufpending all entertainments, till they can be affured of a proper protection ; and alfo of refufing to admit as one of their community a Man capable of taking fuch unwarrantable and wicked means to gain his ends.

JAMES AICKIN.
JOSEPH YOUNGER.
A. J. DIDIER.
J. D.
D. B.
W. SEDGWICK.
WILLIAM ADAMS.
C. SMITH.
CHA. TINDAL.
THO. LANCASHIRE.
SIMEON QUIN.
THO. YOUNG.

THE

G O F F.

AN

Heroi-Comical Poem.

IN

THREE CANTOS.

✦✦✦✦✦✦✦✦✦✦✦✦✦✦✦✦✦✦✦✦✦✦✦✦✦✦✦✦

Cetera, que vacuas tenuiffent carmina mentes,
Omnia jam volgata.   VIRG.

✦✦✦✦✦✦✦✦✦✦✦✦✦✦✦✦✦✦✦✦✦✦✦✦✦✦✦✦

The Second EDITION.

✦✦✦✦✦✦✦✦✦✦✦✦✦✦✦✦✦✦✦✦✦✦✦✦✦✦✦✦

E D I N B U R G H:

Printed for JAMES REID, Bookfeller in *Leith*.
M.DCC.LXIII.   (Price Four-pence)

Far left
Collection of pamphlets, broadsides and caricatures relating to disturbances at the Play-House on 24 January 1767, when it was attacked and seriously damaged by a mob
Sold 23.3.84 at Christie's Glasgow for £5,616 ($8,143)
From the collection of Sir Ivar Colquhoun of Luss, Bt.

Left
Silver-gilt Open Championship medal presented to Jack Simpson for winning the 1884 Golf Championship at Prestwick
Sold 11.5.84 at The Old Course Hotel, St. Andrews, by Christie's Glasgow for £5,940 ($8,197)

Far left
THOMAS MATHISON
The Goff. An Heroi-Comical Poem in Three CANTOS
Second edition, 24 pages, disbound
Edinburgh, James Reid, 1763
Sold 11.5.84 at The Old Course Hotel, St. Andrews, by Christie's Glasgow for £10,800 ($14,904)

Left
Pack of heraldic playing cards,
*c.*1688
Sold 31.5.84 in London at Christie's South Kensington for £1,500 ($2,070)

Right
ADOLPHE MOURON CASSANDRE
Normandie
1935
Lithograph printed in colours
on thin wove paper, linen
backed
Sold 6.2.84 in London at
Christie's South Kensington
for £1,400 ($2,016)

Far right
CECIL BEATON
Footlights Review, 1925
Dress design for one of the
two sisters, from a collection
of 600 drawings and
watercolours by the artist
Sold 7.6.84 in London for a
total of £173,577 ($243,000)

Right
Full-length portrait study of
Houdini
Signed 'Stone walls do not a
prison make, Harry
Handcuff Houdini' and dated
1 October 1907
Sold 9.12.83 in London at
Christie's South Kensington
for £95 ($137)

Far right
WILLIAM HEATH ROBINSON
*A Cloud Dispeller designed by the
1st Lord discovering a Heinkel
Bomber hiding in a Cloud*
Signed and inscribed
Pen and black ink and grey
washes
Sold 4.6.84 in London at
Christie's South Kensington
for £700 ($994)

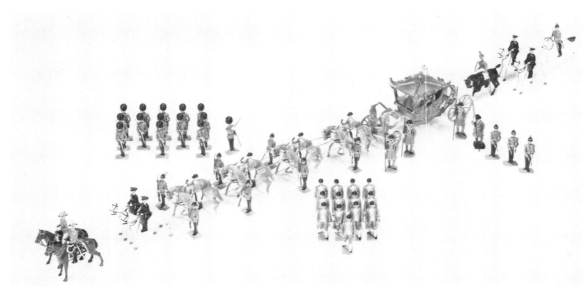

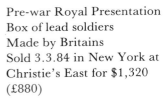

Pre-war Royal Presentation
Box of lead soldiers
Made by Britains
Sold 3.3.84 in New York at
Christie's East for $1,320
(£880)

Above
Edward the Black Prince
By Courtenay
Sold 3.3.84 in New York at
Christie's East for $1,430
(£953)

Far left
Post-1877 Victorian officer's
lance cap of the 21st
(Empress of India's)
Lancers with embossed metal
plate
Bearing a brass plaque
engraved 'L.W.H. Tringham,
Esq., 21st Lancers'
Sold 21.12.83 in London at
Christie's South Kensington
for £1,400 ($1,974)

Left
1768 pattern Grenadier's fur
mitre cap, the embossed
metal plate decorated with
the Royal crest and 'G.R.'
within a motto
Sold 21.12.83 in London at
Christie's South Kensington
for £2,400 ($3,384)

George III ivory and silver-mounted vegetable slicer
London 1816
Sold 24.4.84 in London at Christie's South Kensington for £550 ($770)

Victorian stamping machine
By S. Mordan
London 1884
Sold 20.2.84 in London at Christie's South Kensington for £1,600 ($2,304)

Iron punishment mask or 'scold's bridle' with shaped nasal bar, pierced cheek mask and tongue plate
Sold 13.6.84 in London at Christie's South Kensington for £450 ($630)

George III corkscrew
Probably by John Reilly
London 1816
Sold 23.1.84 in London at Christie's South Kensington for £1,700 ($2,380)

Costume from the Wardrobe of the D'Oyly Carte Opera Company

EMMA CLARK

One could be forgiven for forgetting that one was attending an auction at all; there was music, singing, laughter and even applause. Christie's South Kensington were selling the D'Oyly Carte Wardrobe. For the second time, Christie's South Kensington took over a theatre for three days to sell an enormous collection of theatrical costume. The first time was the sale at the Old Vic in December 1981. This time, on 24 January 1984, it was the turn of the Lyric Theatre, Hammersmith, to provide a charming setting for the sale of over 1,500 costumes and accessories from the wardrobe of the D'Oyly Carte Opera Company, which had disbanded in 1982. A tremendous success, the sale made a total of £31,820 ($44,548) with no lot left unsold.

Starting at 6 o'clock in the evening, and with a champagne interval 90 lots later, the sale attracted enthusiastic buyers from all over the world; collectors, theatrical costumiers and museums keenly bidding on every lot from Pooh-Bah's elaborate and weightly outfit (£380/$532), to a quantity of crinolines and petticoats (£120/$168). The 'Lord High Auctioneer' was Christopher Elwes, whose task was very much enlivened by a company of singers led by Jonathan Ouvry. As each lot was announced one or more singers appeared on the stage dressed in the appropriate costume, singing a line or two from the opera. Thus as lot 44 was announced, the Pirate King (see opposite) strode on to the stage proclaiming:

> But I'll be true to the song I sing
> And live and die a Pirate King

which no doubt helped boost the bidding to a very healthy £260 ($364). Costumes from all the operas except the last two made up the bulk of the sale, most dating from about 1940 to 1975. Various designers were commissioned by the opera company, including Peter Goffin (*H.M.S. Pinafore* 1961, *Ruddigore* 1949, and others), Luciana Arrighi (*The Gondoliers* 1968) and Osbert Lancaster (*The Sorcerer* 1971). Lancaster's beautifully tailored suits were much sought after, one theatrical costumier securing Sir Marmaduke Pointdextre's outfits for £240 ($336). The first lot in the sale, Aline's wedding dress (see opposite), clearly illustrates Gilbert's notion that 'no lady of the Company should be required to wear a dress that she could not wear with absolute propriety at a private fancy dress ball'.

From Bruno Santini's silvery fairy dresses in *Iolanthe* (The Castle Howard Museum securing five lots from this opera) to the Henry VIII style hats from *The Yeomen of the Guard*, bought by the Theatre Museum for £140 ($186), the stage of the Lyric Theatre was transformed. This vast array of costumes hanging from the 'fly-bars' made a truly magnificent spectacle. It was Charles Ricketts's enormous and elaborate kimonos (commissioned for the 1926 production), with strikingly coloured appliqué-work, that aroused most interest at the sale; the highest price, £480 ($672), was paid by an American collector for the Mikado's costume.

All the costumes were in remarkable condition, carefully maintained and restored under Dame Bridget's personal care, and, although a sad occasion for many people, as Lord Wilson of Rievaulx wrote in his foreword to the catalogue, 'Fortunate are those who succeed in buying ... a memento of one of Britain's greatest series of contributions to style, to colour, and to our famed light music.'

Aline's wedding dress from
The Sorcerer
(Osbert Lancaster, 1971)
Sold with another similar for
the understudy

The Pirate King's costume
from *The Pirates of Penzance*
(adapted from
George Sheringham's
designs)
Sold with others similar

Both sold 24.1.84 at the Lyric
Theatre, Hammersmith, for
a total of £400 ($560)
From the collection of the
D'Oyly Carte Opera
Company

German ivory and mother-of-pearl fan
The paper leaf painted with a *Fête Champêtre*
*c.*1730
11¾ in. (30 cm.)
Sold 22.5.84 in London at Christie's
South Kensington for £2,200 ($3,190)

Tapestry cushion cover of Susannah and the Elders
By Sheldon
Late 16th – early 17th century
15 in. (38.1 cm.) square
Sold in London at Christie's South Kensington
for £3,600 ($5,220)

Pair of high-heeled lady's
shoes of white kid
embroidered with flowers in
pink, green and yellow silk
and bound with blue ribbed
silk
Possibly Italian *c.*1730
Sold 18.10.83 in London at
Christie's South Kensington
for £3,000 ($4,500)

Top
Banyan of ice blue satin
brocaded with exotic flowers
and balconies in purple, pink
and yellow
*c.*1710
Sold in London at Christie's
South Kensington for £8,200
($12,300)

Embroidered linen night-cap
thought to have been worn by
King Charles I at
his execution on 30 January
1649
English *c.* 1630 – 50
Sold in London at Christie's
South Kensington for
£13,000 ($19,500)

Royal Relics

SUSAN MAYOR

At Christie's South Kensington on 18 October 1983 a memorable sale took place. The embroidered linen night-cap believed to have been worn by King Charles I at his execution in Whitehall on 30 January 1649 was bought by the private collector Mr George Apter for £13,000 ($19,500).

The night-cap, which dates from about 1630 – 50, certainly is of the correct period. Contemporary prints of the scene show the monarch wearing a night-cap of similar cut. It had previously been exhibited as that worn by the Martyr on the scaffold in the exhibition of the Royal House of Stuart at the New Gallery in 1889, catalogue no. 376, by George Somes, Esq. In size, the cap is unusually small, but then the King himself was diminutive in stature. The superb quality of the needlework enhances the likelihood that the provenance is correct. Certainly the strong bidding at the sale suggested that many collectors believed the authenticity of the legend.

The following lot was a collar of Milanese lace, also believed to have been worn by Charles I on the scaffold, and presumably removed prior to execution. This was similarly exhibited at the Royal House of Stuart exhibition, catalogue no. 374. After spirited bidding, the collar was knocked down for £1,300 ($1,950).

Group of three Bébé dolls and a shoulder-headed Marotte doll
Sold 3.5.84 in New York at Christie's East for a total of $19,558 (£13,970)
From the collection of the Raggedy Anne Antique Doll and Toy Museum

Wine

Magnums of Ch Lafite
1874
Sold 28.6.84 in London
for £500 ($725) and
£780 ($1,131)

Buoyant Wine Sales

MICHAEL BROADBENT, M.W.

One of these days it might be my ill luck to report a depressed market, prices down, turnover down and our competitors ahead. Happily what I have to report is yet another buoyant season with prices well up for just about every class of wine, a solidly satisfactory increase in turnover and a very high percentage sold. Furthermore, we still hold our dominant position in the highly specialised wine auction market.

THE OVERALL WINE AUCTION SCENE

Perhaps the scale of our activity can be best summarised by stating that Christie's three London-based wine auctioneers, Alan Taylor-Restell, Duncan McEuen and myself have, between us, conducted 45 wine auctions during the season, no fewer than 15 being two-session all-day affairs, made up of over 22,000 lots with an overall value just short of £6.5 million ($9.1 million).

During the season we have also published, or been co-publishers of, eight books on wine, including our annual Price Index, the Stanley Gibbons of wine.

CLARET AND OTHER FINE WINE AT KING STREET

Our King Street sales are the heart of the business and it is no exaggeration to claim that in volume and range they are the pivotal centre of the international fine wine market. What is perhaps not realised is that in addition to direct overseas buying (even in our good but unremarkable End of Season Fine Wines sale, one third of the buyers were from overseas: from 16 countries as far apart as Saudi Arabia, Malaysia and Liechtenstein) a substantial number of English merchants buy on behalf of, or with a view of selling to, American clients.

It is, happily, at King Street that we chalk up our greatest success. For the past two seasons we have simplified life for clients and ourselves by holding two major sales each month, one devoted to Bordeaux, and one to other fine wines, the latter including small private cellars of claret and old Sauternes. The results of the past season are as follows:

Type of sale	number	sold total	% sold
Fine wine and vintage port	12	£2.1 m. ($2.9 m.)	97%
Claret and white Bordeaux	10	£1.9 m. ($2.6 m.)	95%

An additional sale for the family of a château proprietor brought the King Street seasonal total to £4.1 million ($5.7 million) at 23 sales.

CHRISTIE'S SOUTH KENSINGTON

Although the early evening monthly sales of bin ends and inexpensive trade stock are popular and well attended, there has been a certain dullness owing mainly to the lack of an office there to deal with day-to-day matters. This has now been remedied. In June a separate department was set up under the management of Tony Thompson, who previously worked on the King Street staff.

Sales for the past three seasons have been hovering around the £400,000 ($560,000) mark, though the percentage sold has improved. With a man on the spot and lively South Kensington management we expect wine sales there to take on a new lease of life.

Left to right
Ch Lafite 1878, £640 ($928)
Ch Margaux (Pillet-Will)
1893, £180 ($261)
Ch Mouton-Rothschild 1947,
DM, £1,800 ($2,610)
Ch Montrose 1870, £290
($420)
Ch Lafite 1874, £540 ($783)

All sold 28.6.84 in London

OVERSEAS SALES

United States: In spite of the obvious potential for sales in New York, our efforts to obtain a permit, despite many concessions on our part, have continually been blocked by vested interests. The spirit of free enterprise, the encouragement of healthy competition, their claim to be the international centre for finance and commerce, all these trite 'truisms' fall rather flat in the face of opposition from intransigent retailers and wholesalers and archaic liquor laws. Our most recent application made some progress, but was not put on the statute table. We try again later this autumn.

In the meantime our wine auctions are flourishing in more liberal-minded Chicago, our four sales this season having topped $1 million (£714,285) once again. Here I should like to pay tribute to Jacqueline Quillen and the small but exceptionally capable in-house team headed by Michael Davis.

After two sales with an American auctioneer at the helm, Christie's was once again invited to conduct the annual Heublein auction of Fine and Rare Wines. Alan Taylor-Restell flew to Atlanta in May to preside. His professionalism was much appreciated, but it would seem that the interest in this purely promotional event is becoming more limited.

The Napa Valley Wine Auction, however, is going from strength to strength. Beautifully staged and set, efficiently organised, and exceptionally well attended (last-minute hopeful bidders were being turned away), the 4th Napa sale in June made a total of $407,000 (£301,481), of which at least $300,000 will be donated to two Napa Valley hospitals. The highest price paid was $21,000 (£15,555) for the first case of Schramsberg/Rémy Martin alambic brandy.

Some of the outstanding prices of the 1983/84 season:

Vintage Port

believed 1834, Roriz	£125 ($181) per bottle
1935 Sandeman	£80 ($116) per bottle
1945 Taylor	£1,450 ($2,102) per dozen
1945 Croft	£1,100 ($1,595) per dozen
1955 Taylor	£640 ($928) per dozen
1970 Noval, Nacional	£1,050 ($1,522) per dozen

Claret

1854 Ch Lafite	£1,600 ($2,320) per bottle
1878 Ch Lafite	£640 ($928) per bottle
1921 Ch Cheval-Blanc	£480 ($696) per bottle
1945 Ch Haut-Brion	£640 ($928) per magnum
1945 Ch Pétrus	£6,850 ($9,932) per dozen
1946 Ch Mouton-Rothschild	£2,300 ($3,335) per bottle
1947 Ch Mouton-Rothschild	£1,800 ($2,610) per double-magnum
1961 Ch Lafite	£3,300 ($4,785) per imperial
1961 Ch Palmer	£2,100 ($3,045) per dozen

Sauternes

1858 Ch d'Yquem	£620 ($899) per bottle
1868 Ch d'Yquem	£330 ($478) per bottle
1921 Ch Lafaurie-Peyraguey	£100 ($145) per bottle
1929 Ch Climens	£1,300 ($1,885) per dozen
1945 Ch d'Yquem	£260 ($377) per bottle

Burgundy

1937 La Tâche	£360 ($522) per bottle
1945 La Tâche	£420 ($609) per bottle
1949 Musigny, Vieilles Vignes	£420 ($609) per magnum
1955 Bonnes-Mares	£440 ($638) per double-magnum
1966 La Tâche	£1,100 ($1,595) per dozen
1969 Musigny, de Vogüé	£640 ($928) per dozen
1976 Romanée-Conti	£2,100 ($3,045) per dozen

White Burgundy

1955 Le Montrachet, Laguiche	£200 ($290) per magnum
1962 Corton-Charlemagne, L. Latour	£770 ($1,116) per dozen
1978 Le Montrachet, DRC	£155 ($224) per bottle

Hock/Moselle

1921 Niersteiner Kehr TBA	£140 ($203) per bottle
1953 Niersteiner Auflangen BA	£130 ($188) per bottle
1976 Zeltinger Sonnenuhr TBA	£95 ($138) per 2 bottles

Champagne

1928 Bollinger	£90 ($130) per magnum
1955 Krug	£680 ($986) per dozen
1966 Dom Pérignon	£720 ($1,044) per dozen

Tokay

1711 Imperial	£300 ($435) per half-litre

Sherry

1830 Solera, Viejo Oloroso	£260 ($377) per dozen

Madeira

1779 Verdelho	£280 ($406) per bottle
1795 Terrantez	£220 ($319) per bottle
1862 Terrantez HMB	£140 ($203) per bottle

Cognac

1811 Bisquit Dubouché Gr. F. Ch.	£330 ($478) per bottle
1811 Napoléon, Gr. F. Rés.	£360 ($522) per bottle
1844 Hennessy, Gr. Vieille Ch.	£150 ($217) per bottle
1898 Peyrolles, Gr. Ch. Rés.	£210 ($304) per bottle

Whisky

Pantheon Old Liqueur Highland	£67 ($97) per bottle

Chartreuse

Period 1840 – 78 Grande Chartreuse, Green	£160 ($232) per litre

Geneva: This was the first of our regular overseas wine auction ventures and has proved a steady if unexciting market. Two sales are held a season, in spring and autumn. Current sales exceed Sw.fr.500,000 (£157,729).

Amsterdam: Very similar to Geneva in frequency and scope, the turnover in Holland has contracted somewhat as cellars from Germany and Belgium now tend to come to London for sale. The total sold in Amsterdam last season was D.fl.755,381 (£175,763).

THE MARKET AND TERMS OF TRADE

Prices, which increased throughout 1983 and accelerated noticeably in the January to May period, flattened out, albeit at a high level, at the end of the season. This is not unusual. The trade presumably do not like to carry undue stock during the quiet summer period and the recent increases in bank rate have added weight to the argument. American buying, directly and indirectly, has undoubtedly been high over the whole season, but though it is generally realised that at nearly $1.3 to the pound buying in London is hugely advantageous, the counter-incentive of very high American interest rates tends to be overlooked.

However, the sudden imposition by Sotheby's of a 10 per cent buyers' premium on wine has had a far greater effect than could have been foreseen. Vendors in their big 6 – 7 June sale had not been informed prior to the catalogue being sent out, and the level of prices was most visibly depressed. It will remain to be seen whether the vendor, particularly the trade vendor, will be more interested in a 'bird in the hand', a low vendors' commission, than in a 'bird in the bush', a higher sale price.

Christie's wine department are determined to stick to the long-tried convention of charging a fair and reasonable vendors' commission. The trouble is, a buyers' premium not only guarantees minimum earnings but also enables vendors' commission discounts to flourish unobserved. Our future policy will depend on comparative prices, effectiveness of sales (so far we win on both counts) and, dare we say it, commission-cutting competition. But for as long as we can, we will not charge a buyers' premium on wine.

WINE PUBLICATIONS

It is perhaps still not fully realised that Christie's are the most prolific publishers of books on wine. Christie's Wine Publications started in 1972 with its first Wine Review and Price Index. We now have 18 titles in print, including 11 commissioned and published solely by ourselves, and 7 for which we act as co-publishers. A new book on *Madeira* by Noël Cossart comes out this autumn, together with new editions of *Wine Tasting* and Cyril Ray's *Lafite*.

THE FUTURE

In 1966, when wine sales were resumed and a new department set up, I was asked where we should find stocks to sell. The same question has been repeated endlessly. My reply now is that some of the highest-value wines we currently sell were actually being made in the autumn of 1966. In short I see no drying-up of cellars, trade or private, and no diminution of interest in the finest and rarest. If times are hard, a lot of wine floods on to the market, albeit at lower prices; if the economy is buoyant, sellers are tempted and buyers can afford the price.

Christie's have been auctioning wine since 1766. I am sure we will continue well into the future.

Christie, Manson & Woods Ltd.

LONDON
Christie, Manson & Woods Ltd.
8 King Street, St. James's, London SW1Y 6QT
Telephone (01) 839 9060 *Telex* 916429
Cables Christiart, London SW1

SOUTH KENSINGTON
Christie's South Kensington Ltd.
85 Old Brompton Road, London SW7 3JS
Telephone (01) 581 2231 *Telex* 922061
Cables Viewing, London SW7, England

GLASGOW
Christie's & Edmiston's Ltd.
164 – 166 Bath Road, Glasgow G2 4TG
Telephone (041) 332 8134/7 *Telex* 779901

Christie's in the City
Simon Birch
10/12 Copthall Avenue, London EC2R 7D
Telephone (01) 588 4424

Agents in Great Britain and Ireland

NORTH OF SCOTLAND
Sebastian Thewes
Strathgarry House, Killiecrankie
by Pitlochry, Perthshire
Telephone (079681) 216

ARGYLL
Sir Ilay Campbell, Bt.
Cumlodden Estate Office
Crarae, Inveraray, Argyll
Telephone (05466) 633

EDINBURGH
Michael Clayton
5 Wemyss Place, Edinburgh
Telephone (031) 225 4757

AYRSHIRE
James Hunter Blair
Blairquhan, Maybole, Ayrshire
Telephone (06557) 239

NORTHUMBRIA
Aidan Cuthbert
Eastfield House, Main Street
Corbridge, Northumberland
Telephone (043471) 3181

NORTH-WEST
Victor Gubbins
Eden Lacy, Lazonby, Penrith, Cumbria
Telephone (076883) 8800

YORKSHIRE
Sir Nicholas Brooksbank, Bt.
46 Bootham, York
Telephone (0904) 30911

MIDLANDS
The Hon. Lady Hastings, Mrs William Proby
The Stables, Milton Hall, Peterborough
Telephone (073121) 781

WEST MIDLANDS
Michael Thompson
Stanley Hall, Bridgnorth, Shropshire
Telephone (07462) 61891

MID-WALES
Sir Andrew Duff Gordon, Bt.
Downton House, New Radnor
Presteigne, Powys
Telephone (0242) 518999

EAST ANGLIA
Iain Henderson Russell
Davey House, Castle Meadow, Norwich
Telephone (0603) 614546
Stuart Betts, M.C., F.G.A. *Consultant*

COTSWOLDS
111 The Promenade, Cheltenham, Glos.
Telephone (0242) 518999
Rupert de Zoete *Consultant*

WEST COUNTRY
Richard de Pelet
Monmouth Lodge, Yenston
Templecombe, Somerset
Telephone (0963) 70518

SOUTH DORSET AND SOLENT
Nigel Thimbleby
Wolfeton House, Dorchester, Dorset
Telephone (0305) 68748

Christie's at Robson Lowe
39 Poole Hill, Bournemouth, Dorset
Telephone (0202) 292740

DEVON AND CORNWALL
Christopher Petherick
Tredeague, Porthpean, St. Austell, Cornwall
Telephone (0726) 64672

SOUTH EAST
Robin Loder
Leonardslee Gardens, Lower Beeding
nr. Horsham, West Sussex
Telephone (040376) 305

IRELAND
Desmond Fitz-Gerald, Knight of Glin
Glin Castle, Glin, Co. Limerick
Private Residence:
52 Waterloo Road, Dublin 2
Telephone (0001) 68 05 85

NORTHERN IRELAND
John Lewis-Crosby
Marybrook House, Raleagh Road
Crossgar, Downpatrick, Co. Down
Telephone (0396) 830574

CHANNEL ISLANDS
Richard de la Hey
8 David Place, St. Helier, Jersey
Telephone (0534) 77582

Companies and Agents Overseas

Argentina
Cesar Feldman *Consultant*
Libertad 1269, 1012 Buenos Aires
Telephone (541) 41 1616 or 42 2046
Cables Tweba, Buenos Aires

Australia
Sue Hewitt
298 New South Head Road
Double Bay, Sydney 2028
Telephone (612) 326 1422 *Telex* AA26343
Cables Christiart, Sydney

Austria
Vincent Windisch-Graetz
Ziehrerplatz 4/22, 1030 Vienna
Telephone (43222) 73 26 44

Belgium
Richard Stern, Janine Duesberg
Christie, Manson & Woods (Belguim) Ltd.
33 Boulevard de Waterloo, 1000 Brussels
Telephone (322) 512 8765 or 8830
Telex Brussels 62042

Canada
Murray Mackay
Christie, Manson & Woods International, Inc.
Suite 803, 94 Cumberland Street
Toronto, Ontario M5R 1A3
Telephone (416) 960 2063 *Telex* 065 23907

Denmark
Birgitta Hillingso
20 Parkvaenget, 2920 Charlottenlund
Telephone (451) 62 23 77

France
Princesse Jeane-Marie de Broglie
Christie's France SARL
17 rue de Lille, 75007 Paris
Telephone (331) 261 12 47 *Telex* 213468

**Monsieur Gérald Van der Kemp,
President d'Honneur of Christie's Europe**
is based in our Paris Office

Hong Kong
Amona Kwok
Room 602, Business Centre
Furama Hotel
1 Connaught Road Central, Hong Kong
Telephone (852) 5 220 955

Italy
Christie's (International) S.A.
Palazzo Massimo Lancellotti
Piazza Navona 114, Rome 00186
Telephone (396) 654 1217 *Telex* Rome 611524
Tom Milnes-Gaskell
Maurizio Lodi-Fè

MILAN
Giorgina Venosta
Christie's Italy S.r.l.
9 via Borgogna, 20122 Milan
Telephone (392) 794 712
Telex 316464

TURIN
Sandro Perrone di San Martino
Corso Matteotti 33, 10121 Turin
Telephone (3911) 548 819

LUCCA
Bruno Vangelisti
Via S. Donnino 8, 55100 Lucca
Telephone (0583) 43715

Japan
Sachiko Hibiya
c/o Dodwell Marketing Consultants
Kowa Building No. 35, 14 – 14 Akasaka
1-chome, Minato-ku, Tokyo 107
Telephone (03) 584 2351 *Telex* J23790

Mexico
Ana Maria de Xirau *Consultant*
Callejon de San Antonio 64
Delegacion Villa, Alvaro Obregon 01000
Mexico D.F.
Telephone (905) 548 5946

The Netherlands
Christie's Amsterdam B.V.
Cornelis Schuytstraat 57
1071 JG Amsterdam
Telephone (3120) 64 20 11
Telex Amsterdam 15758
Cables Christiart, Amsterdam
Harts Nystad

Norway
Ulla Solitair Hjort
Riddervoldsgt 10b
Oslo 2
Telephone (472) 44 12 42

Portugal
Antonio M.G. Santos Mendonça
R. Conde de Almoster, 44, 1° Esq.
1500 Lisbon
Telephone (351) 19 786 383

Spain
Casilda Fz-Villaverde y Silva
Valenzuela 7, Madrid 28014
Telephone (341) 232 66 27
Telex 46681
Cables Christiart, Madrid

Sweden
Lillemor Malmström
Artillerie Gartan 29
11445 Stockholm
Telephone (486) 620 131
Telex Stockholm 12916

Baroness Irma Silfverschiold
Klagerups Gard
23040 Bara
Telephone (040) 440360

Switzerland
Christie's (International) S.A.
8 Place de la Taconnerie
1204 Geneva
Telephone (4122) 28 25 44
Telex Geneva 423634
Cables Chrisauction, Geneva
Hans Nadelhoffer
Richard Stern
Georges de Bartha

ZURICH
Maria Reinshagen
Christie's (International) A.G.
Steinwiesplatz, 8032 Zurich
Telephone (411) 69 05 05
Telex Zurich 56093

West Germany
Jörg-Michael Bertz
Alt Pempelfort 11a
4000 Düsseldorf
Telephone (49211) 35 05 77
Telex 8587599
Cables Chriskunst, Düsseldorf

Isabella von Bethmann Hollweg
Wentzelstrasse 21, D-2000 Hamburg 60
Telephone (4940) 279 0866

Charlotte Fürstin zu Hohenlohe-Langenburg
Reitmorstrasse 30, 8000 Munich 22
Telephone (4989) 22 95 39

United States of America
Christie, Manson & Woods International, Inc.
502 Park Avenue, New York, N.Y. 10022
Telephone (212) 546 1000
Telex 620721
Cables Chriswoods, New York
David Bathurst *President*

CHRISTIE'S EAST
219 East 67th Street, New York, N.Y. 10021
Telephone (212) 570 4141
Telex 710-581 4211
J. Brian Cole *President*

CALIFORNIA
Christie, Manson & Woods International, Inc.
342 North Rodeo Drive
Beverly Hills, California 90212
Telephone (213) 275 5534 *Telex* 910 490 4652
Russell Fogarty

SAN FRANCISCO
Ellanor Notides
3667 Sacramento St.
San Francisco, Ca. 94118
Telephone (415) 346 6633

FLORIDA
Helen Cluett
225 Fern Street, West Palm Beach, Fla. 33401
Telephone (305) 833 6952

MASSACHUSETTS
Edgar Bingham Jun.
32 Fayette Street, Boston, Mass. 02116
Telephone (617) 338 6679

MID-ATLANTIC
Paul Ingersoll
P.O. Box 1112, Bryn Mawr, Pa. 19010
Telephone (215) 525 5493

David Ober
2935 Garfield Street, N.W.
Washington, D.C. 20008
Telephone (202) 387 8722
Nuala Pell *Consultant*
Joan Gardner *Consultant*

MID-WEST
Frances Blair
46 East Elm Street, Chicago, Illinois 60611
Telephone (312) 787 2765

TEXAS
Linda N. Letzerich
2001 Kirby Drive, Suite 702
Houston, Texas 77019
Telephone (713) 529 7777

Carolyn Foxworth
7047 Elmridge Road
Dallas, Texas 75240
Telephone (214) 239 2093

Index